# ICE

## IS WHERE YOU FIND IT

BY

*Captain Charles W. Thomas, USCG*

THE BOBBS-MERRILL COMPANY, INC.

Indianapolis     *Publishers*     New York

*First Edition*

The opinions or assertions contained herein are the private ones of the writer and are not to be construed as official or reflecting the views of the Commandant or the Coast Guard at large

CHARLES W THOMAS
Captain, U. S. Coast Guard

The *Northwind* in the Antarctic pack. Note pressure ridge ahead of ship.

# Dedication

To the world's three outstanding Ice Admirals I respectfully dedicate
this book:

        Richard E. Byrd, Rear Admiral, USN (Ret.)
        Edward H. Smith, Rear Admiral, USCG (Ret.)
        Richard H. Cruzen, Rear Admiral, USN

# Acknowledgment

I AM GRATEFUL to those whose names appear below for their indispensable assistance:

First, to my wife, Anna Magnella Thomas, for her encouragement and understanding and for the benefit of her knowledge acquired over eight years in Greenland.

To Kensil Bell for teaching me to write without a dictionary and for assisting me in research.

To Frank L. Ryman, JO1, USCG; Lieutenant William J. Braye, USPHS; Marjorie Arnett Braye; Lieutenant Howard Robinson, USCGR; Mr. William Dings, Joan Hays and Mrs. Rosemary B. York for their editorial critique.

To Miss Cecilia Donovan for her secretarial help.

To Mildred Sloan and Elaine Mead for their help in making official records available.

To Captain Samuel F. Gray, USCG, and his associates in the Public Information Section of the Coast Guard, for making available historical documents and pictures bearing on the Service.

To Captain R. H. Rice, USN, for permission to use data published by the author in the U. S. Naval Institute *Proceedings*.

To Rear Admiral Richard E. Byrd, USN (Ret.), for his kindness in writing the foreword to this book.

To Betty Kellet Nadeau of the Department of Micropaleontology at Washington University for putting up with a poor student during his struggle to make a deadline.

To the Seattle *Times* for permission to use its photograph of the author on the dust cover.

Finally, to The Bobbs-Merrill Company, Inc., for publishing this account of Coast Guard and Navy shipmates who shared with me the wonders and perils of the Polar Seas.

# Contents

CONTENTS—*Continued*

# List of Illustrations

# *Maps*

# Foreword

I AM GLAD to write this Foreword for *Ice Is Where You Find It*. I admire the author, and I am much interested in his subject.

The ice of the Polar Sea has a strange attraction. Like a woman, it can be beautiful, capricious, fascinating and dangerous—especially dangerous.

For at least a thousand years, ever since Eric the Red explored the polar ways to the Western Hemisphere, man has been trying to conquer the frozen seas. None has ever completely succeeded. Many have lost their lives in the effort. And undoubtedly many more will die going up against the polar-sea ice.

Ships of past generations were often caught in the clutches of the ice and drifted with it for a while until they succumbed to the irresistible squeeze of its jaws, and often the personnel either went down with the ships or were marooned on the ice to die. Modern ships, too, will be caught in the Polar Seas, and some may be sunk, but the casualties will be fewer because of the rescue potentialities of powerful icebreakers and helicopters or planes.

The "wind class" icebreaker of today, the development of which is due to the exigencies of war, is as much ahead of the old underpowered wooden ice ships as the automobile is ahead of the horse and buggy.

And someday the challenge of the ice will finally be met by man to complete the conquest of the seas. Man is a peculiar animal. If there is anything around him to conquer, he must have a try at it. But he does not want to live in the cold and forbidding climates, and he does not want to fight there or die there. Luckily man is a very adaptable animal, because he is going to *have* to learn to fight and live in the Polar Regions, especially at the top of the world. For the Arctic Ocean and the shores that it washes are destined to play a big role in history.

The North Pole is the center of parallels of latitude which pass through the great population and industrial centers of the Northern Hemisphere. If the Northern Hemisphere were spread out flat, the North Pole, as well as being the geographical center of it, would also come close to being the center of human activity of that vast area.

Development of the land areas (especially in Russia) and methods being evolved to navigate the seas within the Arctic Circle are going forward with an ever-increasing acceleration as the world in effect continues to shrink in size.

The Arctic Ocean of the future may become the Mediterranean of the past.

And I know of no person more fitted to take a part in this pioneering effort in the Arctic for this country than Captain Thomas. He has had a notable career in the service of the Coast Guard and Navy. Experienced ice navigators are rare. So far as I know they can be counted on the fingers of one hand. The modern icebreaker of the wind class was a war development, the first one having been finished in 1944. And it takes considerable experience to enable the ice skipper to take full advantage of helicopters, planes and electronics in order to achieve the fullest capabilities of the modern icebreakers. Captain Thomas has had that experience.

When we needed an ice skipper to navigate unprotected ships through the ice of the Ross Sea at the bottom of the world we decided that Captain Thomas was the man for the job.

It was his task to convoy three naval supply and command ships with thin unprotected hulls through 500 miles of the ice of this sea. To steam such ships into ice fields was unorthodox and indeed a ticklish business. Thomas, backed by the courage of Rear Admiral Richard Cruzen, made that experiment a success. It was a landmark in ice navigation.

Recently when I needed information about the ice pack in certain strategic areas within the Arctic Circle the first person I called on to supply this information was Captain Thomas.

The author of this book has a notable record. Aside from being a top ice navigator and Coast Guard officer, Captain Thomas is a capable marine engineer, sea-fighter, diplomat and scientist. His versatility is amazing. But what in this connection surprised me most was to learn of his talent as a writer on subjects other than professional ones. I think *Ice Is Where You Find It* proves my point. It is a fascinating book.

Richard E. Byrd.

Rear Admiral, USN (Ret.)

# Introduction

DURING the last great Ice Age—from which we are now just emerging—Nature scooped up water from the sea and piled it on the land in the form of ice. For this reason, up until 25,000 years ago, the depth of the oceans was some 200 feet less than it is today.

The remaining frontiers of the Ice Age are now confined to Greenland and to the Antarctic Continent. On Greenland the ice is so deep that its depths never have been sounded. It covers more than eighty per cent of the island (the world's largest island), an area of more than 700,000 square miles. The Greenland Ice Cap mounts to an elevation greater than 10,000 feet; and as it creeps slowly down toward the sea under the force of its own weight it grinds away mighty mountains of granite, diorite and basalt. Occasionally a lone spire peeks above the surface of the ice. These rugged projections are known as nunataks.

So vast is this great Greenland ice sheet that if it were suddenly to melt, the waters of the world's oceans would rise more than twenty-three feet! Such a catastrophe would flood the terminal facilities of every seaport in the world.

Beneath the Ice Cap lies a land area formed in the Pre-Cambrian Era, the earliest of all geological ages—over 500,000,000 years ago.

Heavy snowfall builds up the great Ice Cap in winter. With the approach of summer the Cap begins flowing outward, pushing through gaps in high mountains to break off, or "calve," into the sea as icebergs.

But the trend of glaciation throughout the world reflects the emergence of the earth from the Pleistocene period. The climate grows generally milder. The rate of glacial wastage exceeds that of supply. The glaciers flow more sluggishly or become inactive and retreat. The valleys they once occupied are filled with till which becomes stratified and leeched to a point where the soil supports vegetation. This has occurred in the southwestern part of Greenland. There,

where temperatures are higher and sea ice less severe, the older glaci-
ated valleys are covered with grass, providing grazing lands for
cattle and sheep and lending themselves to cultivation.

It is in the southwestern part of Greenland that man first established
himself on the island's inhospitable shores. It might be supposed that
these men were Eskimos, although there is no proof of this.

From the standpoint of meeting life's elemental needs, the Eskimo
is the most successful race throughout the northern latitudes of the
world. He probably evolved on the Arctic coast of Siberia and through
the centuries spread westward as far as Lapland and eastward to
Alaska, across northern Canada and on to Greenland.

There, in Greenland, his eastward migration came to a halt, just as
his westward migration came to a halt in Lapland. No Eskimo ever
migrated eastward—or westward—to Iceland, Jan Mayen Island or
Spitzbergen. *Why?*

I have never examined a work on ethnology in which the answer
to this question may be found. But I believe the answer is obvious to
anyone who has lived among Eskimos for any length of time.

Seal hunting is the Eskimo's chief means of livelihood, *but he never
paddles his kayak to sea beyond the sight of land.* True, his paddling
often takes him outside the bays, inlets and fiords on to the sea. But
unless he can see land other than that from whence he came *he will
go no farther.*

When the Eskimo reached Greenland in his eastward migration he
came to Denmark Strait, the body of open water 180 miles wide
separating the Blosseville Coast of Greenland from the Icelandic
Claw. At sea level, in a kayak, it is impossible to sight land across this
strait.

Admittedly the 6,000-foot heights of Glamujokull and Drangajo-
kull on the Claw are visible on a clear day from corresponding elevations on the Blosseville Coast. But to the seal-hunting Eskimo there
never was an economic necessity to go inland or to engage in mountaineering. Moreover, a dread of inland dwellers and other spirits*
deterred him from venturing into the interior.

Thus bound to the low coastal area of Greenland by natural econ-

---

* See Part Three, Chapter 20, page 177.

omy and by superstition, it is probable that no Eskimo ever scaled the near-perpendicular wall of Greenland's most rugged coast. Consequently he lived in ignorance of any land beyond—and his eastward migration stopped.

On the other hand, such an adventursome seafarer and mountaineer as the Norseman would not hesitate to climb an Icelandic coastal mountain. He would survey the sea area about him from such a vantage point and be impelled to undertake its exploration. It is not mere conjecture that the existence of Greenland was known to Icelanders long before the days of Erik the Red.

A pile of rubble near the present-day village of Karsiorsuk is believed to be all that remains of an ancient farmhouse which the Danes aver was Erik's abode. This ties in very logically with the sparse information we have of Erik's voyage.

On his return to Iceland in 984 Erik tried to entice settlers to the new land where he had spent his exile. To sell his colonization project he called the country "Green Land." The name was certainly inappropriate, but it conveyed an impression of widespread fertility—and Erik was a master salesman.

In the tenth century A.D. such institutions as the Better Business Bureau and the round-trip ticket were nonexistent. So in the spring of 985 Erik sailed again for Greenland with twenty-five ships. In them he carried 500 or so "customers." According to Vilhjalmur Stefansson, about fourteen of the twenty-five ships reached their destination with approximately 350 settlers. The other ships were either lost or forced back to Iceland by violent gales.

Erik's colony is believed to have been initially established as Frederiksdal in southwest Greenland. But by the end of the twelfth century colonization had spread over the coastal area of what is now Julianehaab Colony. There were sixteen villages with a total population of approximately 9,000.

Through the efforts of Leif Eriksson, son of Erik the Red, the Christian Church became firmly rooted in Greenland. The Icelandic form of government was adopted with the *Althing* as the representative body. The Renaissance had not yet dawned on medieval Europe, so the colonists could hardly have been expected to keep a written record of their laws. Consequently a *Law Singer* served as clerk of the assembly. He was required to memorize all the laws the *Althing* enacted and to recite them at each annual meeting, or whenever the occasion demanded.

In 1261 Greenland became a colony of Norway. But growing supremacy of the Hanseatic League, the Black Death and various political causes brought about a decline in Norwegian-Greenlandic commerce during the fourteenth century. In 1412 Greenland was completely cut off from intercourse with Europe.

Little is known about the Greenlandic colony throughout a void of some three hundred years. Then in 1721 Hans Egede, a Norwegian missionary, voyaged to Greenland under the Danish flag. Egede believed that the descendants of the Norse settlers were still established on the island. He reasoned that they were Roman Catholics (as all Western Europe had been before the time of Martin Luther) and hoped to convert them to the Lutheran faith.

Hans Egede found no trace of the Norse colonists or their descendants. Only Eskimos inhabited the island. But to Egede a soul was a soul, and he set about learning the native language and making converts to his church.

Egede's interests were not confined to proselyting. His foresight impelled him to explore the resources of Greenland in order that a new economy might be built on the ruins of Erik the Red's empire. Wherever Egede traveled in southwest Greenland he examined the Norse ruins in an effort to gain some clue to the fate of the colonies. He concluded at length that the colonists had migrated to the east coast of Greenland, about which little was known.

In 1724 Egede prevailed on the Norwegian government to send an expedition to east Greenland to investigate his belief. However the expedition of two ships failed to penetrate the ice along the east coast north of Cape Farewell.

Egede then established a colony at Frederikshaab from which to base a trans-Ice Cap expedition to the east coast. But it was 161 years before the first successful crossing was made.

Meanwhile in 1728 the Danish crown, which maintained sovereignty over Norway, appointed Claus Paars governor of Greenland. Trading stations were established and colonization expanded, with Sukkertoppen and Julianehaab added in 1775. Further development of Greenland was accomplished by Povl Egede in the latter part of the eighteenth century.

Povl, Greenland-born son of Hans Egede, carried on the work of his illustrious sire and established a geodetic survey of some parts of Greenland. He persisted in his father's belief that descendants of the Norse colonists were living in east Greenland. The Danish government voted him the equivalent of $6,000 to conduct an investigation by ship. But, like the expedition organized by Hans Egede, Povl's failed to reach the coast.

Very little was known about the southeast coast of Greenland until recent times. In 1883-1885 Gustav F. Holm explored the shore between Cape Farewell and Cape Ryder. Visiting Angmagssalik, he found a settlement of 431 Eskimos and later established a trading station there. The only trace that could be found of the Norse colonists was the crumbling ruins of their ancient farms.

Since 1774 the administration of Greenland has been in the hands of the Danish government. The prime concern of Denmark has been to keep 18,000 native Greenlanders alive, in good health and as nearly self-supporting as possible. Foreigners and Danes alike are excluded, except with the consent of the Greenland Administration. Trade is a monopoly of the crown.

The Lutheran Church is the state religion of Greenland.

The government operates trading posts through which native produce is exchanged for commodities which the Administration considers necessary to the Greenlanders. Spirits are forbidden. In four sections tobacco and coffee also are denied.

Until 1940 there were three Inspectorates: two on the west coast and one on the east coast, each having a governor. In that year events took place which shattered the political structure of Greenland.

## The Birth of The Greenland Patrol

It was at five o'clock in the morning on April 9, 1940, that German troops, without warning, poured over the Danish frontier at Flensburg. In perfect synchronism with this land operation three Nazi cruisers came to anchor in the port of Middlefart. While, as strategists knew, the move was primarily a preparation for the invasion of

France, the New York *Times* farsightedly stated: "The blow has been so violent that it has sent its tremors as far as Greenland."

Few Americans outside President Roosevelt's inner circle realized the full significance of this statement at the time. To most people in the United States Greenland was a land of snow and ice "somewhere up near the North Pole" and certainly of little importance to us. Neither did they grasp the significance of a visit to President Roosevelt by the Danish minister in Washington within twenty-four hours after the German occupation of Denmark. As a result of that meeting the President stated that the interests of the United States in Greenland were purely humanitarian.

There can be no doubt of official Washington's genuine concern over the plight of Greenland's population. Beyond this, however, Greenland had suddenly assumed vast strategic importance to the United States. The island lies athwart the shortest air route between the United States and Europe. Also it is immediately north of the shortest steamer lanes between the Western and Eastern Hemispheres. Whoever controlled Greenland would control these air and surface-ship routes. And in 1940 it was beginning to appear that Germany might attempt to acquire this control.

There was still another factor in Greenland of vital importance to the United States. At Ivigtut on the southwestern coast is the world's only commercially available supply of cryolite, a mineral necessary to the extraction of alumina from bauxite. Already in 1940 the United States' aluminum industry was feeling the pinch of a short supply. Our annual peacetime production of the lightweight metal totaled approximately 327,000,000 pounds.* It took little imagination to realize that we would require far greater quantities if war came. And we probably could not produce those quantities unless we had access to Greenland's cryolite.

None of this appeared in the news in the spring of 1940. Rather, the press and radio told only of a United States consulate being established provisionally at Godthaab, Greenland. This announcement was made on May 1. A little more than a week later the public was told that the United States Coast Guard icebreaking cutter *Comanche* was

---

* Wartime production of aluminum in the United States eventually totaled as much as 900,000,000 pounds annually.

departing New York for Greenland, laden with Red Cross supplies and carrying as passengers the newly appointed consul and vice consul.

Three months later the Coast Guard cutters *Duane, Cayuga, Campbell* and *Northland* also were operating in Greenlandic waters—transporting supplies, furnishing medical aid, carrying mails and providing a variety of technical services. In short, the work of the Coast Guard's Bering Sea Patrol was shifted to Greenland.

Meanwhile—on May 3, 1940—Greenland had established its own provisional government, designated as the Greenland Administration. It was not a separatist movement; the United Greenland Councils reiterated their allegiance to King Christian X of Denmark. However the Councils (consisting of native Greenlanders and Danes representing North, South and East Greenland) called on the United States to recognize the German occupation of Denmark as a threat to established public order in Greenland.

A year passed. Then on April 9, 1941—the anniversary of Germany's invasion of Denmark—the United States and the Greenland Administration signed an agreement for the defense of the island.

Stated briefly, the agreement gave the United States permission to take sufficient steps to keep Greenland from being converted into a springboard from which Hitler could hurl his forces against the Americans. The terms authorized the improvement of harbors and anchorages, the installation of aids to navigation and the construction of roads, airfields, communication facilities, fortifications and bases.

The physical features of Greenland opposed every effort directed toward implementation of the agreement. Mountains, ice and violent weather conditions during most of the year created problems of the greatest magnitude for our naval and military commanders. Moreover Greenland was a totally raw land, without a single road, telephone, telegraph or any other type of modern development. The harbors and coastal waterways were virtually uncharted. And inland areas were equally unknown. Native Greenlanders and Danish residents who had spent a lifetime on the island had little or no knowledge of conditions beyond the relatively few small settlements established along the shores of fiords.

The first task confronting the United States was a survey of the habitable portion of Greenland. This job was handed to Commander E. H. (Iceberg) Smith, USCG, in command of the cutter *Northland* and Commander C. C. (V.P.) Von Paulsen, USCG, in command of the cutter *Cayuga*. Both ships departed New York on April 7, 1941, to seek potential bases and commence a hydrographic survey. But a few weeks later the *Cayuga* was withdrawn for delivery to Great Britain under the Lend-Lease Act.

The *Northland* continued alone. Dr. Hobbs of the University of Michigan had previously located a flat place at the head of Sondrestrojm Fiord just above the Arctic Circle. The discovery of the Narsarssauk site, 500 miles to the southward and about forty miles inland, which ultimately became the principal United States base in Greenland, was largely a matter of luck. A thorough survey by sea and air of the formidable, rugged terrain had virtually convinced Commander Smith that the Sondrestrojm site was the only one available along the entire western coast. But because of its location so far to the north it would create difficult logistic problems.

On putting in at Julianehaab to discharge a native guide whose services would no longer be required, Commander Smith went ashore to pay his respects to Mr. S. Andersen, the colony manager. When Mr. Andersen heard of the fruitless search for a site in the southern part of the island he remarked that native Greenlanders spoke of a place which they called Narsarssuak, which in the Greenlandic language means "flat place, level, big." Mr. Andersen sent for a man named Hough, a Greenlander who served as Julianehaab's village carpenter. Hough had been a hunter in his youth and recalled having seen the place known as Narsarssuak. He described it briefly and gave Commander Smith directions for finding the spot.

The *Northland* got under way the next morning. The report of the expedition later stated, "Everyone expected little of the new location." But when the *Northland* came to anchor off Narsarssuak, the report continued, "All hands began breaking out survey equipment, as it appeared to be what we had been looking for."

Investigation quickly confirmed the first enthusiastic impression. Narsarssuak was a gravel plain about three miles long and one mile wide gouged between mountains by a retreating glacier. There was ample depth of water in the fiord to accommodate large ships and a suitable spot for constructing a crib dock. Ashore there was a good water supply and sufficient space for aircraft runways and parking areas, hangars, barracks, shops, fuel-storage tanks and all other buildings necessary to a large-scale base headquarters.

Commander Smith's survey expedition was now completed. The South Greenland Survey Force was dissolved and its ships transferred from Coast Guard to naval operational control. Admiral Harold R. Stark, Chief of Naval Operations, established the East Greenland Patrol and the West Greenland Patrol as subdivisions of the Atlantic Fleet. The *Northland* was ordered back to Boston for alteration of her peacetime armament to wartime condition. Smith sailed from Greenland on May 20, 1941.

This, in brief, is the background which impelled President Franklin D. Roosevelt to initiate a secret memorandum to the Chief of Naval Operations in 1941. The President wrote:

I think the Nazis will attempt to establish weather stations on the east coast of Greenland, probably in the vicinity of Scoresby Sound. I suggest that you have the *Northland,* the *Bear* and one other iceworthy ship patrol the east coast of the island to prevent their setting up weather stations, bases or other military works.*

So the Northeast Greenland Task Unit was born of the pen of the President himself. It consisted originally of the Coast Guard's *Northland* and *North Star* and the Navy's *Bear,* all under command of "Iceberg" Smith. Later the *Bear* was shifted to a West Greenland Task Unit.

With the threat of war growing, the importance and activity of naval forces in Greenland grew. On September 11, 1941, President Roosevelt issued his shoot-on-sight order, stating in part: "The time has come when the Americans themselves must be defended. . . . Attacks in our own waters, or in waters which could be used for further and greater attacks on us, will inevitably weaken American ability to repel Hitlerism."

The day after the President's order the East Greenland Patrol

---

* This is quoted from the original to the best of my memory. Wartime security prevented making a verbatim transcript.

struck its first blow in defense of those waters and made the first United States capture of World War II—that of the *Buskoe*—at Cape Hold With Hope.

The *Buskoe* flew the Norwegian flag, but her oversize radio apparatus aroused suspicion. Commander C. C. Von Paulsen, the *Northland's* skipper, sent Lieutenant Leroy McCluskey with a patrol to reconnoiter the surrounding area. McCluskey found a well-concealed building, slipped up on it and surprised three German radiomen asleep in their bunks. This abortive enterprise proved to be a Nazi attempt to relay messages from the German Naval Command to the U-boats which infested the North Atlantic.

Less than three months after the *Buskoe* affair the United States was at war with Germany. The East Greenland Patrol and West Greenland Patrol were merged into the Greenland Patrol and command was vested in Commander Smith. He in turn was made responsible to Commander Task Force Twenty-Four, Atlantic Fleet, at Argentia, Newfoundland.

Smith now faced an acute problem. He was charged with insuring the safe and timely arrival of all transport requirements to and from Greenland. Stepped-up construction with urgent demands for troops and equipment had tripled shipping. Escorts were in demand everywhere, and there was a fleet of seaworthy trawlers fishing out of Boston. Of course they would be far from ideal for escort duty—too slow and too small—but even an armed trawler is better than no escort. Then, too, Smith counted on experienced Coast Guard crews to make up for material deficiencies.

Smith asked Vice Admiral R. R. Waesche, Commandant of the Coast Guard, to get him ten trawlers. Admiral Waesche cut red tape to obtain them at once, then manned the vessels with picked crews. These wooden ships with iron men gave splendid service for more than a year—until replaced by steel cutters and gunboats.

The Greenland Patrol reached its maturity in 1943. Its far-flung activity was spread a quarter of the way around the world—from Jan Mayen to Churchill on Hudson Bay. The versatile nature of Greenland Patrol operations, from combat in the east to mere drudgery in the west—all in ice—tells more clearly than words that no job was too big for Rear Admiral Edward H. Smith, USCG.

*Part One*

THE SABINE ISLAND EXPEDITION

*1943*

# Chapter 1

## *THE ICE WORM*

NOWHERE on earth can you find such extremes of calm and fury, the beautiful and the terrifying, as in the Polar Regions. There, at both ends of the globe, lie awesome lands of incisive contrasts.

The polar quiet is unbelievable. It can be so deep and impenetrable that a man's shout is lost in the endless, frozen wastes. Then, with the suddenness of an exploding bomb, the silence can be broken by the screaming fury of frigid winds, the terrible roar of crashing ice fields and the thunder of calving glaciers.

Unparalleled beauty is unfolded for the polar traveler. Deep fiords are carved incoherently through sheer, jagged mountains. Clean blue water breaks sharply against the frothy white fronts of snow and ice. Across the cold and cutting night sky the Auroras flash with spellbinding, riotous color.

The terrifying is always there in the Polar Regions. You can feel it everywhere: about the ship, in the air, in the ice that constantly stalks one with the power to crush any puny intruder who disputes its rule.

The United States Coast Guard cutter *Northland* rode lazily across swells of polished emerald, bound from Reykjavik, Iceland, for Sabine Island, northeast Greenland. The quiet of the pilot house was unbroken, save for the sibilant rhythm of the steel hull plowing through salt water and the muffled escape of exhaust from her stacks.

*Clang! Clang!*

I jumped as the ship's bell brassily announced that another hour was only a record in the log.

A flurry of hourly reports to the officer of the deck broke the calm of the pilothouse.

"Sir, all secure about the decks," the coxswain of the watch reported.

"Sir, revolutions nine-five for one o'clock" sounded hollowly through the voice tube from the engine room.

"Sir, horizon clear!" the lookout high in the crow's nest shouted.

"Sir, air temperature twenty-one, sea temperature twenty-nine," the signalman on watch reported.

I, the captain of this ship, stood by, ignored in this bit of seaman-like routine. *A smart ship,* I told myself. But I was still an "ice worm." This was new business to me, this Arctic work.

Our mission to Sabine Island was a vital one. It had been determined a few months before that a Nazi weather-reporting station was located there. Now in the summer of 1943 we were to destroy it.

Our task unit consisted of the *Northland,* the USCG cutter *North Star* and the U. S. Army-chartered Norwegian sealer *Polar Bjorn.* The *North Star* and *Polar Bjorn* were now at Reykjavik, preparing for the voyage to northeast Greenland. The task-unit commander, Captain C. C. Von Paulsen, USCG, was on board my ship. This was comforting because he was an experienced ice man.

"Did you hear that, Captain?" Lieutenant Norman von Rosenvinge, USCGR, the officer of the deck, asked. "Sea water twenty-nine degrees!"

I started a little as Von Rosenvinge's voice broke into my thoughts. Then I seized the opportunity to display a little of my book knowledge. "Yes, better keep a sharp lookout ahead for ice blink, Mr. von Rosenvinge."

"Aye, aye, sir."

The term *ice blink* is given to the weird reflection which is the first evidence of ice over the horizon. It is an aura visible for several miles, even during the night.

On our starboard beam the sun hung close to the horizon, casting a tint of gold over the gray-and-white dazzle camouflage covering the *Northland* from stem to stern. An hour before, Lieutenant Freeman Harmon, USCG, the ship's navigator, had "shot" the sun at its lowest "dip" and determined our midnight latitude. Harmon's calculations showed that we were well above the seventy-fifth parallel.

*Well above the seventy-fifth parallel,* I thought. *Fine!*

From this point our destination was only a hundred miles or so to the southwestward—roughly in the vicinity of the seventy-fourth parallel. We had run well to the north of our goal because we must reckon on the southward sweep of the ice pack fetching us down to latitude seventy-four by the time we reached the Greenland coast.

Permanently on the march out of the polar basin, the ice pack drifts southward along the entire length of east Greenland. This is the principal avenue of escape for frozen masses of sea water from circumpolar circulation.

Smooth, young sea ice forms at an ordinary thickness of nine feet or less. Then the extraordinary fury of wind and sea breaks it up and piles layer on layer in numberless angles. Freezing integrates the masses to form what the Danes call *storis* or "big ice"—ice which has built up through upheaval to a thickness of ten to forty feet or more; ice whose surface is hummocked and scored, then further heaped with frozen snow.

By the time the *storis* enters the southward flow of the East Greenland Current, repeated freezing has welded it into enormous fields of rocklike hardness. But it is an ever-changing formation. Compact fields break into floes sometimes separated by clear water or water filled with fragmentary ice called *brash*. Such open spaces are known as *leads* or, if sufficiently long and narrow, *channels*. Often two large fields are separated by a slender ribbon of water which is known as an *ice canal*.

As a result of unceasing turbulence polar ice—*storis*—may produce eerie shapes of haphazard dimensions, often objects of exotic beauty or fantasy—particularly after a flow has broken into smaller units called *floebergs*. These separated ice masses frequently resemble their glacial counterparts—icebergs—but are apt to be more irregular because of their softer structure.

History is rife with accounts of ships which entered the pack, bound for the east Greenland fiords, but failed to navigate this procession of ice. To make good his westing through the pack, the navigator must run well north of his coastal objective in order to compensate for drift.

"Ice blink on the horizon ahead, sir!"

This report from the lookout quickened my pulses.

"This is it!" commented the officer of the deck.

"Better tell the task-unit commander," I suggested.

The news would bring Captain Von Paulsen to the bridge, even though to him it would be routine. For "V.P.," as the task-unit commander was affectionately known, was no longer overawed by the pack after spending many of his thirty-odd years as a Coast Guard officer in the Arctic. Before taking command of the Northeast Greenland Task Unit he had been skipper of the *Northland*—now *my* *Northland*—and he knew her intimately from truck to keel: her whims, her capabilities and her behavior in ice. Now I was conscious of a feeling that I did not want V.P. on the bridge. His presence topside always made me feel like a newlywed whose bride's ex-husband was along on the honeymoon.

The impression I had received of the ice was both confusing and terrifying. "Crush you like an eggshell if you're not careful!" everyone told me. "Just use ordinary horse sense. There are no rules" was Von Paulsen's curt advice. But I doubted whether I possessed even meager horse sense. Now, with the apparently formidable wall of ice looming unbroken on the horizon before me for the first time, my legs felt shaky.

Lieutenant von Rosenvinge, obviously reading my thoughts, reassured me. "Always looks worse from a distance, Captain."

Perhaps the *Northland* would not be crushed after all! She had worked through the pack before, but in a "good" ice year. Despite this optimistic thought, I realized that the ice forecast for 1943 was "bad." Then I remembered that my ship, which had been built in 1926 to replace the historic Coast Guard cutter *Bear*, was designed for the less rigorous ice of the Bering Sea. She had been the first steel ice vessel in the service of the United States, and old-timers still predicted with wagging heads that she would never weather a real pinch.

"No give to her sides. Should have been built of wood," the old ice sailors lamented. "Diesel engines are no good for ice," they went on. "No heat for keeping the stuff out of your injection! Not enough power. Diesel electric! Bah! Newfangled gadgets! They ought to have put Scotch boilers and reciprocating engines in her! She's got too much top hamper and deckhouse. Top-heavy tub!" And so on.

Captain Von Paulsen was the only representative of the old school who had a nice thing to say about my ship. "It's not the ship—it's her skipper," V.P. counseled. He was now on the bridge beside me, his faithful pooch Eight Ball, a dusky little spaniel, draped unceremoniously over his master's forearm. An agile man, this veteran officer. A six-footer, straight as an arrow and strong as an ox, whose physical stamina combined with a keen sense of humor made him an ideal polar traveler. His brush of close-cropped hair, now turned to silver, and his fame as a pioneer of naval aviation had long ago earned him the nickname "The Flying Dutchman."

"Skipper, do you see that dark surface-cloud a trifle on your port bow?" V.P. asked, lowering his glasses. "That's a water-cloud and indicates a lead. Head for it!"

Within an hour we were chugging through a well-defined lead between broken floes of *storis* thirty feet thick and hard as a rock! *Squoosh! Squoosh!* each floe sang as it gently rose and fell to the lap of a northeasterly swell. As the ship pushed deeper into the lead the ice completely damped out the sea action. It was like steaming into a harbor carved in a boundless white waste. Only a cat's-paw, a ripple, furrowed the surface.

"Launch your plane and have Hershey make an ice reconnaissance," Captain Von Paulsen suggested, judging correctly that at this point the lead was sufficiently wide and ice-free for a take-off by our plane, a single-motored Grumman J2F-5.

Hershey—Ensign Paul Hershey, USCG—the plane's pilot, took off and returned within two hours to deliver a report in a jargon completely foreign to me. He talked about compact fields, close-packed ice, moderate pack, open pack. I heard frequent reference to old ice, polar ice, young ice, brash ice, floebergs, icebergs and ice lakes.* What *I* knew about ice was contained in a couple of trays in a refrigerator.

But V.P., understanding perfectly, plied Hershey with questions.

"Looks bad?" I asked meekly after the pilot had left.

"Not too good, Skipper. But you never can tell definitely until you get there," V.P. answered. "Remember, *ice is where you find it!* So just keep pushing, and watch the weather!"

By late afternoon the breeze resolved to blow from the north. Dark clouds moved in, blotting out the blue overhead and the warmth of the sun. They bore with them a rare combination of snow and fair visibility. Our lead wound through a mosaic of broken floes. Suddenly I felt we had been transplanted by a magic spell to some distant part of the world—to the state of Iowa as I had known it in my childhood.

This, at any rate, was how it appeared to me as the *Northland* seemed to be twisting through the tortuous channel of a lazy river. On both banks the low, flat countryside was clad in the grayish white of an early winter evening. Snow-laden trees, fences, farmhouses, barns, expansive fields unfolded before us. One might expect to see little lights wink on one by one, to shimmer across the snowy landscape. The cattle should be in the warmth of their barns on such an evening.

Then the illusion was broken. There on the windward shore three bluish creatures were lumbering our way with a most unbovine gait.

---

\* *Brash ice:* Finely broken ice, fragmentary sea ice.
  *Close pack ·* Seventy to one-hundred-per-cent ice coverage of surface water.
  *Compact field ·* More than one square mile of unbroken ice.
  *Floeberg:* Fragment of a floe of polar ice large enough to resemble an iceberg.
  *Growler:* A small piece of glacial ice, a small iceberg.
  *Heaping ice:* Ice heaped into an irregular mass which rises above the surrounding ice.
  *Ice Lake (or Pool).* A body of relatively open water surrounded by ice.
  *Moderate pack:* Thirty to seventy-per-cent ice coverage of surface water.
  *Open pack:* Less than thirty-per-cent ice coverage of surface water.
  *Polar ice:* Ice which originates in the polar basin and is built up through rafting and freezing. Characterized by a hummocky surface and generally more than ten feet thick. Often called "hummocky ice" or "old ice."
  *Turret ice* Ice heaped into a mass resembling a tower or turret.
  *Young ice ·* New or virgin ice with a smooth surface. Generally less than ten feet thick. Variant. bay ice.

Boat-deck scene, U. S. Coast Guard cutter *Northland*

Troop-laden boat approaches Sabine Island, Northeast Greenland.

Advance of joint Army-Navy landing force on Sabine Island.

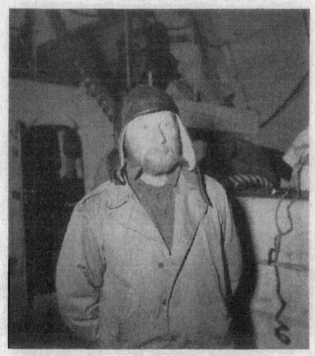

Dr. Ralph Sensse as he appeared when captured.

As the ship drew closer their color changed to cream. Frightened by the invading sea monster, the mother polar bear promptly herded her two young into a radical change of direction, and the three lumped away with added speed.

The river once more became an ice channel separating endless fields of polar ice. Familiar homey objects turned into pressure ridges, hummocks and eerie piles of turret and heaping ice. If those two fields were to close on us, our ship would be crushed. The thought scared me. I ordered an increase in speed from "two thirds" to "standard." The propeller beats quickened.

Soon the end of our channel was in sight. Beyond it lay an ice lake with shores of marshlike softness, but a film of new ice separated the lake from the pack.

In that lake was sanctuary. The yielding ice forming its banks would cushion us from the surrounding tough polar ice. The ship *must* reach that ice lake by breaking through. This was a most imprudent undertaking with the wind on our starboard beam, for it would keep the ice squeezed tightly against the ship's sides. But there was no choice here. I ordered: "Full speed ahead!"

We must swoop down on that intervening ice with all possible momentum. The big motor whined, Diesels roared, tongues of flame shot upward from our exhaust stacks. Trembling with increased power, the *Northland* lunged forward.

Our bows rode high on impact with the ice. On the bridge we clutched the grab-rod or anything handy to keep from being thrown off our feet. Forging ahead with slackening speed, the ship settled each time the ice crumpled beneath her weight.

Again and again we climbed on the ice, crushed it, moved on. But the *Northland* was becoming exhausted, and each successive onslaught was more feeble. Now as the bows mounted we instinctively exerted a forward thrust with our bodies, as though to aid the ship. But it was useless. The *Northland* slid slowly to a standstill.

I let the propeller churn awhile to wash broken ice clear of the wake before backing off and charging again. Huge blocks of ice bobbed in the current astern and raced aft to fetch against their fellows jammed into the channel we had cut.

I ordered: "Full speed astern!"

Nothing happened.

I rushed to the bridge-wing, looked down at the ice and saw we were fast. "Full speed ahead!" I shouted.

Still no motion.

Pressure slabs were already forming along the *Northland's* sides, softly hissing as they mounted steadily like a rising tide. I realized in alarm that we were in a tough spot! The soft ice would spend itself against our sides, our deck structure and our top hamper. Then the polar ice would move in and—Taps!

"I want Captain Von Paulsen here in a hurry!" I exclaimed desperately. V.P. was the only one to whom I could turn. He was a pillar of strength.

When the task-unit commander reached the bridge I looked at him helplessly. Words were not needed. He nonchalantly scolded Eight Ball for some trivial offense, then sauntered to the port bridge-wing and drew a deep breath on his cigarette. I was at his heels. He flipped the butt carelessly to the ice. It fell about ten feet from the ship's side.

"You'll have to blast, Skipper. Where that cigarette butt lies. Opposite the section of maximum pressure. I'll lend a hand." V.P. gathered up his little dog and left the bridge.

On the ice the unit commander toiled with pick and shovel alongside the gunner's mates. The crew leaned over the bulwarks and watched attentively while the little group dug a hole in the ice. The miners progressively detonated single demolition blocks until a depth of about six feet had been reached. Then they prepared a charge of eight blocks and covered it with debris and fresh water. It quickly froze solid in the surrounding ice.

"Get those plane wings covered pronto!" V.P. shouted as he climbed the Jacob's ladder to the deck.

When everything was ready the officer of the deck rattled the engine-room telegraph to full-speed-ahead. Deep in the engine room the black gang coaxed all possible power to the wheezing motor. The ship must be prepared to move the instant the ice pressure was relieved.

"All hands stand clear!" I shouted. "Let 'er go!"

With a muffled roar the charge burst, sending a shower of ice fragments rocketing skyward, plummeting onto the decks. Good thing the plane wings *were* covered!

On both sides of the ship the rails were manned by eager men. They gazed anxiously at arbitrary reference points on pressure slabs: huge pieces of ice which by this time had mounted nearly to eye level. Underfoot the deck thumped wildly to the rhythm of the beating propeller. The ship was moving! The trick had worked!

Inch by inch the vessel slipped through whispering blocks of ice. She slowly gained speed. Then as we advanced faster with each revolution of her propeller huge lumps of ice toppled on edge like a crumbling house of cards. The hissing increased in volume, became a dull roar. Gathering momentum, the ship labored into an ice pool.

Fine! Now we could work up speed to batter through the remaining distance to the lake. Quickly the *Northland* sped through the pool and charged into the ice beyond.

"Rudder amidships!" I ordered.

V.P. cupped his hands to his mouth, shouted across the bridge. "Watch your . . ." His words were lost in the clamor of the impact.

Again the bows rose high. But this time the ice beneath did not break. Instead the forefoot sought the less resistant ice to port. The ship shuddered and lurched violently to the left, where her weight smashed through the ice with a thud like a wrestler thrown from the ring.

Suddenly the propeller stopped dead still. It paused briefly, then resumed its churning with full force.

That fleeting instant was long enough for V.P. to speak his piece. "Motor tripped out when the prop struck ice. Lucky! Now mind your rudder!"

I could see it now. Bows swinging to port had caused the stern to thrust the propeller smack into hard ice. *Lucky* was right! If the electric motor had ground on instead of tripping out, either the screw or the ice would have had to give. And it would not have been the ice that gave! Then, without propulsion, the ship would have been left helpless in the grip of a merciless pack.

I was so humbled by my own incompetence and by V.P.'s sharp admonition to "Mind your rudder!" that I gave no order to either helm or engine room until we plowed into the ice lake.

How did one judge ice thickness in time to give rudder to compensate? Why had Coast Guard Headquarters back in Washington put a greenhorn in command of the *Northland?* I was convinced that I would never learn the ice business.

I could imagine officers and crew members on the bridge telling their messmates how their stupid captain had nearly lost his propeller, how he had nearly sent his ship's company to its death. The word would spread through the ship. Everyone would be outwardly respectful, but inwardly contemptuous of his commanding officer.

Well, I decided, I would somehow get out of ice just as soon as this expedition was over. To hell with Greenland! To hell with the Arctic! It would be the South Pacific for me. *That* was where I belonged.

Even as I slipped my ship alongside a billowy bank and ordered our ice anchors planted these thoughts coursed through my mind. Smarting with embarrassment, I retired to my stateroom like a sulky child, feeling very sorry for myself.

# Chapter 2

## *SABINE ISLAND*

LIEUTENANT REGINALD F. BUTCHER, USCG, was executive officer of the *Northland* and therefore second in command. For nearly half his life "Butch" had been as bald as a doorknob. It was only his inability to accomplish the adornment of a well-groomed head of hair which precluded for him such a nickname as "The Beau Brummel of the Greenland Patrol." For Butch never showed up without polished black shoes, shiny visor, glittering brass buttons and gleaming gold stripes. His spotless white starched collar and eternally pressed blue uniform stamped him with a trademark that set him apart from the ship's other officers, particularly V.P., whose well-worn uniforms look as though they hadn't seen a pressing iron since years before the outbreak of hostilities.

How did Lieutenant Butcher manage to sleep in his clothes (a wartime and Arctic requirement) and maintain an appearance worthy of an admiral's inspection? I have never found out.

But Butcher was no fop. He had fought his way up the ladder from the ranks. He was an ace seaman—not the swashbuckling bellower of the old school, but an officer who exemplified quiet efficiency. To him, as to V.P., the *Northland* had no bounds of capability. She could have broken her way across the Greenland Ice Cap just as readily as she could break through a paper bag.

While we were anchored in our ice lake, Butcher had the morning watch, which spans the period of drowsy wakefulness between 4:00

A.M. and 8.00 A.M. All through the night we had waited for a lead to open up so we could get under way again toward Sabine Island. Shortly after 4·00 A.M. I was aroused with the watch officer's compliments. A lead was opening, the messenger from the bridge told me, and might Mr. Butcher try to push on?

I instructed the messenger to tell Butcher to get under way. Then, wanting to take advantage of every opportunity to learn the ice business, I climbed sleepily to the bridge.

On the ice a little group of men danced around to keep warm, waiting for the order to dig out ice anchors. The ship faced the north wind, which drove a light snowfall before it and ringed the white fields surrounding our lake with a curtain of bluish haze. Visibility was limited to about a mile. Just ahead of the *Northland* bits of brash were breaking loose from the watery film of ice separating two heavy fields. Driven before the wind, the brash drifted past us and piled up far astern at the end of the lake.

Abeam of the ship on the side on which our anchors were planted a pin point of haze fluttered feebly. Then it took the shape of a familiar lumbering object; a polar bear headed squarely for the *Northland's* bow!

I had barely sighted the animal, it seemed, when I realized that all the men never would have time to scramble up the lone Jacob's ladder to safety. The junior officer of the deck, Lieutenant (j.g.) Dorris Bell, USCGR, grabbed a Tommy gun and followed the intruder through leveled sights.

"Don't shoot!" I said. There was no use infuriating the bear or exciting the men. And I had read that men in motion would scare off a bear.

But apparently this bear hadn't read the same book, for he complacently lumbered past the forward detail at a distance of a few paces. At that point, with the anchor uprooted, the men saw him. The entire forward detail streaked up the ladder and sat panting on the deck. The nimbleness of our fellow men surprised Bell and me more than the amazing speed of the bear.

Both anchors were soon in, and I thought with satisfaction that it would be a feather in my cap to surprise Captain Von Paulsen, now asleep in his stateroom, with a substantial number of miles made good by the time he awakened. He would be pleased to find that the skipper had brought the ship so much closer to her destination without his mentor's aid.

Lieutenant Butcher had the con; that is, he was immediately responsible for the ship's movements by giving orders to the wheel and to the engine room. The junior officer of the deck took station aft to signal the bridge if ice threatened to foul our propeller. For myself I chose the important job of spotting leads. Routine checking of compasses fell to the lot of the quartermasters. They entered comparative readings of gyro and magnetic compasses in a book every quarter-hour, notifying the officer of the deck only in case of undue variation.

Butcher handled the *Northland* with masterly icemanship. How I envied him as he slewed and wormed through places which seemed impossible to squeeze by! But it was said that lead spotting required just as much skill as ship handling. And wasn't I doing a splendid job, too? I asked myself.

The answer apparently was "Yes!" when shortly before eight o'clock we had smashed through fourteen ice miles of pack. Then we entered an ice lake strikingly similar to the one in which we had spent the night. Further progress appeared to be blocked, so out went the ice anchor. The *Northland* would lie here until another lead opened up.

Feeling very proud of myself, I descended to the cabin, where Captain Von Paulsen was at breakfast. I sat down and waited smugly for him to inquire about mileage during the four-to-eight watch.

But V.P. did not talk shop. He said nothing about the ship, the ice or Greenland. Instead his conversation was far away. I don't remember where; probably he discussed tropical ornithology, a subject dear to his heart.

"We made fourteen miles this morning!" I blurted out finally.

V.P. looked only mildly surprised. "Really? Now, I could have sworn we were in the same ice lake as yesterday."

"It does look it," I agreed. "But—ha! ha! . . ."

V.P. got up, napkin in hand, and looked out the porthole at a jettisoned oil drum bobbing in a patch of brash and slush. "I thought that was the same oil drum you hove overboard last night."

I sprang to the telephone and buzzed the engine room. No, the answer came back over the phone, they had not cast away any drums since the eight-to-twelve watch last night.

I felt the blood rush to my face and beads of perspiration break out across my forehead as the truth dawned. The leads I had followed this morning had taken us around in a *complete circle*—a circle fourteen miles in circumference.

V.P. read my thoughts. "Don't worry, Skipper," he consoled. "I had to learn the hard way, too. Just remember that you must never follow a lead which doesn't run in the approximate direction you wish to travel." He reared back in his chair and laughed.

I joined the laughter. But mine was artificial, not from the belly!

Later that morning a lead opened up for us. We got under way, and from noon on the *Northland* corkscrewed through dreary, interminable channels carved through endless fields of white under a gray, overcast sky.

Then with the unpredictable suddenness so characteristic of the Arctic the ice fields were gone. The sun peeked through a window of blue near the northern horizon, shooting its rays beneath a ceiling of clouds and casting a fiery path across an ebony sea. Here and there bergs and floes drifted aimlessly, cloaked in doubtful shadows behind fronts of sparkling splendor.

The spell of the scene was broken by a shout from the battle lookout on the flying bridge. "Submarine! Bearing zero-five-zero!"

The officer of the deck jumped to the rail and focused his glasses down the bearing. "Looks like the real McCoy, Captain," he said. "No motion! Probably thinks we're a berg. Here, have a look."

Until the officer of the deck passed this judgment I had ruled out the possibility of a sub penetrating the pack. Now I peered eagerly. There was no mistaking the familiarly cigar-shaped hull with a "cash register" conning tower. A Kraut job, sure enough! She lay close under a big berg. Previous experience with enemy planes had taught us to shoot first and ask questions afterward. I reached for the general alarm and depressed the handle.

Within thirty seconds a salvo from the three-inch "ready" gun shrieked across the ice-studded water and enveloped the silhouette in a column of spray and ice particles.

When the splash dissolved, the outline of a submarine was unbroken. I immediately knew we had thrown steel at a dark shadow produced by the overhang of the berg. "Cease firing! Secure!" I ordered.

Weird light had played tricks with our eyes. But at least we had had good gunnery practice. More important, though, the false sighting helped reassure me that the ship's company was on the alert. This was especially important now. For we were within approximately forty miles of our destination—and the enemy!

Our intelligence of the Nazi occupation of Sabine Island had come about through a sequence of dramatic events running back several months to the spring of 1943.

Sometime prior to this—probably as long ago as August 1942—the Germans had established a meteorological station on the island as an aid to their U-boat wolf packs generally operating off Cape Farewell, Greenland, and along the sea routes to Iceland. The station was to supply these submarines with advance information about the weather which breeds over Greenland and then moves out into the Atlantic. It also was to serve as a relay point for messages from the German Submarine Command in Europe. Quite naturally the presence of this outpost was carefully concealed by the enemy.

But men living together in isolation and close confinement are apt to become restless and crave adventure and action, even to the point of rashness. In the case of the enemy force on Sabine Island this desire for activity took the form of a raid on the headquarters of the Greenland Army at near-by Eskimonaes.

The tiniest army in the world, the Greenland Army was allied to the United States in our war against aggression. It was a full-fledged military unit, though suggestive of the fighting forces of the Land of Oz in that it boasted a preponderance of officers. Four of its total strength of eight personnel enjoyed commissioned status. Three were non-commissioned officers, one was a private.

But the elements of the Greenland Army were tough, aggressive men: rugged Danes hardened by years of long, cruel northeast Greenland winters. They had been trappers before the war. Now they were banded into a well-knit miniature task force whose mission it was to deny a determined enemy a foothold on one of the world's most desolate coasts.

Paradoxically the Greenland Army was large from a standpoint of bivouacking facilities, which consisted of more than a hundred huts forming a network of relay stations. These were spread along several thousand miles of coastline between Cape Steensby and Scoresby Sound. They dated from prewar days when trapping had been a lucrative monopoly of the Danish crown, which subsidized the best of housing for the trappers in need of refuge from biting winter blizzards. Many of the huts—now stations of the Greenland Army— were equipped with radio so that the roving patrolmen might maintain contact with their headquarters at Eskimonaes on Clavering Island.

Perhaps there was a grain of justification for the decision of the Nazi commander of Sabine Island, Lieutenant Hermann Ritter, German Naval Artillery, to assault the Greenland Army. He may have felt it necessary to attack and either destroy or capture the patrolmen before they discovered and attacked him.

At any rate the Nazis on Sabine Island moved in force against Eskimonaes in the early part of April 1943. A pitched battle followed. The three Danes holding the headquarters station were greatly outnumbered and confronted with the overwhelming fire power of the Germans' automatic weapons. Escaping in the night, the three retreated to the southward. Then the Nazis razed the station and started back to Sabine Island. But now their secret was out!

Meanwhile Sergeant Eli Knudsen of the Greenland Army had been reconnoitering in the north. As he was returning to Eskimonaes he inadvertently ran into the Nazi raiding force bivouacked at Sandotten. With his ears covered by his parka hood Knudsen could not hear the German command to halt. Seeing the enemy's automatic rifles leveled at him, he turned to get in the first shot, but was killed before he could squeeze the trigger.

Marius Jensen, acting commanding officer of the Greenland Army at the time, had been one of the three to escape from Eskimonaes. He circled north to warn Knudsen, but he was too late. When he saw the slain Dane's dogs and sledge he thought they were being driven by Knudsen, and unluckily he walked into a Nazi trap.

As a prisoner of war Jensen was ordered by the Germans to guide them back to Sabine Island. But the wily Dane convinced Lieutenant Ritter of the advisability of traveling in two parties. One of these parties, consisting of the main body of Germans, was directed by Jensen to take a long, roundabout route. Then Jensen and Lieutenant Ritter set out on a shorter route. As soon as the two were alone the big Dane overpowered his captor and took *him* prisoner!

There followed a fabulous journey to the southward, more than three hundred miles over the ice. Jensen and his prisoner arrived in Scoresby Village about May 18 after forty days of living side by side on the trail, eating together and sharing the same sleeping bag!

Meanwhile the other two Danes who had escaped from Eskimonaes with Marius Jensen had reached Scoresby Village. Their news of the attack and of the German occupation of Sabine Island was flashed by radio to Greenland Base Headquarters at Narsarssuak on the southwest coast. This culminated in orders to Captain Von Paulsen's task unit to proceed to Sabine Island when ice conditions permitted and destroy the enemy station.

It was to fulfill this mission that the *Northland* had worked her way through the *storis* and was now immediately off the coast of northeast Greenland, approximately forty miles from our destination. Aboard our ship was the regular commanding officer of the Greenland Army, Captain Niels O. Jensen, a Dane who had spent many years as a trapper in the area patrolled by the troops he had been sent to lead. We also had Corporal Hans Jensen as a passenger.

Captain Jensen's remaining troops were disposed as follows: one (sergeant) in the *North Star*, three lieutenants, one corporal and the Army's lone private at Scoresby Village awaiting transportation via *Polar Bjorn* to such place as Captain Jensen ultimately would select for his base headquarters. Of sledge dogs there were twenty-one in the *Northland* and sixty in the *North Star*.

In placing Captain Jensen in command of the Greenland Army the Greenland Administration had made a wise selection. For Niels, as we came to call him, was well qualified as a leader: experienced in Arctic living and travel, skilled as a technician, mechanic, meteorologist, marksman and dog driver. Moreover Niels possessed remarkable physical stamina, exquisite manners, sunny disposition and a magnetic personality. Forty years of clean living hung lightly on his sinewy body.

It was approximately 11:00 P.M. when we in the *Northland* discovered with one salvo from our "ready" gun that our "submarine" was merely a shadow on a berg. Throughout the rest of the night, which remained as bright and clear as daytime due to our northerly position, we wove our way through scattered ice around the south end of Little Pendulum Island and into Pendulum Strait, the body of water separating Little Pendulum and Sabine islands.

At 4:00 A.M. the ship was fully awake. An atmosphere of tenseness spread over her, from the cooks and messmen busy in the galley over bubbling pots of black coffee, to the restless gun crews gulping the potent contents of their mugs at battle stations, to the fire-control party high on the flying bridge. This was "Der Tag." The *Northland* was approaching her objective and making ready for the assault.

The company of joint landing force detailed to attack the Nazi stronghold was completing its preparations to go ashore. There was a platoon of United States soldiers and another platoon of our own bluejackets. The commander of this force, Captain Melvin Jensen, USA, was already aloft in our ship's plane, scouting the situation.

At the moment I was intent on the navigation of the *Northland,* weaving among the heavy floes spread over Pendulum Strait. A mile or so ahead I could make out an unbroken wall of ice spanning the narrows. That would be the place where we must disembark our troops.

"Planes approaching! Several! Bearing one-six-four. Distant seven miles!" air-search radar suddenly reported.

*Bombers! German jobs!* I thought in alarm, realizing we had been in view of Sabine Island throughout the night and could have been sighted by the enemy entrenched there.

Before anyone could reach for the general alarm a flashing light burst from the° lead plane. It was the challenge signal—the correct one. This was a bombing squadron under Colonel Bernt Balchen, USA, Arctic flyer, sent from Iceland to support our attack. It occurred to me then that we had hit our ETA (Estimated Time of Arrival) right on the button!

Balchen's formation circled low over Sabine Island, then steadied on a southerly course. "No sign of life," he signaled by blinker light. Our own J2F-5 returned from her reconnaissance to confirm this report.

However the operation must proceed. Neither Balchen's nor our plane's observations could be accepted as definite assurance that the island was unoccupied. We thought it entirely conceivable that the enemy, hearing the approach of aircraft, would scatter and conceal himself in camouflaged tents which would be difficult to detect from the air.

I maneuvered the *Northland* to the shore-fast ice spanning the narrows, nosed into it and planted an ice anchor—and the landing force poured over the side to begin its advance.

# Chapter 3

# THE PHANTOM INTRUDER

THE "Battle of Sabine Island" will probably never be recommended as a study reference to future students of warfare. It reminded me of something I once had read about the King's horses and the King's men who went after a lion and caught a mouse. The mouse *we* caught, a forlorn little German doctor, looked as though he had just been booted off a boxcar in a Middle Western tank town.

This capture of ours—an amazing story in some respects—took place in the course of a series of rather anticlimactic events.

The Nazis had vamoosed!

Where had they gone? We did not know. But the tons of valuable equipment left behind in disorder, and in carefully stowed and hidden caches as well, bore witness to a hasty evacuation.

A few spars poking through the ice in Hansa Bay marked the grave of the German ship which evidently had brought the station's personnel to northeast Greenland from Europe. She had probably been sunk by Colonel Balchen's bombers during a raid from Iceland in May 1943, less than two months before we arrived at Sabine Island in the *Northland*.

Had the enemy sent another ship to remove the station's personnel after this attack? If so, wouldn't they have taken more of their gear aboard instead of leaving it here? Had large planes been flown in to remove the men to Norway? This appeared most unlikely, for there was positively no place on the island for landing and taking off a big plane. How about a water landing? This might have been possible.

46

Yet quantities of ice drifted in Pendulum Strait, and there was considerable risk involved even in the use of our little J2F-5.

And so the "Battle of Sabine Island" became the "Mystery of Sabine Island"—a mystery which was to deepen within a couple of days.

With our patrols ashore and sweeping over the northern part of the island in a thorough search for the enemy, I decided to join Captain Von Paulsen and Niels Jensen, whose boundless energies impelled them to augment our reconnaissance parties. I had just finished dressing when my two companions entered the cabin. V.P. leveled his little finger at me and broke into a paroxysm of laughter.

"What's the joke?" I asked. Surely I was well clad, for I had put on long-handled woolies, heavy socks, jungle-cloth trousers, woolen shirt, blouse and parka. In brief, I was well-padded against the cold. Moreover, my shoe packs would keep my feet warm and dry.

"Oh, dear me!" V.P. gasped derisively, brushing tears of mirth from his eyes. He turned to Jensen. "Niels," he said, "show the skipper how to dress for the kind of job we have to do. Come on," he added coyly, "take 'em off, Queenie!"

Shyly, in the manner of a modest chorus girl applying for a job, the commander in chief of the Greenland Army went into a partial strip tease. As he did so, the task-unit commander emphasized each garment. "No hat or headgear," V.P. pointed out. "Woolen OD shirt. A flannel CPO shirt would do," he said to me in an aside. Then he turned to Niels. "Tsk! Tsk! Where's the insignia of your rank, Niels?"

Rank in the Greenland Army was denoted by a white band with red borders sewed on the right arm. Insignia was in blue: captain, two stars; lieutenant, one star; sergeant, three vertical bars; corporal, two bars; lance corporal, one bar; private, none. Actually no one wore his badge of rank, although everyone had it in his possession. Plain U. S. Army woolen OD's were uniform with the brassard intended to comply with international law concerning armed forces.

Without waiting for the embarrassed Dane to reply about his insignia, V.P. continued his lecture to me. "Woolen OD trousers like mine," he said, indicating his own trousers and those Niels was removing. "Long-handled woolies. That'll do, Niels," he finally said. "Now, explain why you wear woolen socks and tennis shoes."

Captain Jensen dressed while he told us in precise English, "In this country one must keep weight pared to a minimum. Even though it is freezing outside, we will perspire when we start scrambling over rugged land. Porous wool next to the skin is even better than close-knit wool because it will allow the steam to escape, so to speak, and still keep you warm.

"The streams here have a lot of drainage to accomplish in a short time," he continued. "They run deep, so you will dip your boots. Since your feet will get wet anyway, it is best to wear something which will give a good footing and allow you to travel swiftly. In winter we wear kamiks—knee-length Eskimo boots made of sealskin. Leather is bad when frozen. Now——"

"If I don't miss my guess," V.P. interrupted, "the skipper has a pack made up strictly in accordance with the Landing Force Manual, U. S. Navy, to take ashore."

I blushed at V.P.'s deduction.

"The regulation pack is no good here," V.P. declared. "Niels, break out your rucksack."

The Dane reached into his rucksack and drew out three cans of pemmican, a sweater, mittens, a change of socks, flashlight, soap, razor and a small coil of nine-thread Manila. Then he exhibited a light-weight eider-down sleeping bag. A first-aid kit and a knife were secured to his belt. Finally he picked up a carbine and a bandolier of ammunition and slung them over his shoulder.

"And now, in conclusion," V.P. said, "never burden yourself with a lot of heavy clothing and useless gear. You'll only have to throw it away. Then when you stop you *will* be in a jam, because you won't have anything to sleep in or keep you warm. Maybe you'll even be careless enough to throw away your rations."

Save for a woolen helmet to substitute for my deficiency in hair, I succeeded in dressing to V.P.'s satisfaction.

The sun had long since dipped below the lofty mountains ranging about Pendulum Strait by the time V.P., Niels, Lieutenant von Rosenvinge and I went ashore. In their shadows the air was frosty and penetrating. But after a few minutes of scurrying over frozen hillocks I was ready to swap my clothing for a fig leaf.

The steep slopes of Sabine Island are surmounted by cliffs of coal-black basalt topped by a plateaulike region studded with a few mountain peaks. From below, the cliffs have the appearance of a castle wall rising to an elevation of perhaps a thousand feet.

Niels scrambled up these natural battlements with the agility of a mountain goat. V.P. and I followed, puffing like a couple of locomotives. We reached the top and stepped over to a promontory which commanded a sweeping view over three cardinal points of the compass. V.P. plopped down on a rock, drew out a pair of binoculars, raised them to his eyes and moved them ever so slowly across the scape.

Even without binoculars, I was enthralled by the raw grandeur of the vista. To the northward, unbroken ice covering Hochstetter Bay reflected and magnified the glare of the midnight sun. To the east and south, deep fiords and the sea beyond were etched in indigo with bergs and floes drifting aimlessly like curds of milk on an inky surface.

I drew a sharp breath. *A battleship*—out there beyond Little Pendulum Island—slowly stealing southward.

Could it be the German *Von Tirpitz?* It looked like her!

Wartime regulations compelled us to study the silhouettes of every type of enemy ship and airplane, and we had looked at a miniature outline of the *Von Tirpitz* so often that I suspect we were as familiar with her appearance as the Krauts themselves.

A narrow ridge of mountains which formed Little Pendulum Island hid the formidable capital ship from those aboard our own *Northland* lying complacently beneath us.

I could not help, in that anxious moment, but admire the tactical skill of a hostile captain. He was keeping his ship off our radar scope by remaining behind the mountains of Little Pendulum. When he rounded Cape Desbrowe he would be unmasked, but with mighty guns poised he would pour on a few devastating salvos and blast the unsuspecting *Northland* out of existence!

Breathlessly I gripped V.P.'s arm and pointed to the menacing dark gray hull.

"Well, I'll be—!" V.P. said. "It's a dark berg! Take my glasses and see for yourself."

I took his binoculars for a close-up view.

V.P. continued, "Those black bergs can be deceiving at a distance because they always look like something familiar. Stefansson says to use your glasses for at least fifteen minutes in the Arctic before you draw any conclusions—or words to that effect. It's a good rule."

Lieutenant von Rosenvinge drew up, dragging one foot after the other and panting heavily. He removed his rucksack from his shoulders, spread it for a pillow, flopped down and rolled over on his side. Suddenly he sprang to his feet and pointed inland, down a little slope. "There's something you missed!"

Perhaps fifty yards from where we stood a camouflaged tent was pitched. It blended so cleverly with the surrounding boulders that it was difficult to identify even at that close range. Three Mauser rifles were carefully stacked in front.

We approached cautiously and peeked inside the tent. It was patently an observation post, equipped with a telephone, rations, sleeping bags and a primus stove. Three heavy German military overcoats were laid out with meticulous care beside the other gear as though awaiting inspection. The discovery of this observation post and so much other material left behind lent credence to our supposition that the enemy might have been evacuated by aircraft. But this was pure conjecture, and the element of doubt still existed.

We continued our march along the ridge until we reached a breach in the basalt wall. Then Von Rosenvinge, who was in the van, made some remark about reclining in the shade of a tree. Actually his comment was about twenty million years too late, for we had wandered into the midst of a petrified forest!

Logs, stumps and fragments of what once had been trees lay about in the chaos of a ravaged woodland. What catastrophe in the distant Pre-Pliocene had leveled these trees and eventually turned them to stone? As sailors, we did not know; but we did know we were seeing with our own eyes proof that Greenland once had been tropical—or certainly a far warmer region than it is today. The nearest trees now are on Iceland—and only on the north coast. Even there they are rare.

We returned to the ridge of basalt. The fiord scene below had changed completely in little more than an hour. Gone was the dark blue of open water. In its place a white mosaic of ice covered the surface of Pendulum Strait.

I grabbed the binoculars and looked anxiously for the *Northland*. She was nowhere in sight. Maybe the ice had crushed her when it moved in! I was worried.

"Your ship is in good hands," V.P. observed calmly. "Butcher obviously reached for sea room when he saw the ice crowding in. There's nothing for us to do but go back to the observation post. We'll have some breakfast, get some shut-eye and wait for Butcher. He'll be able to bring the ship back before long." He turned to Niels. "How long do you think it will take Melvin Jensen and the landing force to comb this north end of the island?"

The Dane thought awhile, then replied, "They should be finished before supper tonight."

"O.K.," V.P. said. "We'll get them back aboard tonight and search the south half of the island tomorrow." He then told me that, with the troops and bluejackets aboard the *Northland* once more, we should sail at midnight for Walrus Island off the south end of Sabine. Anchored in the lee of Walrus by morning, we would again disembark the troops and bluejackets for a sweep over Sabine Island to Hansa Bay.

Back at the German observation post we opened up our supply of K-rations and then turned in after a quick meal. Sometime later I was awakened by the wail of a newborn wind swooping down from the north.

I looked out of the tent. The sky was clouded and threatening, and flurries of fine snow were swirling through the air. I rushed to the vantage point on the promontory.

In the fading visibility I could see no ice in Pendulum Strait except two grounded bergs lying close to shore. Behind them the *Northland* rode serenely at anchor. I looked at my watch, noted the second hand ticking. Only about two hours had elapsed since we had gazed on an ice-packed fiord. I recalled V.P.'s words: "Ice is where you find it!"

# Chapter 4

# THE FORCE OF CORIOLI

THE ice moved out of Pendulum Strait within two hours, and Butcher returned with the *Northland*. We got the troops and bluejackets aboard by nightfall, then got under way for Walrus Island according to plan.

Thus far there had been no sign of the enemy, other than his abandoned stores and equipment. But we were on the verge of two more discoveries which proved more puzzling than helpful.

Niels Jensen made the first of these when he went ashore at Germania Havn. On the beach Niels found his old boss sledge dog Tykke, alive, well and overjoyed to see his master again.

Tykke had been captured by the enemy during the skirmish at Eskimonaes in the spring. Had he managed to escape from them? Or had they abandoned him? If they had abandoned him, why? A husky can be a valuable asset on an overland journey in Greenland. And even if this were not the case, soldiers of all armies are inveterate collectors of mascots and pets. If it had been at all possible, we conjectured, the Nazis would have taken Tykke with them when they evacuated.

Where had they gone? How had they gone? If only Tykke could talk, he could probably solve the mystery of Sabine Island.

Before the second discovery turned up, however, I was confronted with an immediate and desperate situation, one which stemmed from a scientific phenomenon and added to my education in ice navigation.

I had turned in for a little nap and was awakened by a soft rap on my stateroom door. "Sir," the messenger said, "Mr. von Rosenvinge says a field of solid *storis* is drifting past the south end of Walrus Island. The wind should fetch it clear of us, but he will keep an eye on it."

"Very well," I mumbled and had barely turned over to get more sleep when I heard another rap on the door. This time it was urgent.

"Sir," the messenger said anxiously, "Mr. von Rosenvinge wants you quick."

I fairly flew to the bridge. One quick glance made the situation clear. The wind was from the southeast. Close to our starboard side the heavy ice field Von Rosenvinge had reported was bearing down on the ship. This field was perhaps a square mile in area and roughly thirty feet in depth. A corner had apparently grounded on the south point of Walrus Island. Still, it was drawing nearer every second. It seemed to me it should be drifting before the wind. Why, then, this erratic behavior? There was no time now to speculate. We must act quickly.

Anticipating our having to get out at once, Von had sent the special sea detail to its stations. Already the anchor was being hove in. And now the ice field was brushing the ship's side, forcing her slowly toward the rocky Walrus Island shore.

I tried to calculate. The anchor was planted in twenty-one fathoms of water to seventy-five fathoms of chain. It would take at least ten minutes to break out. Would there be time? I glanced over our port side. The bold rocks along the shore were getting closer. Our exit to southward was blocked. We would have to maneuver around to escape to the north end of the island. Ten minutes was not time enough!

I ordered the officer of the deck to spin the ship's head into the field and push—with full power. The attempt failed to halt the steady advance of the ice. Moreover our chain was fouled now. The windlass strained, then ground to a stop. The anchor detail threw on a deck stop to hold the chain secure.

"Leadsmen aft!" Von shouted. The men left the chains and raced to the fantail. The lead was cast astern. Von jangled the telegraphs to full-speed-astern. The vessel shot aft. The chain slackened and stretched taut. The ship jerked to a near-stop, then began dragging the anchor protestingly astern, and the *Northland* continued to move slowly toward the rocks at her rear.

"Half three!" the leadsman shouted. It was time to stop.

Before sternboard was completely checked, a dull thud from under the stern told us the ship had backed into rocks. The stop was thrown off the anchor chain, and the windlass began heaving it in. *Clink! Clink! Clink!* Link after link came pouring through the hawse. It seemed tantalizingly slow.

I gave orders to prepare for slipping the anchor chain. Lieutenant Rolfe Hallencrutz, chief engineer of the *Northland,* appeared to anticipate my wishes. He rushed to the forecastle with an acetylene torch. Again the ice was upon us. It appeared as though we had lost the race. To slip the cable was all we could do. Yet I hated to lose a bower anchor. It might mean the difference between success and failure for the expedition.

Von threw the engines to full-speed-ahead. The rudder was put hard right. The ship pivoted dizzily to starboard, then fetched to with a jerk on the anchor chain.

"Slip!" I told Von hoarsely. The OOD repeated the order.

Hallencrutz, his burning torch in hand, protested with gestures. "Please, sir," he pleaded, "let me cut the chain. You've got five hundred and fifty dollars' worth in the chain locker. I'll save the government that much money."

I could not suppress a laugh. "Hold everything!" I told Von. Coast Guard poverty in bygone years had indeed left its mark on my chief engineer.

The OOD jerked the telegraphs to stop and ordered the detail to heave 'round again. After a few turns Ensign Maurice Rucker, in charge of the detail, shouted joyously, "Anchor's aweigh!"

The ship was headed the right direction—to the north—to get out of her trap. But there was a very narrow span of water separating the threatening field from an ice foot or ledge of shore-fast ice. Lieutenant (j.g.) Dorris Bell in the motor surfboat was already sounding through this gap. "Three and a half!" he signaled. Three and a half fathoms of water! We might still make it. Von rang up half-speed-ahead and pointed the bows for this exit.

"Goose 'er, Von!" I shouted. The OOD looked puzzled. "Goose 'er!" I repeated. "Haven't you ever goosed anyone?"

"Only old ladies, Captain," Von answered, moving the telegraph to full-speed-ahead. "The *Northland's* old, but she ain't no lady!"

The ship sprang toward the thin margin of water, now filled with brash. She crashed into it and calved off part of the ice footing. Still, she squirmed on, but with slackening speed. A dull bump under keel told me she was sliding over a rock.

"Rock your rudder!" I yelled. The helmsman shifted his rudder slowly from port to starboard. The ship gathered speed. After a few agonizing seconds we were through—and safe.

A few hours later we were back at our Sabine Island anchorage. Squad by squad, bluejackets and troops filed onto the ice footing opposite the ship. We began ferrying them aboard. At length Von Paulsen and Jensen arrived. With them was a nondescript stranger whose weary eyes and unkempt beard gave some hint of the hardships he must have endured.

"Who's your friend?" I asked V.P.

"Assistant Surgeon Rudolph Sensse of the German Navy," Von Paulsen answered. "We found him sitting complacently on a rock during our sweep across the island. Guess he was waiting to be captured."

V.P. had questioned the prisoner at some length in German. Scraps of information linked with inference pieced together a story like this:

Dr. Sensse was the Gestapo man of the Sabine Island garrison. He was responsible, not to Lieutenant Ritter, but to some higher echelon of command. His job was to bring back information about the land and the people who lived in it. Sensse had been ranging over northeast Greenland when Colonel Balchen bombed the Sabine Island installation. He had been south as far as Scoresby Sound. Returning to Sabine Island, he attempted to drive his dog team across Clavering Strait. His dog team plunged through the melting ice, carrying his sledge with it.

The doctor managed at length to make his way to Hansa Bay, only to find that his comrades were gone. He had seen the *Northland* arrive and the landing force disembark and advance on Hansa Bay. Finally he had decided to give himself up rather than face starvation.

I had the prisoner placed under guard and quartered him in the sick bay. Next I related to Von Paulsen the incident of the charging ice.

"You've learned another lesson—the hard way," V.P. commented. "Maybe I should have told you. In the northern hemisphere ice always drifts to the *right* of the course of the wind—about forty degrees in this latitude. The phenomenon is called Corioli's force. It's the deflecting force of the earth's rotation."

# Chapter 5

# PERILOUS ROUTE
# TO ZACKENBERG

V.P. HAD a theory. He reasoned that if Dr. Sensse's companions—the German Sabine Island force—had not been evacuated by plane, they would have retreated northward and established themselves at some predetermined place to await a relief ship from Norway.

Following out this line of reasoning, our task-unit commander concluded that the Hochstetter Bay region, immediately north of Sabine Island, would have been selected for such a rendezvous. If this were the case, it was evident the enemy would be pinned down for some time to come. Hochstetter Bay was solid with impenetrable ice. There was no possibility at the moment of any ship—an enemy vessel or our own *Northland*—making an entrance. Once the ice broke up, however, the situation would be altogether different. We could then conduct a search—and, of course, an enemy vessel could attempt a rescue of the Nazi force.

Meanwhile we could—and should—be getting on with our work in and around Gael Hamke's Bay to the southward. It was there, as well as in Hochstetter Bay, that we were to establish the Greenland Army and stock a number of its stations with supplies.

There was a chance, of course, that the ice in Hochstetter Bay would break up while we were working in the vicinity of Gael

Hamke's. For this reason V.P. decided to set up an observation post ashore and man it with a small force from the *Northland's* company. This group would keep the Hochstetter area under surveillance. If they saw any indication of a breakup or had any intelligence of an enemy vessel approaching, they would contact the *Northland* by radio, and we would come up from Gael Hamke's at our best possible speed.

A careful consideration of the nature of the terrain indicated Pendulum Island as the spot best situated for observation purposes. The northern end of this island rises steeply from the sea, and its 700-foot elevation commands a view across the entrance of Hochstetter Bay between Bass Rock, an islet adjacent to Pendulum, and Cape Philip Broke on Shannon Island.

V.P. apprized me of this plan after he had completed his questioning of Dr. Sensse. He instructed me to proceed with the establishment of the observation post as soon as ice conditions permitted.

In the interest of saving gasoline for J2F-5 I took Mr. Harmon, the ship's navigator, ashore with me to make an ice reconnaissance from the heights of Mount Germania on Sabine Island. We had a good view of the ice and waters surrounding Pendulum Island and spotted a lead inshore which ran the full length of the seaward side. With this encouraging information we returned to the *Northland* and got underway.

It was 10:00 P.M. on July 24 when the ship arrived off the channel separating Bass Rock from the northern end of Pendulum Island. V.P. announced that Bass Rock should not be overlooked as a possible enemy hiding place.

Since the islet was accessible to a landing force by a short trip on foot across the ice, we disembarked troops and bluejackets under Captain Melvin Jensen, USA. But this search proved fruitless, as Jensen and his men made a thorough investigation of the entire islet and the two cabins which the Danish government had erected there many years ago. In one of these cabins, incidentally, Ejnar Mikkelsen and a companion had lived for two years while awaiting rescue after their ship, the *Alabama,* had been crushed in the ice in 1910.*

After the return of the landing force we set about the business of

---

* See *Lost in the Arctic,* by Ejnar Mikkelsen.

putting the observation party ashore on Pendulum Island. The weather, meanwhile, had taken a sudden turn for the worse. A northerly wind, springing up quickly, darkened the skies and soon brought a heavy snowfall.

As the motor surfboat left the ship's side I could not help but feel a pang of sympathy for Ensign Martin O'Hara and his four men who comprised the observation group. The night was raw and dismal, and, although Mr. O'Hara and his men were warmly clad, the prospect of groping up the steep sides of Pendulum Island, burdened with radio equipment and supplies and lashed by a bitter wind and a stinging snowfall, was certainly not a cheerful one.

The motor surfboat returned at 2:15 A.M. After hoisting it in we got under way once more, feeling our way southward along the island wall, bound for Gael Hamke's Bay.

A blanket of snow swept past the stacks and swirled about the bridge, bringing with it the unmistakable smell of fuel oil—an odor inevitably present on the bridge when the ship raced before a gale. Occasional gusts of wind played a howling crescendo on the rigging. At such times we scarcely could see beyond the bridge rail. But then, as the wind's cry diminished to a dull moan and the thick, driving haze of snowfall momentarily lightened, we could sight the shadowy cliffs of Wollaston Foreland near by on our starboard hand.

Closer by on our port hand—very much closer by—was ice: hard, polar ice in compact fields. Sizable floes which had been detached from these fields and blown into the narrow channel of open water loomed here and there ahead of the ship.

The floes, so haphazardly strewed across our course, gave Mr. Harmon, the officer of the deck, considerable concern as he peered anxiously through the clear-vision (rotary) window. Now and then he snapped a sharp order to the wheel and the ship suddenly swerved off to avoid a collision. Normally we would have taken things slowly. But this was no time for caution! Astern, the northerly blow was pushing a wall' of ice ever closer to shore, shutting off our retreat. *We had to go ahead.* And we had to go at full speed, for there was danger of the compacted fields on our port hand moving in across our bow, piling up against the shore and blocking the way, before we reached Cape Borlase Warren. Once around the cape, we expected to be out of trouble, for we could scurry into the safer, spacious waters of Gael Hamke's Bay.

Borlase Warren had a reputation for treachery. Because of this, I knew I was undertaking an imprudent thing by making a go for it in a gale. But the *Northland* had a heavy work schedule. Ice conditions in Hochstetter Bay precluded, for the present, a search for the enemy or stocking the Greenland Army huts in the area. Therefore, I reasoned, it was logical to move down to Gael Hamke's and go to work rather than remain idle while we awaited favorable ice to the north.

This had seemed sensible to me a few hours ago. But now—with the life of my ship threatened by treacherous wind and ice crowding us close to shore in unsurveyed waters—I was beginning to doubt whether my reasoning would prevail before a general court-martial, if the *Northland* foundered.

Up until now I had been aware of a tall figure huddled against the forecastle bulwarks. I recognized him as our passenger, Corporal Hans Jensen of the Greenland Army. He was to be set ashore at Gael Hamke's Bay with a stock of supplies and the twenty-one sledge dogs quartered on our deck.

Hans was preoccupied and unmindful of the swirling snow and the muffled chant of the leadsmen perched in the chains. To my sailor's mind it was unbelievable that anyone could be so disinterested in such a vital matter as the depth of the water through which we were slipping at full speed.

On the bridge-wing I drew my parka about me as I watched each of the lead lines zoom thrice through the zenith of its arc before the leadsmen made their casts into the frothy water immediately ahead. I cupped my ear to catch the report from the man in the starboard chain.

"By the mark five!" the man called, announcing we were in thirty feet of water.

I darted across to the port better to hear the leadsman on that side. "An'na quarter five!" the man shouted.

This meant slightly more than five fathoms of depth, perhaps thirty-two feet at the most. I knew, of course, that the *Northland* drew nineteen feet, and I thought to myself: *This is too damned shallow for unsurveyed waters!*

As the leadsmen coiled their lines for the next soundings my eyes returned to Corporal Jensen. In sixty-odd years of life he had mastered but two words of the English language, acquiring these only since sailing in the *Northland*. The words were "chow" and "down." I still believe they had been impressed on Hans more by instinct than by learning, for "Chow Down" is the Navy announcement that food is ready to be served on the mess deck.

The crew referred to Corporal Jensen as "Trader Horn" because, though beardless, he had a striking resemblance in other ways to the original of that name. He was a hunter. He also was a hermit in the classic sense, a stoic who kept to himself and minded his own business: feeding and caring for the Greenland Army's dogs.

I suspected Hans had been miserably unhappy away from the isolation of northeast Greenland. He wanted nothing more, I'm sure, than to return to the lonely surroundings he knew and loved so well. There he could serve his only lord, master and idol, the Greenland Army's commander in chief, Captain Niels O. Jensen.

If all went well, Hans would soon have his wish fulfilled. We were to put him ashore at Zackenberg, the location of a Greenland Army hut several miles inside Young's Sound, which is an arm of Gael Hamke's Bay. Knowing this, knowing he was almost home, he was preoccupied and seemingly unaware of the driving snow, bitter cold and warning calls of the leadsmen.

Watching Hans now and then and occasionally thinking of the life he had lived set me to comparing him with Ensign O'Hara and the *Northland's* four men at the observation post on Pendulum Island. How much better fitted by experience and temperament was Hans for such duty. It must be dreadfully cold and uncomfortable for our men and somewhat terrifying, too—perched up there on that rocky promontory 700 feet above sea level and sheltered only by a tent in this young blizzard. Yet I had every confidence in Mr. O'Hara, a game little officer with a keen intellect and a quick Irish wit. If anyone could carry out the task, he could.

I was thinking of Mr. O'Hara when a report from the radarman jolted me back to our immediate situation.

"Cape Borlase Warren! Range, five hundred yards—slightly on the starboard bow, sir!"

My heart sank at that. Then when a few more propeller beats brought the ghostly aura of the ice into view and I saw an undulating line of foam licking at the rocky shore I knew we were in a fine kettle of fish. There was ice right up to the cape! Our chances of getting by looked slim.

"Mr. Harmon!" I called. But no order was necessary. The officer of the deck had anticipated my course of action and given a slight change of rudder to the helmsman.

"I'm heading her over now, Captain," Mr. Harmon said. Then he called to the helmsman, "Now steady her where that floe joins the main pack!"

A big floe was jammed between the pack of polar ice and the rocks at the foot of the cape. Fortunately the pack and the floe did not seem to be welded together. To us on the bridge there appeared to be a narrow crack between the two. Somehow we must pry our way through that crack—if there was enough water to float the ship.

"An'na half four!" the starboard leadsman shouted.

Four and one-half fathoms, approximately twenty-seven feet of depth. With the *Northland* drawing nineteen feet we would have only inches to spare!

I began to have my doubts about getting through and looked around for V.P. But the task-unit commander had slipped away. When I finally spotted him he was on the forecastle with two gunner's mates huddled close by. The three were taping the terminal connections to a wrecking mine, a fifty-four pounder, preparatory to blasting, if necessary. I looked aft and saw the plane crew already drawing the heavy protective tarpaulin over our J2F-5.

The forthcoming battle promised to be like the one we had been through at Walrus Island, except that the floe now blocking our way was much harder than the shore-fast ice back there at Walrus.

Mr. Harmon gently nosed the vessel into the crack and called for full power.

The leadsmen had their lines coiled and were blowing on their hands to warm them. Unable to drop their leads into the water, they watched the ice directly beneath their feet as the ship pried alternately right and left.

There was a nerve-racking grating under the keel as the bottom scraped across rocks. I imagine I must have had a weak grin on my face as I tried to find some humor in the situation by thinking that the rocks were harder on the barnacles fouling our bottom than they were on the *Northland's* steel plating.

The ship slowed almost to a standstill and then slipped free. But it was evident her momentum had been spent, for she dragged slowly to a full stop even though her propeller churned wildly with every ounce of power the engine room could give us.

Now we *were* in a fix!

Mr. Harmon looked at me appealingly. There was no water, no film of slush and brash, between the ship and the ice. Instead there was the compacted field on the port side, the big flow jammed tightly against the shore on the starboard side—and the *Northland* was wedged solidly between the two, caught in the jaws of a mighty, tightening vise.

"Just keep her turning over at full speed," I said to Mr. Harmon with a confidence I did not feel.

I stepped to the bridge-wing and looked for V.P. He and the gunner's mates were already on the ice, receiving a mine being lowered from the deck. With the charge safely in their hands they scooted about thirty-five feet beyond the bows and lowered it into the crack we were trying to slew through.

*He'll blow the bow off the ship!* I thought. But this was not new business to V.P. He knew what he was doing.

After one of the gunner's mates had driven an iron spike into the ice and secured the holding line which kept the mine at the most advantageous depth the three returned aboard. The ship remained motionless all this while, though her propeller still was churning at full power.

V. P. gave us the highsign. We piped all-hands-clear and threw the switch. There was a muffled roar ahead. Then chunks of ice rained down on the ship—*and we were moving!*

True, we barely were inching along, but our speed gradually was accelerating. Blasting had saved us again. I breathed a prayer of thanks for having a boss who not only knew that ice is where you find it, but knew how to cope with it after you've found it!

Free of the ice vise and with Cape Borlase Warren astern, the

*Northland* wove among large floes separated by fairly wide avenues of water. Here in the shelter of mountains towering above us on the north shore of Gael Hamke's Bay the gale subsided to a temperamental breeze. Overhead, patches of blue peeked through racing clouds.

We set a course for Sand Island. Rather, we set a course for where Sand Island was presumed to be. Even under favorable conditions this islet, which is little more than a shoal, can rarely be seen except at very close range. But unless it *is* seen, a ship is not likely to enter Young's Sound without mishap, for the islet is situated more or less squarely in the mouth of the sound.

Today—as I was to learn to my chagrin and also to the advancement of my knowledge of Arctic navigation—Sand Island was covered with snow and engulfed in an unbroken field of fiord ice.

We were steaming at six knots with a quartermaster chanting soundings to the rasp of an obstreperous fathometer. His voice was mechanical, routine. "Twenty! . . . Twenty-one! . . . Nineteen!" he called, giving the depth of the water in fathoms as he read the recordings. No one on the bridge paid much attention. Depths such as these gave us ample water under our keel.

"*S-seven!*" the quartermaster announced nervously.

At this sudden indication of shoal water the bridge became tense, alert.

"*Five!*" the quartermaster called anxiously.

The officer of the deck leaped to the telegraph and drew back the handle to full-speed-astern.

"The fathometer does not register, sir!" the quartermaster cried.

The screw current suddenly became very muddy. Then a violent jerk threw us off our feet, and the bows vaulted under the impact of the forefoot plowing into bottom sand.

When I got to my feet I ordered the engines stopped. They were getting us nowhere, for we were hard-and-fast aground. And with the engines running under such conditions we were likely filling our injection with ruinous, emerylike silt.

There was nothing we could do except sit and wait for high tide.

*Suppose the tide is high now!* I suddenly thought. Knowing we might never get off if that were the case, I hurriedly fanned the pages

Capt. Niels O. Jensen and Lieut. Harmon examine ruins of Sledge Patrol station at Eskimonaes.

Conference on shore, Eskimonaes.

Laying the foundation for the direction-finder structure, Jan Mayen.

Only a narrow stretch of beach separates North Lagoon from the sea.

of the *Nautical Almanac* and *Bowditch's American Practical Navigator,* nervously making computations.

I finally closed the books with a bang. We were O.K —but I had learned something else. We must watch our tides carefully and avoid navigating uncharted waters at high tide. Aground at high water, we might never get off.

The shock of striking bottom had aroused V.P., who was taking a nap in our stateroom. When he came onto the bridge he looked about and called for a boat.

"I'll take Niels and a few men ashore yonder," he told me. "We'll walk up the fiord to Sandotten and bury Eli Knudsen's remains. After you get afloat you might try breaking through the fiord ice to the Greenland Army hut a couple of miles up the sound. You can pick us up there. We won't be back for supper," he concluded, patting his shotgun.

"Won't you need picks and shovels?" I asked.

"No use. The frost line is less than a foot deep here. We couldn't dig a grave. We'll cover Knudsen's body with rocks. That is, we will if the Krauts didn't leave it where the wolves could have a feast. By the way, Skipper, have you heard from O'Hara?"

"No, sir. Can't get through to him," I answered. "Probably on account of the storm outside."

"Hmm. Maybe."

Within an hour the rising tide lifted the *Northland* clear of the shoal on which she was aground. We felt our way cautiously to the south end of Sand Island and started into Young's Sound. Here we ran into solid fiord ice—about three feet thick. It was quite rotten, however, and had the appearance of Swiss cheese. I decided to try breaking through and charged at it with full power.

After the first jab at the ice the *Northland* made virtually no progress. The groove we were trying to lengthen rapidly filled with seething debris, hissing defiance at each lunge.

This was odd, I thought, because the ice should crack easily between the holes which honeycombed it. I hated to call quits, but we were accomplishing nothing. We'd jab, stop and bounce, jab, stop and bounce again. It was like trying to stab an India-rubber man.

Eight bells martialed the first watch to the bridge. Lieutenant von

Rosenvinge, assuming the duties of officer of the deck, led the procession of reports. The relieved OOD pointed to the abortive slice we had cut out of the ice and informed Von Rosenvinge we were getting ready to anchor.

"Captain," Von Rosenvinge said to me solemnly when he had taken the deck, "may I send for an office desk and a swivel chair?"

Before continuing with the conversation which followed this absurd request it probably is necessary to explain briefly the already evident familiarity between the lieutenant and myself, a familiarity which extended to V.P.

Both of us—V.P. and I—had taken a warm personal liking to Von Rosenvinge and appreciated his brilliant mind and his particular brand of humor. As his seniors we had broken down to some extent the usual barriers between officers of the various ranks. This could be done with safety in Von Rosenvinge's case, for he had more than enough good common horse sense to observe the proper decorum at the proper time.

"Well, slap my top and call me 'Cappy,' " I mocked. "Why do you want a desk and a swivel chair?"

"If you please, sir, I just want a cozy place to sit while I learn to compute tides."

"Extraordinary, Holmes," I said. "But why?"

"Elementary, sir," Von Rosenvinge answered. "I'm just a lawyer in a sailor's suit, but I always observed before you came aboard and took command that we broke ice against the tide, the current or the wind. Maybe breaking *against* the tide—or *against* the current or *against* the wind—keeps your channel clear of ice so that you don't have to punch at a cushion."

"You damned juris juggler," I growled. "Instead of beating around the bush, why didn't you come right out and tell me I'd forgotten one of the fundamental rules of ice breaking?"

I stomped off the bridge in feigned disgust, but, truthfully, my disgust was partly real. In my eagerness to make up the time we had lost while aground on Sand Island I had overlooked the obvious. The tide was running with us. Consequently the ice we broke piled up ahead of our bows instead of washing astern. We would have to wait until the tide began ebbing, or until we had a wind from dead ahead.

Either the ebbing tide or a wind from ahead would carry the broken ice past us, keeping our channel clear as we progressed.

It was a strange sensation the following morning—like soaring over a sea of clouds, a sea spread between massive mountain walls beneath a sky of spotless blue. In the distance ahead Mount Zackenberg rose majestically above the flat sea cloud which covered Young's Sound to bridge level. Its snow-capped peak and eastern face were turned to cherry red by the crimson glow of rising sun. *Like a strawberry sundae,* I thought.

We had lain overnight at Sandotten. Breaking through the mile or so of fiord ice at the entrance to the sound had been easy work, once the tide started to ebb.

Captain Von Paulsen and party found that Knudsen had already been buried—mysteriously so, in a remarkably fine grave. (We learned later that Dr. Sensse paid this final tribute to a brave man.) Relieved of its morbid task, the party had gone to work with shotguns. The boat bearing them to the ship was filled to the gunwales with ducks and wild geese.

As the sun mounted higher and burned away the sheet of fog I noticed the familiar figure of Trader Horn standing in the eyes of the ship, his gaze fixed ahead. He may have been drinking in the emerald grandeur of Zackenberg Valley, with its purple flakes of lichen blossoms, its glistening threads of sparkling streams. I suspect, though, he was looking for the little hut our chart showed should lie near the shore at the base of the mountain. That little shack was home to Hans. And no home-coming of a prodigal to his loved ones could have meant more than a return to Zackenberg to Corporal Jensen.

Now, as we neared the shore, he did a strange thing. Wheeling abruptly about, he motioned us to go back. While no soundings were charted, the fathometer showed twenty-one fathoms—plenty of water—so I hadn't the slightest idea of the purpose of his wild gesticulation.

Mr. Butcher had the con; he jerked the annunciator handles back to full-astern and shouted to let go the anchor. The chain was rattling out through the hawse when the forefoot struck a submarine ledge with an impact that nearly sent us sprawling. The *Northland's* bows rose high, while her stern settled to a sickening drag. For several minutes the propeller throbbed madly in a futile effort to back her off. I realized with a shock the tide should be forenoon high! And we were stuck!

"Heave 'round!" Butcher ordered quietly. The anchor cable straightened in an after lead. The windlass groaned and stopped.

"Mark five!" from the leadsman. Five fathoms under the sounding position. The shelf must be quite steep.

Forward, the men fitted capstan bars to the windlass and bent their weight against them. That did it! Slowly the vessel slid into deep water and bobbed onto normal trim.

I lost no time telling Captain Niels Jensen how his corporal had saved my ship. Without a timely full-astern bell she would have grounded hard and fast, probably never have gotten off.

"He remembered the time the *Polar Bjorn* did the same thing," said the Danish captain. "Luckily the *Godthaab* was here to pull her off. You'll always find alluvial deposits off drainage basins in this part of Greenland. Shun them as you would the devil."

I sat right down and made an appropriate entry in the ship's standing orders. Now to get Trader Horn and his dogs ashore!

# Chapter 6

## I MAKE A BET WITH V.P.

*A bull will never attack a man unless the man is showing red.*

My mind kept repeating this old wives' tale as I raced down a mountainside with a half-ton of enraged beast charging after me.

I wasn't showing him red. If I was showing any color, it was yellow—for I was genuinely frightened and wishing I had brought a rifle from the ship instead of a camera. Likely, though, I would have disposed of the rifle as I had disposed of the camera—flung it aside in order to run with my speed unhampered by excess gear.

That morning, shortly after Corporal Hans Jensen and his dogs had been put ashore, V.P. had decided to send a patrol across country to Cape Berlin. It was a job for a couple of soldiers. But two American lads, turned loose on their own in this part of the world, would be like babes in the wood. Therefore Hans was directed to accompany them as a guide.

One of the *Northland's* men—a member of the Brooklyn Fire Department before the war—volunteered to substitute for Hans and carry on with the Dane's Greenland Army duties while he was off with our patrol.

This man's job would not be easy. In addition to feeding and caring for the twenty-one dogs he must tend a gill net which Hans had rigged across the mouth of a river discharging into Young's Sound. Salmon were running in big schools. Consequently the net would have to be emptied frequently. Moreover the man was required to clean, salt and barrel the fish for the use of the Greenland Army's men and dogs during the coming winter.

The soldiers detailed to make the patrol watched the old Dane packing his rucksack, their young faces unable to conceal their contempt and pity. "We'll have to carry our own packs and the old man's, too, before we get back," one complained.

"You said it!" the other grumbled. "And we'll have to carry *him*, besides!"

Hans could not have understood their words, but he must have sensed the meaning of their grousing. He paused, gave them a withering look and then resumed his packing.

The little reconnaissance patrol disappeared among the rocks and lichens on its march across the peninsula. The day was clear, sunny and baseballish. When half the *Northland's* crew received permission to go ashore for exercise the younger men welcomed the opportunity to play a few innings.

Someone mentioned a musk-ox hunt. This caused the older men to take notice, and there was a rush to the armory to draw rifles. As a member of this latter group, but lacking the fortitude to kill even a chicken, I drew a camera. Of actual hunting—stalking or tracking, that is—there was little to be done. It is easy to spot musk oxen in northeast Greenland almost any place where moss grows in sufficient quantity to satisfy their dietary requirements. No trees or brush offer the big, lumbering animals concealment. The hunter need only look for black dots against the slopes. If these move slowly from time to time, the hunter knows he has located a grazing herd. The actual shooting is about as much sport as killing a steer in a slaughterhouse. If there is any art at all in taking the beasts, it lies in enticing them close to your boats while they still are on the hoof. Otherwise the hunter may have to lug the half-ton carcasses several miles over difficult terrain.

Captain Niels O. Jensen thoroughly understood the business of luring the animals to any desired spot, as did Tykke. Together Niels and Tykke climbed uphill toward a herd we had sighted a mile or so away from the beach. I tagged along to photograph the activity. Meanwhile the riflemen formed an ambuscade near our boats by taking positions behind boulders on both sides of a gulley.

The herd paused in its grazing when Niels, Tykke and I approached. Ramlike horns flashed toward us as the bulls snorted and stomped the ground with their forefeet. A coat of long, shaggy hair conceals the profile of the musk ox's body. To say they have the appearance of a freak of Nature is putting it mildly.

Tykke began his canine chore. Dashing into the herd, he snapped at the cows and calves, rounding them up into a compact group. The bulls faced the danger by forming a defensive semicircle in front of these weaker members of their families.

While the dog darted nimbly at the flanks of the bulls, Niels slipped to the rear. I was supposed to go with him. But I chose to stand at a little distance atop a knoll where I felt I could get better snapshots.

Tykke was fast and skillful, adroitly dodging as one or another of the bulls occasionally made a short, sudden lunge in an attempt to horn him.

With everything in readiness Niels fired his pistol into the air, and the stampede was on! Tykke rushed down the ravine toward the waiting riflemen with the entire herd thundering after him—except one bull.

This creature, apparently having a mind of his own, made toward me with an ominous snort. I trotted off to one side. The bull changed course accordingly, and I realized the big brute really *was* after *me!*

I felt wobbly in the legs, but managed to move off a little more to one side. In my boyhood I had read books whose heroes were skilled and fearless hunters. These supermen knew precisely how to handle such a situation. They would merely slip around the animal and sever a tendon in one of his hind legs. I had my sheath knife in its case on my belt, but I could think of only one thing to do. And that probably was the worst thing. *I ran!*

Soon my feet and legs were growing very heavy. I was gasping for breath. From the increasing loudness of the thundering hoofs I knew that the distance between the bull and me was closing rapidly. Worst of all, my flight was diverging from the stampeding herd and the armed men who could save me.

Should I take a chance and cut sharply to the right in an effort to get within range of the rifles? This seemed my only hope. Nevertheless I dodged behind a rock, changed direction abruptly, then glanced back. Maybe the bull couldn't turn very quickly.

He either couldn't or wouldn't, for he made no turn at all. Very likely I had had only a temporary fascination for him. But my vanity wasn't a bit injured as I saw him galloping downhill without the slightest change in his course.

I lay down on the moss and gulped air. Then Niels drew up, puffing heavily. "My pistol jammed after that first shot," Niels explained. "I followed you while I was freeing it, but you and your friend got out of range. It's best to give these creatures a wide berth unless you are armed. Sometimes they're unpredictable."

"Amen!" I panted.

That evening we had raw musk-ox-burgers garnished with raw egg, served by Von Rosenvinge in the accepted mode of northeast Greenland. I was somewhat concerned at first about eating uncooked meat, but my fears were overcome when I learned that in uncontaminated northeast Greenland the bodies of animals are totally free of disease-carrying parasites. Their meat can be safely eaten raw—and, in the case of musk ox, eaten with more enjoyment than when it is cooked.

V.P. attended our dinner. Impaling a juicy morsel on his fork, he looked at it and asked distractedly, "Von Rosenvinge, you damned shyster, answer this one for me. Why is it, with all those good-looking cows present, that bull chased the skipper instead of one of the ladies?"

"The answer is very simple, sir," Von Rosenvinge said. "It must have been a lady bull!"

"Ah! Shed-dup!" I growled, and changed the conversation.

I can't recall now the topic I hit on to divert the others from my "bull fight"—or bull *flight,* as they were calling it. Whatever the topic was, it led to another. Then, in the rambling fashion of many dinner-table conversations, *that* led to another. Sooner or later we got around to one of V.P.'s favorite subjects: discipline. He lectured us for several minutes.

A ship's crew, especially in the Arctic, must wage a never-ending battle with the elements, V.P. said. Every member of her company must subordinate his ego to the good of all. But with too much discipline a ship's rank and file loses all initiative. The men become

The armed German trawler *Externestiene* cornered in the Greenland ice pack.

Predawn roundup of German prisoners, Little Koldewey, Northeast Greenland.

so dependent on their officers that they won't raise a hand in self-preservation unless given an order by someone with gold lace on his sleeve.

V.P. summed up his theories in words to this effect: Disciplinary training must cultivate teamwork and strict obedience to orders among the members of a ship's crew. But discipline is never fully effective unless the men realize that the officers who give the orders are capable of carrying them out themselves. And the officers must demonstrate that they *are* capable of carrying them out. Moreover the officers must inculcate self-reliance in their men—and trust that self-reliance to a certain degree.

Among any group of United States Coast Guard officers a discussion of this nature is bound to touch on two elementary discipline-building exercises which Service Regulations require as weekly drills. These are infantry drill and boat drill. Both are important. Many officers consider one more important than the other, and the relative virtues of each drill have been the basis of heated argument in the service since the eighteenth century.

I mentioned this to V.P., fully knowing he championed boat drill—and knowing he realized I favored infantry drill.

We argued our points.

"Dammit!" V.P. finally said. "There's only one way to find out. The patrol to Cape Berlin won't be back for two days. We'll have to wait here. Take half your crew ashore and drill 'em as infantry. Take the other half and give 'em boat drill. I've got two little round iron men that say you'll come over to my side before this cruise is ended!"

"Taken!" I told him.

I didn't realize at the time that there was a man in the *Northland's* company who would have a more or less direct bearing on the outcome of our bet. This man was Paul J. Travers.

Sometime early in the year 1942 Travers had stood in a long line of naval recruits slowly filing past a classifier's desk. The man with brass buttons behind the desk was sizing up each recruit, recording his history and determining his future in the Navy by perforating cardboard forms with a paper punch.

"Name!" Brass Buttons snapped.

"Travers, sir."

Brass Buttons saw a tall, slender young man with black, curly hair. From a pile beside him he picked up a blank, unpunched cardboard form and scrawled Travers' name and service number across the top. "What's your age, Travers?"

"Twenty-six, sir." Travers answered the routine questions. He was a clerk by occupation. He had studied business administration at Boston College for a year. He hoped to get a rating as storekeeper in the Navy.

Brass Buttons, busy with his punch, seemed unaware of Travers' answers. Abruptly he said, "That's all! Next man!"

Maybe Brass Buttons punched the wrong space. Maybe he was endowed with a spark of genius. I don't know. But after Travers finished "boot" training the Navy sent him to a school and he graduated with high marks as aerographer's mate, third class.

When Travers reported to the *Northland* for duty he found he was a pioneer. There never had been such a rating aboard. Therefore its proper rung on the social scale of the berth deck never had been established.

Travers was Navy. The rest of the men were Coast Guard. This made no difference, for the crew's caste system in both services is equally rigorous. Travers, with his rating unclassified by the enlisted men, circulated freely among all ratings. He was accepted by Jim Sloan, radarman, first class, who was the dean of the berth deck, sage of the forecastle and at the top of the ship's social ladder. At the bottom of the ladder the lowly cooks always had a hearty smile, a cup of coffee and a sandwich ready for Travers. At the same time Travers could carry on intelligent discussions of art with Norman Thomas, specialist, third class, the *Northland's* staff artist, whose paintings of the Arctic scene and of life at sea in wartime were winning acclaim in New York art circles.

There was no organization in the northern latitudes to aid in scientific weather prognosis at the time Travers was with us. It was not until later that we had weather-reporting stations sufficiently far north to supply the necessary information for charting isobars, isotherms, wind vectors and fronts. Consequently we had no use for a trained aerographer. We needed a goose-bone weather prophet.

This was what Travers became as he kept an eye on the clouds, the anemometer and the barograph. Between times he filled in as quartermaster, signalman and even junior officer of the deck.

Travers never volunteered a forecast. But when he was asked for one he delivered it in a most unorthodox manner. The professional meteorologist almost always begins with the word *if*. "*If* the high now central over Squedunk moves east," he will say, "we *may* expect strong northeasterly winds, *provided* the low approaching from the west is not deflected by the mountains."

This was not Travers' way of forecasting. He left no doubt. "It will blow from the north with whole gale force before midnight," he would say.

These were the words I heard from Travers on the morning of August 1, 1943, three days after V.P. and I made our bet.

Meanwhile I had carried out the terms of the bet. While we lay off Zackenberg, half the crew were strenuously exercised at the oars and repeatedly drilled in lowering and hoisting the boats and clearing away and coming alongside.

There is no denying it was hard work. Yet it also was useful work. The men probably didn't appreciate this, however. They must have thought only of their weary muscles and envied their shipmates on shore, who were marching back and forth in the various patterns of formation and frequently breaking into extended order.

This also was hard but useful work. From aboard ship I could hear hear such commands as "By the right flank, march!" or "Column half left, march!" echoing across the fiord all day long. I suspect the boat crews were being envied, too.

At this time I was beginning to feel some concern for Ensign O'Hara and the four men on Pendulum Island. We had instructed them to keep in touch with the ship by radio. Four days had passed since we put them ashore, and there had been no word from them. The stormy weather had undoubtedly interfered with radio reception, but it seemed to me we should have received a signal by this time.

The little reconnaissance patrol guided by Corporal Hans Jensen also added to my uneasiness. According to our reckoning, the three should have been back about noon of this third day since they had left the ship. But noon had passed, and the fiord and valley had been engulfed in the evening shadows for several hours. Still there was no sign of Hans and the two soldiers. Perhaps the youngsters had been right. Hans was getting older, probably no longer capable of enduring a three-day march over difficult country.

It may have been coincidence or I may be psychic, for this is what I was thinking when a messenger knocked on my stateroom door.

"Sir, the officer of the deck says three men on shore are standing this way," the messenger announced.

I hastened to the bridge, broke out my glasses and turned them shoreward. Three figures appeared in the lenses. One was traveling considerably faster than the other two. His pace was sprightly, and he paused now and then for the laggards to catch up.

When the three approached the Greenland Army hut the man in the lead quickened his step and turned toward the dogs tethered near by. He looked them over for a moment. Then without removing his rucksack from his back he turned to several fish barrels, peered inside each one and finally strode to the hut and entered.

Several minutes later a boat came alongside the *Northland*. A soldier climbed unsteadily to the deck and slumped onto a bitt head, exhausted. "Phew!" he said wearily. "We couldn't make old Trader Horn understand what 'slower' and 'stop' meant. And we didn't know the Danish words. We were going to carry *him*. What a joke! What a guy!"

With the two soldiers back aboard—they had found no sign of the enemy, incidentally—we got under way and stood farther up into Young's Sound, coming to anchor off Tyroler Fiord early in the morning of August 1.

On this day we received a dispatch from the *North Star*. She had left Reykjavik, Iceland, five days before—on July 28—to rendezvous with us. But, according to her dispatch, she was beset in the ice near the seventy-fourth parallel. Fortunately the ice was soft; probably she could break out. Her commanding officer, Lieutenant Commander H. T. Diehl, USCG, would have to use his own judgment, V.P. said, and ordered a dispatch to this effect to the big wooden vessel.

There still was no word from Ensign O'Hara. This bothered me. I also was bothered by Travers' weather prophecy that morning: "It will blow from the north with whole gale force before midnight."

As I have said, I do not know how Travers arrived at his prophecies. He had been jokingly accused of uttering eerie quotations from some obscure, occult manuscript and also of keeping a frog in a jar hidden deep in the recesses of his locker.

To date Travers' average was 1,000 per cent. This was why I was disturbed, even though my own weather eye disagreed with him. The day was beautiful with a cloudless blue overhead. Sunlight playing on the multistriped cliffs of Tyroler Fiord added a chromatic polish to their breath-taking splendor. Above these cliffs lofty copper-hued cones vainly tried to hold back the relentless march of inland ice toward the sea.

I say "vainly tried to hold back," for here and there the inland ice in the form of mighty glaciers squeezed through the gaps between those mountainous cones. Over the centuries the glaciers had carved vertical fissures in the sheer walls of rock and thus were able to slide down to the fiord. And there, at the water's edge, huge icebergs calved free from the glaciers with a roar like the discharge of numerous cannon.

Now and then we laid to while a boat laden with supplies darted clear of the ship, headed toward a little hut on shore, and then returned with hastened strokes. I sensed that the bustle of increased activity reflected Travers' reputation as a seer. Everyone aboard—officers and men—wanted to accomplish as much work as possible before Travers' bad weather struck.

The Greenland Army station at Rivet on the western side of Clavering Island was one of the most important in the chain. It was a junction point for numerous sledge routes extending in several directions. For this reason the Rivet Station required more than the usual amount of supplies. Also it was equipped with a two-way radio powered by a Diesel generator. Servicing the station would require about two hours.

Rivet was last on the day's agenda. We found an anchorage with fair holding ground about a mile offshore. With this, and with the weather holding calm and clear, we had little to worry about. Only a few detached clouds scudded from the north.

The time was now about 8:00 P.M. Travers had only four hours, more or less, in which to make good his prophecy, and his stock was already beginning to tumble. But he clung unwaveringly to his statement of the morning. The wind would blow from the north with whole gale force before midnight!

V.P., Von Rosenvinge and Ira Beal, chief gunner's mate, piled into the motor surfboat and headed down the fiord on the trail of a herd of musk oxen. They wanted me to go, but my enthusiasm for that pastime had been deflated at Zackenberg. Moreover there was a report of genuine green grass growing at Rivet. This I wanted to see. So I joined the little group of men who were to handle the supplies our motor cargo boat carried ashore.

The work of unloading and stowing the supplies in the hut was finished, and the men had long since returned to the ship. Captain Niels O. Jensen and I stayed behind to repair the decrepit, old-fashioned radio equipment. Two Greenland Army skiffs lay bottom-up near the beach. Captain Jensen wanted to take these to another station, so we decided that each of us would row one back to the *Northland.*

I began to get uneasy after a while. I had glanced outside the hut and noticed a change in the weather. There seemed to be a real threat. Dark nimbus clouds raced beneath a gloomy sky and smashed into the surrounding mountains, blotting out their peaks and the great inland ice beyond. Nevertheless a surface calm belied an immediate break. There was still time to return to the *Northland,* and, as her commanding officer, I belonged aboard in the event of a blow.

I made known my fears to Jensen.

"You need not wait for me, sir," he said. "I want to finish soldering these connections. I'll return in the morning, if necessary."

We launched one of the skiffs, and I hopped in, starting the mile-long row to the anchorage. The skiff had been out of water for a long time. This made it leak badly, and I was obliged to stop frequently and bail. By the time I was well over halfway to the ship I felt I could ease my stroke. I stopped rowing to bail again and glanced toward the *Northland.*

My glance must have become a stare of terror, for a dark, sinister curtain of cloud was sweeping toward the ship and toward me with express-train speed.

There was no time to bail now. Even before I could turn and start rowing, I saw the *Northland* disappear in the cloud as though she had been blasted off the earth. Then the blow struck my skiff. In literally the winking of an eye, visibility closed to a few yards, and the sea was lashed to a boiling fury by a screaming wind driving sharp missiles of sleet into my back. Seas whipped over the gunwales, adding to the water level inside the skiff. Making headway was impossible. My only chance lay in running before the blow and hoping I would eventually land on the beach.

I tugged on one oar, trying to skew the skiff around and bring her stern to windward. She was halfway around when a comber poured in over the gunwale. I felt her begin to sink. Slowly she eased over on her side and tumbled me out. Free of my weight and emptied of water when she capsized, the skiff bobbed to the surface, bottom up.

By this time I had reached down and turned the knobs which inflated my rubber life belt with $CO_2$ gas, thankful I had made a habit of wearing the belt in obedience to a wartime order. With the belt inflated and keeping me afloat, I grabbed the keel of the skiff and endeavored to drape my body across her bottom so I could drift with her to safety. But it was no use. I slid off at every attempt because of the inflated belt bulging around my waist.

Authorities reckon a life expectancy of various lengths in water of twenty-nine degrees Fahrenheit. All estimates are under ten minutes, the average about six minutes. I could not hope to hold on many more minutes—certainly not enough minutes for the skiff to drift to the beach.

There was no use shouting. My voice against the gale and seething sea would be like a popgun competing with a cannon. My hands were numbing, my whole body was numb and I was gasping for breath.

I sensed something to windward and made an effort to shake off the numbness and squint hopefully. There *was* something white looming faintly through the blinding sleet.

I remember thinking it might be a growler and dimly realizing a chunk of ice could not drift fast enough to overtake the skiff. Then the white bulk took recognizable shape. It was a surfboat!

"In bows! Way enough!" That was Harmon's voice.

Several husky hands scooped me into the boat.

"Thanks, Harmon," I gasped when I had caught my breath.

"Three-stripers are a dime a dozen, but skiffs are rare up in this country. Don't lose that one."

"We'll take the skiff *and* the three-striper, sir," Harmon said. He began explaining. "The OOD was keeping a bearing on you. When he saw the storm coming he sounded the man-overboard alarm. With his bearing and—" Harmon pointed to the boat compass—"I knew exactly where to look for you."

I somehow managed to check over the *Northland's* officers and recalled this would be Lieutenant Edward C. Murphy's watch. Murphy, a Yankee, had been skipper of a down-east schooner until the war. He couldn't read without his glasses, but, sailor that he was, he never missed a trick on the bridge. Good teamwork, this. If it had not been . . .

I began shivering violently. It might have been nervous reaction. But I was cold, too. Desperately cold.

After a late dinner I reached across the table and handed V.P. a two-dollar bill. He took it in silence. We both knew my rescue by a well-drilled surfboat crew had cinched the argument.

"I could have saved the skipper those two bucks if he had heeded my advice," Von Rosenvinge said. "It would have been absolutely free advice, too."

"Listen, you damned ambulance chaser," V.P. growled, "your legal advice isn't worth——"

"The skipper doesn't need a lawyer," Von Rosenvinge interrupted. "He doesn't need legal advice. He needs a Tibetan Lama's prayer wheel. I'll see that one is fitted to the sausage grinder in the galley."

V.P.'s expression became serious. "The propeller," he said gravely, "is where any ice pilot wants to have a prayer wheel."

# Chapter 7

# THE GRAVE ROBBER OF
# CLAVERING ISLAND

V.P. WAS a man of many interests. The Arctic, of course, received a large share of his serious attention. So did tropical ornithology, zoology, geology, anthropology and the works of Charles Dickens. These last two—anthropology and Dickens' works—were responsible for his making a contribution to the map of the Arctic regions.

This occurred in 1941 before the United States entered World War II. V.P. was commanding officer of the *Northland* at the time, and she was serving as flagship for an expedition composed of United States Coast Guard cutters operating along the coast of western Greenland.

The commander of the expedition (then Commander E. H. Smith, USCG) temporarily detached V.P. from the ship and sent him off on a survey mission. Several days later the motorboat carrying the survey party returned. As it chugged in alongside the *Northland* the expedition's commander, eager to learn the results of the mission, rushed to the gangway and looked over the side. He saw V.P.'s unkempt figure standing in the cockpit, surrounded by human bones and an assortment of Eskimo relics.

"We picked 'em up on an island," V.P. explained after he had climbed aboard the *Northland*.

"What island?" the expedition commander asked.

"I don't know, sir," V.P. answered. "It hasn't any name."

"Well, if it hasn't a name, you get the privilege of giving it one. What will it be?"

V.P. gave the matter serious thought, probably taking into consideration the fact that he had not picked up the bones and relics, but had *dug* them up. Then his mind turned to one of Charles Dickens' characters: Jerry Cruncher, the grave robber. That settled it!

"Cruncher!' V.P. told the expedition commander. "Call it Cruncher Island, sir."

And so today—and for all time, perhaps—the name Cruncher Island is suitably inscribed on all charts showing an island at the mouth of Sondrestrojm Fiord on the west coast of Greenland.

In view of his interests, northeast Greenland was a happy hunting ground for V.P. This was especially true of the Gael Hamke's Bay region.

Captain Douglas Charles Clavering and Sir Edward Sabine, two British explorers, had visited Gael Hamke's in 1823. On the island now bearing Clavering's name they had found a small but thriving and apparently permanent Eskimo settlement. These are the only human beings reported in modern times as living north of the sixty-ninth parallel on the eastern coast of Greenland.

So far as is known, almost a half-century passed before another white man called at Gael Hamke's Bay. This explorer—Captain Karl Koldewey, in command of a German expedition consisting of two ships, the *Germania* and the *Hansa*—went ashore on Clavering Island in 1870. He found the Eskimo settlement in ruins and lacking any evidence of recent habitation.

Koldewey and his party made history by wintering on Sabine Island, the first white men to undertake this rigorous experience in northeast Greenland. During the months they remained in the country, members of the German expedition traveled overland as far northward as the seventy-seventh parallel—to the vicinity of the Koldewey Islands—and engaged in considerable other exploratory work ashore. They found no trace of living inhabitants.

However, in addition to confirming the one-time existence of the village reported by Clavering, Koldewey discovered primitive Eskimo ruins at Cape Rink, which juts into the northern reaches of Hoch-stetter Bay. Koldewey also reported that the abundant herds of rein-deer seen by Clavering—one of the Greenlander's chief sources of food—had disappeared completely.

What had happened to Clavering's Eskimos? Had they or their descendants been wiped out by disease? What had happened to the herds of reindeer? Had the disappearance of the reindeer any con-nection with the disappearance of Clavering's natives? Lacking rein-deer meat, had the natives died of starvation? This seems unlikely, for the Greenlander also obtains much of his food from the sea.

Had the Clavering Island people migrated to the southern extrem-ity of Greenland? Or had they marched across the inland ice to seek a less harsh existence on the west coast? This latter is not tenable. The Greenlander shuns the great ice as he does the polar sea.

Many noted Arctic authorities have puzzled over the disappearance of the Clavering Island people. Greenlanders can throw no light on the question, for they did not begin recording the history of their migrations until 1867, nearly a quarter-century after Clavering's visit and shortly before Koldewey arrived.

V.P., while perhaps not so well known as some Arctic authorities, had a burning desire to unravel the mystery or, at least, contribute to its ultimate solution. I did not share his enthusiasm and told him so when the *Northland* came to anchor in Deadman's Bay, an indentation on the southern coast of Clavering Island, appropriately named be-cause it had been used by the Eskimos as a burial ground.

The cabin which V.P. and I jointly occupied resembled a charnel house and a miniature museum. Little by little, since he had re-linquished command of the *Northland* and assumed the larger duties of task-unit commander, he had added to his collection of Cruncher Island bones, geological specimens, native clothing, utensils and weapons. I did not enjoy the prospect of further discommoding my-self for the convenience of a bunch of human skeletons. ·

"Dammit, Skipper," V.P. said, "if my relics aren't good enough for the cabin, everything I collect from now on will go into Von Rosenvinge's stateroom. It's so full of junk—and I mean his stuff *is* junk—that he won't even notice a few skeletons."

I am still wondering what standard V.P. used to discriminate between junk and relics. It seems to me he must have had a very fine line of distinction. As for Von Rosenvinge, he had no distinction at all. His quarters were a nightmare!

Individually and collectively, the executive officer, the first lieutenant, the wardroom steward and I had endeavored to inculcate a spirit of tidiness in the lawyer-sailor. We finally gave up. Our surrender produced license.

At sea the door to Von Rosenvinge's room could be opened in safety only on the downroll. Anyone opening it on the uproll would let loose into the companionway an assortment of junk of all descriptions. It is unbelievable but true that Von Rosenvinge even went so far as to share his bunk with a varied assortment of books and materials for which he had no earthly use. "It makes a good Dutch wife," he rationalized. "Keeps me from rolling out at sea."

Actually V.P. and his crew of gravediggers who went ashore at Deadman's Bay armed with the implements of their trade were only a sideshow to the main event. A new Greenland Army headquarters station had to be erected to replace the one razed by the Nazis' Sabine Island force in April.

It was necessary, however, that the headquarters continue to be situated on Clavering because of the island's strategic location in respect to the Army's operations and communications. Captain Jensen believed a suitable position—one so strong that a handful of men could hold out against a battalion—was available at Deadman's Bay or near by. We had come to anchor in order that Captain Jensen might reconnoiter the vicinity and find such a location, if it existed.

We expected—and hoped—that the *North Star* would break free of the ice and discharge her construction-material cargo and passengers at Deadman's Bay, or at the site finally chosen by Captain Jensen, in time for the Greenland Army to have the new station well along toward completion before winter set in.

The *Polar Bjorn* was still at Reykjavik, awaiting delivery of radio equipment for the new station. She was to bring this up to northeast Greenland along with five of Captain Jensen's men. Then she was scheduled to call at Scoresby Village en route and pick up Captain Jensen's one private soldier, a native Greenlander, and proceed to our rendezvous.

Shortly after the *Northland* reached her anchorage in Deadman's Bay a breeze swept down through the defiles dividing the mountains towering above the shore. It swept the waters clean of the relatively small pack ice, but it had no effect whatsoever on the movements of the gigantic bergs floating all around us.

This was not unusual, for bergs will drift into the wind or across the wind as often as they drift with it. The uninformed may question this statement, saying it doesn't seem possible that the wind would not effect the movement of an object which presents a surface as vast as that of an iceberg. It must be remembered, however, that the portion of a berg protruding above water is only a fraction of its total bulk. Consequently underwater currents exert their force on the major portion of a berg. It is *not* the wind which determines the course of a berg.

Now and then one of the bergs would nestle against the *Northland's* side, as though resting for a moment, and then drift slowly on. I recalled the fear with which I had initially regarded bergs. This was shortly after I had relieved V.P. as commanding officer of the *Northland*.

We had been anchored in Kusinga Bay on the west coast of Greenland at the time, and there probably had been as many bergs in the vicinity as there were here at Deadman's Bay. Whenever one drifted close to the ship I called for steam and shifted anchorage. So it was shift, shift, shift—until I became so sick of moving around that I resorted to ice pikes, which I had the men use to fend off the bergs.

But no one in the *Northland's* company paid bergs the slightest attention now. I was convinced—and I still am—that, because of the pressure exerted by the hull, a ship the size of the *Northland* need never have any fear of a berg capsizing the ship.

Deadman's Bay, being free of pack ice, gave us an opportunity to use our J2F-5, which could become air-borne only by taking off from the water. Since we had still had no word from Ensign O'Hara and his four men on Pendulum Island, I ordered Ensign Paul Hershey, the pilot, to make a flight to the northward in order to observe, if possible, how O'Hara was getting along and to make a food drop to the party.

After leaving Rivet we had tried desperately to fight our way up

Pendulum Island. But polar ice jammed across the entrance to Gael
Hamke's Bay had defied our efforts. We had then attempted to follow
a shore lead around Cape Borlase Warren. After the ship had nosed
onto the rocky sea bottom at the cape I had abandoned the attempt.
The narrow squeak we had had when we came south around Borlase
Warren was still fresh in my mind!

I anxiously awaited Mr. Hershey's return, hoping for the best, but
subconsciously half fearful, too. Fortunately the pilot brought good
news when he returned. All was well on Pendulum Island, so far as he
could discern from the air. The little party was living in what appeared
to be a stone hut. Needless to say, the food drop had been eagerly received.

I felt considerably better. Now my only concern was V.P. and the
contents of the graves I knew he and his men were opening.

With the beginning of the month of August we began to enjoy a
brief period of darkness along about midnight. At Deadman's Bay the
blackness was accentuated by the shadows of the mountains towering
around us. As a result the boat returning with V.P. and his ghouls
and Captain Jensen was virtually alongside the ship before it was
sighted.

When I received word of the task-unit commander's arrival I hurried to the gangway, prepared for the worst. V.P. sprang aboard and
proudly pointed to a neat pile of Eskimo utensils in the bottom of the
boat.

"Where are the skeletons?" I asked.

V.P.'s face dropped. Probably I had reminded him of the keen disappointment he must have felt throughout the day as his men dug up
spot after spot in the burial area without success. "Ah!" he growled.
"Some damned grave robbers got there first!" Then he quickly
changed the subject, telling me that Captain Jensen's scouting mission
had satisfied him of the desirability of Deadman's Bay as the site for his
new headquarters.

We should get under way for Eskimonaes within a few hours, V.P.
added. At the old Headquarters there we would take on all salvageable
equipment which the Nazis had left behind and transport it back here
to Deadman's Bay.

Eskimonaes was a shambles of death and destruction. Carcasses of machine-gunned dogs lay strewed among charred debris of the two-story station which the Germans had razed a few months before. An outhouse which stood apart from the burned structures and a few drums of gasoline were the only things the enemy had spared.

Why? It struck us as odd, particularly since the outhouse was stuffed with over ten thousand dollars' worth of furs.

After a reconnaissance of the surrounding country failed to turn up any clue to the mystery we loaded all salvageable materials on board to take to Deadman's Bay. In the meantime I decided to take on fresh water from a near-by creek.

I had often boated water, as had most sailors for the past milennium. It was a back-breaking job. The boats had to be swabbed, filled with fresh water, then towed to the ship. There they had to be hoisted and the water siphoned into the ship's fresh-water tanks.

Captain Von Paulsen chanced to see preparations being made and asked me what was up.

I told him.

"Don't be an old fogie, Skipper!" he said. "You have a thousand feet of fresh-water hose and two portable pumps in this ship. Warp your stern in to the creek and *pump* the water on board."

I did as he advised. In four hours our tanks were full.

During the afternoon Hershey took off in the plane and flew over the *North Star*. She was still stuck fast, but the ice was young and the vessel was in no apparent danger.

On the evening of August 5 we got under way for Deadman's Bay. The ship had no more than cleared the headland when a messenger entered the cabin with a dispatch. It was from O'Hara, only thirty-one miles away. But the message had traveled some 8,500 miles. He had been unable to work the *Northland* direct, hence the electronic detour. O'Hara's radio had raised Presque Isle, Maine, and cleared his traffic. Thence his message had been relayed to Arlington, Virginia, then to Argentia, Newfoundland, to Iceland and finally to us.

I read the dispatch aloud to V.P.: "Ice moving out of Hochstetter Bay.' "

# Chapter 8

## O'HARA'S RESCUE

For four days the *Northland* valiantly tried to batter her way to Pendulum Island to O'Hara and his men. But the ice off-shore was too heavy for her limited power, and the shore lead around Cape Borlase Warren was too shallow to navigate.

Gazing across the mosaic of close-packed ice which penned us up behind Sand Island, I thought of Cape Borlase Warren as my own private hoodoo. Nowhere that I could see was there any possibility of an early escape. I hung up my glasses and gloomily retired to my cabin.

About an hour later the officer of the deck roused me with the announcement that the bay was free of ice.

"No?" I asked incredulously.

"Yes, sir. The ice is gone!"

The ice was gone from Young's Sound, but it was still plentiful around Cape Borlase Warren. In fact, it was so abundant that we required all of eight hours to maneuver around the cape. Not until 6:00 A.M. the following morning did we reach Walrus Island. Then the ice forced the *Northland* so close to shore that one could easily have tossed a pebble against the cliffs which stretched along the eastern side.

At 8:00 A.M. we made anchorage in Lower Pendulum Strait. I immediately sent Mr. Harmon, in the motor surfboat, after O'Hara and his men. He brought them back before noon.

The spunky little Irishman and his detail were chilled to the bone. The tent, the warm clothing, the primus stoves they had taken to the

The shore watering detail slew the musk ox as a humanitarian measure.

Ice mallets were in almost continuous use as December approached.

Coast Guardsmen dine on German canned goods.

island had not been enough to keep them comfortable. But O'Hara
had solved the housing problem. One of his men had been a stone
mason in civilian life. Under his guidance the little party had built a
stone house and covered it with their tent. This had kept them fairly
warm.

"If we had had mortar," O'Hara said, "we could have built a real
house."

In the evening I climbed Germania Mountain and studied the ice
around Little Pendulum Island. It looked favorable for getting into
Hochstetter Bay. When I returned to the ship we pushed northward,
bound for Cape Rink.

During the winter of 1869-1870 Koldewey had banked heavily on
using Eskimos and their dog teams to carry out his exploration of
northeast Greenland. He had hoped to locate the north side of Greenland.

As we have seen he found no Eskimos and no reindeer. Perhaps
this handicap of dog-team transportation was for the best. Foot travel
restricted him to a few degrees of latitude and encouraged greater attention to scientific detail. One of Koldewey's geologists, Lieutenant
Payer, found an outcrop of coal near Cape Rink which paralleled the
shore for several miles. Later geologists investigated and concluded
that the coal was immature. They named the location of the outcrop
"Kolhus."

Yet, coal—even poor steaming coal—can be superior to wood as a
fuel. This was true of Kolhus coal. The Eskimos who once inhabited
Cape Rink never recognized the value of fuel lying virtually in their
back yard. For countless generations the Eskimo has known only seal
oil as a fuel. He selected his village site with a view toward sealing
rather than mining.

Cape Rink, at the junction of Peter Bay, Shannon Sound and Hochstetter Bay, is well situated for sealing. Moreover a two-thousand-foot
mountain rises from Cape Rink, providing the Eskimo a vantage point
from which to view the seal herd.

Long after the Eskimo made his exit from Cape Rink, Danish
trappers chose a site near the Eskimo ruins for a hunting station. Then
when trappers became soldiers the Cape Rink station became an important outpost of the Greenland Army.

Of Cape Rink it might be said that whoever holds this important point commands the approaches to Shannon Island in the east, to Dove Bay in the north and to Eskimonaes in the south. With coal deposits near by and a wealth of fauna at hand, it is a place of significant strategic importance.

The *Northland* anchored off Cape Rink on August 16 after a difficult voyage from Pendulum Strait. Captain Von Paulsen was anxious to investigate the vicinity to determine if a force of Germans had been there. He led a company of Army and Coast Guard men to make a reconnaissance and emphasized an important detail. There was one commodity no Arctic-wise traveler would be without, V.P. declared—toilet paper. The force must be alert for it.

"Germans," the captain concluded, "are fastidious in their habits, so you may have to look some distance from the station."

O'Hara, who had the forenoon (8:00 A.M. to noon) watch, recorded the events something as follows: "Vessel at anchor as before throughout this watch. Captain C. C. Von Paulsen, USCG, ashore with reconnaissance patrol, searching for toilet paper."

Captain Von Paulsen did not return empty-handed. The patrol found a clue, though not such as Von Paulsen expected. This was a German naval officer's uniform which had one gold stripe on each sleeve.

We sent for Dr. Sensse and asked if he had an explanation. The German doctor had one and gave it without hesitating. "I left a uniform here," Dr. Sensse said, "when I made a reconnaissance of this region last winter." There was no further comment, and the doctor refused to say more. We were as much in the dark as before.

For V.P. there was still a matter of unfinished business at Cape Rink. The opportunity for an archeological investigation of the ancient Eskimo village was too much for him to resist. Taking a few crew members with him, he returned to shore and spent the rest of the afternoon seeking human remains and artifacts. The result was the same as at Deadman's Bay—"Some damned grave robbers got there first."

By 4:30 P.M. we were again under way and standing up Ardencaple Fiord, an ancient cirque which cut deeply into the ice cap. This flooded canyon is a waterway of exotic beauty and color with banded cliffs rising sheerly to a height of 5,000 feet in places. Perhaps we could have rationalized a trip to the end of this fiord on the grounds of geological and hydrographic surveying, but there was important work to be done. Coal had to be mined and distributed.

Unless coal was properly apportioned among his many stations Jensen's army was useless. It could not, without mobility, serve as the eyes of the Allied Forces in northeast Greenland. And coal limited its scope of operations. With it Jensen could range at will. Without it he could not move.

At 9:00 P.M. August 17, the *Northland* arrived at Kolhus. We were there to mine coal, then distribute it among stations north of Cape Rink. Coal was heaped on the *Northland's* spotless decks, which sight was too much for Lieutenant Murphy. "First it's dogs!" the first lieutenant grumbled. "Now it's coal! If there's a herd of swine in Greenland, it'll be on our decks before this cruise is ended!"

Leaving Kolhus and rounding Cape Rink, we found that pack ice which had squeezed through Shannon Sound was pressing close to to shore. Because of treacherous outlying reefs along Hochstetter Foreland, further progress to the northward would have been impossible, except for icebergs. It was easy to distinguish grounded bergs from floating ones. Grounded bergs, we knew, marked the shoals. Just give them a wide berth on either side and you have ample water under the keel.

Roseneath Bay, at the approximate midpoint on Hochstetter Foreland, was our immediate destination. It is a crescent-shaped bay which is formed by an out-jutting mountain, linked to the foreland by a sand spit. This mountain rises 1,000 feet and bears such a striking resemblance to a European haystack that Koldewey promptly named it "Haystack."

While Roseneath Station was being fueled I climbed Haystack to survey the ice north of us. It was plain that we were at the end of the line for 1943. Ice completely carpeted Dove Bay and piled against the north shore of Shannon Island. The only clear water in sight was that narrow ribbon along the south half of Hochstetter Foreland through which we had twisted to reach Roseneath Bay. Only a powerful icebreaker could have gone beyond Haystack.

When I returned to the boat Captain Von Paulsen was waiting while

Von Rosenvinge wove among near-by boulders, carrying something white. On reaching us he reverently deposited an Arctic hare at V.P.'s feet.

"I shot it," V.P. explained. "Norman retrieved it."

"Yeah." Von Rosenvinge sighed. "I'm pinch-hitting for Eight-Ball. It's a dog's life I lead, sir."

"A poor substitute," Von Paulsen growled. "Neither Eight Ball nor any other self-respecting dog would lead your kind of life!" Turning to me, the captain asked, "How's the ice?" I told him. "We'll go south," V.P. declared. "Then we will stop at Bastian's Fiord and Cape Maurer on Kuhn Island."

After supper that evening we reached Bastian's Fiord to find a breeze making up from northeastward. This meant the ice would begin moving slowly in toward shore. We would have to be quick about our work at the station.

While we were entering the fiord the fathometer belt broke. There were no spare belts on board. A new one must be manufactured, and, with demands for precision, this might require a day. The fiord was too deep for hand-lead soundings and too treacherous for us to proceed without soundings. These waters had never been charted.

I asked V.P. if his bag of Arctic tricks might cope with the situation.

The captain thought awhile, then said with assurance: "Lower the head of your antisubmarine sound gear halfway, Skipper, then cut in your chemical recorder and begin your submarine transmissions. The echo traces on the recorder will give you the depth under keel in yards. It won't be too accurate, but it will be good enough here."

Captain Von Paulsen's improvised fathometer worked surprisingly well. About two hours later he had another occasion to reopen his bag of tricks.

When we sailed out of Bastian's Fiord the wind was blowing briskly, and the shore lead along Kuhn Island was all but filled with pack ice. Bastian Fiord would soon be invaded and untenable as an anchorage. There was no place to go. Again I sent for Von Paulsen and asked him what to do.

V.P. sauntered to the rail and carefully surveyed the advancing pack. He picked up his binoculars and gazed at a large iceberg a couple of miles down the coast.

"See that berg?" V.P. asked, lowering his glasses. "It is grounded. Make fast to it."

We were soon nosed up against the lee side of the berg, riding comfortably to an ice anchor which our men planted on its white, spreading side. Through the night the wind howled and ice roared as it crashed against the berg, but we were well protected.

I awakened the following morning to find the wind calm and the skies clear. There were only scattered floes about us. The favorable turn of weather enabled us to accomplish our work at Cape Maurer in short order.

The *North Star* was still beset, and it appeared to V.P. that she might not shake loose until too late in the season to reach Deadman's Bay. She might even need our aid in the event of severe ice damage. It was now fairly plain that the Nazis had not retreated northward. Captain Von Paulsen decided to go south to Clavering Sound.

# Chapter 9

# TRAPPED IN HOCHSTETTER BAY

SHANNON ISLAND lies roughly south of Dove Bay, east of Peter Bay and north of Pendulum Strait. It is a low, generally flat island covered with tundra and rock. Its lack of relief on the south end is marred only by Tellepatte, a 500-foot-high basalt hogback on the south end of the island. Tellepatte stretches several miles in a north-south direction from Freden Bay.

Situated at the junction of three wind funnels, with its east coast exposed to the Greenland Sea, the island is buffeted by violent storms and subject to radical changes of weather.

Like most tenderfeet, I paid little attention to physical geographical factors in making decisions. All I knew was that this nineteenth day of August was beautiful, flying weather was excellent and we needed an aero-reconnaissance of the periphery of Shannon Island. Without even consulting V.P. or Niels Jensen, I sent for Hershey and ordered him to fly around the island.

As a sort of afterthought I asked Travers for a weather forecast. The weather prophet studied the sky a minute, then read the barometer and thermometers. At length he announced with finality, "It looks northish, Captain."

"You mean a northerly blow?" I asked incredulously.

"Yes, sir," Travers replied confidently.

Had I not been awed by my aerographer's mate's ability to prognosticate, I would have laughed outright. But it seemed to me there

94

was no likelihood of bad weather within an hour. And one hour was all the time required for our plane to make a circuit of the island. I ordered the aircraft away from our anchorage at Freden Bay.

The impossible occurred. The plane had scarcely faded from sight before clouds began to invade the overhead. First these were fleecy and friendly, but within a half hour black, threatening clouds moved in beneath them. I became alarmed and ordered the radio room to recall the aircraft.

Actually an Arctic-wise pilot like Hershey needed no coaching from the ship. He was already returning when the squall struck. It made up that quickly.

The plane was on the radar, only a few miles distant, flying close to Tellepatte. Suddenly, as dark clouds swallowed this mountain ridge, the plane disappeared from the radar scope. In reporting this O'Hara added: "She's down for certain, Captain. The radar doesn't lie."

I ordered a search and rescue party called away, but before it could assemble, the full fury of the storm burst on the *Northland*. The seas, whipped into a seething white froth, lashed furiously at the ship. A screeching blast struck like the concussion of a mighty explosion. The anchor chain stretched taut. Our world shrank to a mere hundred yards or so. Stinging white pellets flew at the ship. Our boats were powerless to make headway against the wind. I held the rescue party on board.

The radio room tried repeatedly to raise the plane. No response. We could only infer the plane had crashed.

"There's nothing you can do, Skipper. So there's no use worrying," V.P. advised. I wished I could share his complacency.

The *Northland* swung wildly at her anchor chain. On one yaw she struck a submerged object with a terrific jolt. I had the engines set astern and dragged anchor to seaward. We were clear on the next yaw cycle. From a dished-in plate near the keel I concluded that we had swung into a submerged rock.

The storm abated nearly as quickly as it had sprung up. The seas calmed and flattened. The black clouds fled to leeward, leaving the sky milky and cheerful.

From the shadows of Tellepatte our plane buzzed into the air, circled widely and landed near the ship. Hershey stepped out of the cockpit, very much alive and apparently tickled over something.

The pilot explained that he could probably have made the ship ahead of the squall, but, fearing there would not be time to hoist it on board, he had set down on a natural airstrip which paralleled the foot of Tellepatte.

"As an airport," Hershey continued, "it's a natural. Has twin runways and will take the largest plane built and then some!"

This was important news. It fitted into the mystery of the Sabine Island Nazis. It was likely that the Germans knew of this airfield. The station crew could easily have crossed Hochstetter Bay on the ice for evacuation by airplane. There would likely be no tire marks, because snow had obviously covered the island until quite recently. But there would be other clues to confirm or deny this supposition. The matter would bear investigation.

The following day, August 20, was beautiful and cloudless. Large scattered floes of heavy ice drifted lazily about Hochstetter Bay. Warm weather and ice were two prerequisites for fresh water. After months of freezing in near-zero temperatures, salts and other impurities in ice are precipitated. These form crystals which trickle down through the ice and pass out through the lower surface. When ice melts on the surface it drains into pools scattered about the irregular surface of a floe. This water can then be pumped into the fresh-water tanks of a ship.

We were sorely in need of water. While the reconnaissance patrol was ashore to survey the airstrip I selected a suitable floe and moored the *Northland* alongside to water ship.

In northeast Greenland watering day was always a gala occasion. It meant the ship could be scrubbed down with soft, fresh water. Water rations were lifted, and no limit was placed on the consumption of the precious fluid. All hands could take turn about at the showers.

The big old-fashioned cabin bathtub was filled with Captain Von Paulsen, who loved to soak in it for hours. In fact I am convinced that if he were to design a library, it would be furnished with bathroom fixtures of two types instead of the conventional furniture.

Because the visibility was so clear O'Hara secured the air-search

A scouting mission in the bleak northern country.

Sea areas surrounding iceberg-calving glaciers such as this are covered with bergy bits and growlers during the navigable season.

radar while he and James Sloan made necessary repairs. As these two erstwhile educators tinkered with the set amidst a maze of charts and instruction books the drone of heavy motors cut into the yapping of portable water pumps. O'Hara recognized the sound and, without looking for the source, sprang to the general alarm and turned down the handle.

The crew flew to battle stations. Many men wore only long-handled undies. Von Paulsen, clad in his birthday suit with a towel wrapped around his midriff, raced with me to the bridge. My eyes followed the outstretched arms and pointed fingers of the lookouts. A large bomber was directly overhead. It bore the familiar black cross of a German plane. Actually it was 500 feet in the air, but at the time it appeared to graze the mainmast.

Thirty-five seconds were usually required to get the main batteries into action. But with a good portion of the crew on the ice and many more under the showers it took much longer this time. When the first salvo was fired the Nazi bomber was well out of range.

I took stock of the situation. The Nazi plane was northbound, flying in the path of the noonday sun. Our sky lookouts had failed to see him in the glare. On the other hand the camouflaged color of the North-land blended so well with the ice and water about us that the Germans had not spotted the Northland until it was too late to drop bombs or try strafing.

I wondered who was more frightened, the Nazi pilot or I!

The reconnaissance patrol returned with news and clues. While it had found nothing on the order of toilet paper, there were many footprints in places which had been wind-swept while the snow was still on the ground. Moreover the men brought back with them an Eskimo dog so weak from lack of food that it had to be carried. The poor beast had apparently had a tough time of it on the island. A few ugly wounds told of encounters with musk oxen. Probably the dog was so hungry it had been willing to tackle anything. But he was so pitiful and docile that the men took an immediate liking to him. Within a few minutes he had acquired a new name—"Shannon."

A reconstruction of events produced something like this: The Nazis had crossed Hochstetter Bay on the ice and had been evacuated by plane from Shannon Island. Some of the dogs had made their way back to Sabine Island while "Shannon" was left stranded. Obviously some dogs had perished after or before the Germans took off.

V.P. decided to go south to Deadman's Bay. We started out to round Little Pendulum Island.

Before the *Northland* cleared the vague line which marks the entrance to Hochstetter Bay, ice hemmed her in on all sides. For three anxious days the set of the East Greenland Current bore her steadily toward rocky Little Pendulum Island. Yet we were helpless to move until the ice relaxed its grip on the ship. At length the ice did relax, and we battled valiantly against the current to retrace our drift toward Cape Philip Broke.

During the night of August 24, I suddenly felt a sensation which was akin to riding in a flat-wheeled Pullman car. I knew at once that we had damaged the propeller. V.P.'s prophetic words flashed across my mind—*The propeller, gentlemen, is where we need the prayer wheel!*

Investigation revealed that a blade was badly bent. The engine room reported that the shaft could be turned over for six and one-half knots without overheating the spring bearing.

Our situation was bad. In the open sea a damaged propeller is nothing to be alarmed about. Here, in heavy pack ice during a bad ice year, it could mean the difference between life and death. I wondered if we would be able to battle our way out of Hochstetter Bay.

Captain Von Paulsen took the news of our damaged propeller philosophically. "It happens to the best of ice navigators" was his only comment.

It was late in the evening of August 25 when we battered our way into Freden Bay. I had planned to lie there while awaiting favorable ice conditions under which to stand south, but a southerly wind was making up which I knew would pile the ice in on us. The decision to move on to Cape Rink was made none too soon. Advancing ice pushed the ship into Cape David Gray so closely she scraped bottom getting past it.

On the morning of August 26 we anchored in the newly formed skim ice which spread around Cape Rink. Captain Von Paulsen received two dispatches that eased the blow he must have felt when the *Northland* broke her propeller. The first of these was from the *North*

*Star.* She had shaken loose from the pack off Traill Island and was now standing to sea.

The second dispatch was from the *Polar Bjorn.* She had navigated a shore lead past the Liverpool coast and was making fair progress toward Eskimonaes.

Newly formed ice denied us use of the plane for scouting. By August 30 our plight was serious. But the other ships sent good news. The *Polar Bjorn* was standing into Clavering Sound. The *North Star* was making good progress toward Clavering Sound, westbound through a lead along the seventy-fifth parallel.

That afternoon the *Northland* made a tour around her pen and anchored at Cape Rink. V.P. invited me to climb Musselberg, a 2,000-foot mountain rising from the cape. We needed further ice information, and this was our best means of obtaining it.

Musselberg is so-called because the summit is covered with brachiopod fossils. Most of these are molds which fix the orogeny of this part of Greenland as Cretaceous.

V.P. studied the icescape with his glasses for fully fifteen minutes, then began to summarize our situation. "We may have to winter here if we don't get a foehm wind pretty soon, Skipper," he began.

I recalled that a foehm wind is a local wind which blows off the ice cap. In the cirques and fiords it is heated by compression and attains an accelerated velocity. Because it is warm and invariably blows offshore, it is considered a friendly wind. Foehm winds are hailed by ice pilots because they scatter the pack.

"I have been giving a good deal of thought to such a possibility lately," V.P. continued. "By freezing in at Kolhus, the ship with a skeleton crew of twenty-five or thirty men will be assured ample fuel and food. Three transport planes should be able to evacuate all remaining hands from our Shannon Island airstrip."

I agreed it would be unwise to keep a full crew on board the *Northland.* There was insufficient food to sustain it through the winter. Of course the men could scatter in groups over northeast Greenland, but they were inexperienced, and the measure would be ill-advised.

"If we are not out of here in ten days," the captain continued, "I'll advise Admiral Smith. In the meantime there's no use to alarm the men, so we'll keep the matter under our hats."

The following day we were helplessly hemmed in by ice. This may have irritated me and induced a latent mania. My first commanding officer had been mildly superstitious about beards. But with V.P. on board the *Northland* I hesitated to upset the ship's traditional practice of wearing beards. While he never wore one, he did not object to crew members wearing them.

Today I didn't care what V.P. thought. I ordered all beards removed and gave the men a half-hour to do it. Maybe Captain J. S. Baylis, my first skipper, was right. Maybe it would bring on a foehm wind. So off came the beards, and I felt better.

We needed to forestall a meat shortage and at the same time keep the men occupied, so I organized a musk-ox hunt. The hunters were successful in bagging five bulls and brought back each carcass in one piece. This was done by rolling them down a bluff to the water's edge. Our boats took care of transporting them to the ship, and the butchering was done on board without wasting an ounce of meat.

That evening we held a pie-eating contest for the International Arctic Regional Championship. The cooks prepared fresh, juicy blueberry pies for the contestants. Each mess was represented—the crew, the chief petty officers, the wardroom and the cabin. Niels Jensen, the cabin entry was the favorite, but Von Rosenvinge, the wardroom hero, won the sweepstakes.

The award for this classic event was a jawful of musk-ox teeth suspended from a gilded toilet-paper core. Duly inscribed were the words "King of the Choppers." It had to be worn on the seat of the victor's pants, and Von Paulsen was not very gentle about pinning it on Von Rosenvinge. The latter's words of acceptance were: "Ouch!"

Then Von continued, saying, "You have made me very happy. Tomorrow I am going to send you a foehm wind whether Travers likes it or not."

The next day, September 1, a mild foehm wind blew down Peter Bay! It brushed away the ice and allowed us to use our plane. V.P. sent Jensen to the *Polar Bjorn*, anchored at Eskimonaes, where he joined the main body of his Greenland Army. Hershey, on his return, bolstered the spirits of all hands by announcing that we had a good chance of smashing through Pendulum Strait.

Pendulum Strait was plugged at its upper end. But we were determined to force our way through this bottleneck and began, at 8 00 P.M., to buck the ice. This was no time for halfway measures. The situation called for full power, regardless of the spring bearing. We charged again and again, we slewed, we pried, we blasted and we warped. Our attempt to escape from Hochstetter Bay was a desperate one, and of course the bearing became sizzling hot!

It was after 4:00 A.M. when the ice gorge finally lay behind us.

Our escape from Hochstetter Bay was made not an instant too soon. Even as we broke out of the ice gorge the wind shifted to the north. Dawn broke as we reached the lower strait, and the wind was now really howling. Dark clouds flew in and let loose fine, biting pellets of snow. We raced before the wind through white-capped waters until the ship came to the south entrance of the strait. From headland to headland a heavy wall of unbroken ice stretched before us.

The *Northland* was still penned in, but I knew we would have a chance later on to get out of Pendulum Strait. Now there was nothing to do but wait for a turn of weather, so I selected an anchorage behind grounded bergs, close to the Sabine shore.

The engines had no more than been rung off when a dispatch flashed over the radio to the task-unit commander. It was from the *North Star* and read something like this:

Broke rudder stock maneuvering through heavy ice in gale. Position three miles north of Cape James. Wind and ice setting ship toward lee shore. Need immediate assistance.

The *Northland* was helpless to get beyond Pendulum Strait. The *Polar Bjorn* was at Eskimonaes, only twenty miles from Cape James, but we could not raise her by radio. The little sealer carried only one operator, and he was not scheduled to go on watch until noon—some five hours hence.

There was only one thing to do—a slender chance, one which involved a desperate risk. That risk Captain Von Paulsen decided to accept.

# Chapter 10

# BESET

VON PAULSEN's plan was to get a message to the *Polar Bjorn* by airplane! Take-off and landing in the lee of grounded bergs, with ice fragments drifting about, would be hazardous. A metal tube containing V.P.'s instructions to the sealer must be dropped squarely on her deck. These instructions ordered Captain Marø to proceed immediately to the *North Star* and render all possible assistance.

Ensign Hershey was willing to take the chance. In keeping with the traditions of Coast Guard aviation he would risk his own life and that of his radioman in an effort to save 160 officers and men from certain death.

I clung tightly to the bridge rail, watching the plane take off. Puffs of cold spray showered the frail aircraft as it smashed into each white-crested wave. On every impact it seemed to waver between plunging under or skimming on to the next breaker. Finally it was air-borne! But would it clear the top of that iceberg ahead?

There were a few tense, uncertain seconds. Hershey climbed steeply with full power. He cleared the berg—by inches!

In an hour or so the pilot was back, and he landed safely, his mission successfully accomplished. The *Polar Bjorn* was proceeding at full speed to the stricken *North Star*.

For several days unnavigable ice kept the *Northland* penned in Pendulum Strait.

On September 3 word was flashed to V.P. that the *Polar Bjorn* had succeeded in towing the *North Star* to Eskimonaes, where she would begin manufacturing a jury rudder in the shelter of East Bay. In the meantime the *Polar Bjorn* would lighter materials for Jensen's new command post from the *North Star* to Deadman's Bay.

The pressure was off. Yet I knew the *North Star* and *Polar Bjorn* were working against time. They needed our help.

The following morning the ice looked better. I got the *Northland* under way and made a stab at reaching Gael Hamke's Bay through a narrow shore lead which stretched along Wollaston Foreland. The weather was promising when we left Pendulum Strait, but soon after we passed Cape Wynn it took a turn for the worse. The wind made up suddenly from the north and within a half-hour or so was blowing furiously. Ice, torn from the fields among which we sped, began to invade the shore lead.

We were approaching Cape Borlase Warren, and I could see there was no chance to slip past the headland. Retreat was impossible. There was only one thing to do—place the ship in the pack and hope for the best.

Fortunately, with the season far advanced, fields had been broken up into floes. I spun the ship into a sharp turn and headed offshore. We managed to squeeze between the floes for at least a mile. Then the wind, howling with gale force, packed the ice closely about us. The *Northland* was stuck and completely at the mercy of wind and current.

Held fast by the ice, the *Northland* drifted southward for a whole week. At times she moved at the reckless pace of the main current. More often she poked along in the feeble backwash close to shore—too close to shore. There were countless hazards—rocks, islets and shoals and, finally, the broad, bold headland of Cape Hold With Hope. The very ice pressure which imprisoned the vessel helped her past the gauntlet. But this pressure also came near to crushing the vessel.

At times ice pressed up the ship's sides and crowded onto her main deck, threatening to sweep away the deck structure. Sometimes she would heel over to an angle of ten degrees. As we passed Cape Hold With Hope pressure was at its worst.

On the seventh day of her drift the cape gave way to the fiord region. The ice had a place to go—up Franz Joseph Fiord. It relaxed its grip. Free now of pressure, the *Northland* rolled back slowly onto even keel.

In the meantime the *North Star* and *Polar Bjorn*, working twenty-four hours a day, had completed their task in Clavering Bay. The barracks were up, and Jensen and his men would finish the rest of the work. The *North Star* had installed her jury rudder.

The two ships sailed from Clavering Sound and sought leads which would take them clear of the coast. In trying to work offshore, however, both became stuck, the *Polar Bjorn* off Pendulum Island and the *North Star* off Cape Borlase Warren.

With his entire fleet beset there was ample cause for V.P. to be alarmed. But Captain Von Paulsen never worried over big things. However he was duty-bound to keep Admiral Smith, Commander Greenland Patrol, informed of the disposition of his task unit. This he did—in a matter-of-fact report by routine dispatch. Then he settled back to await developments.

Admiral Smith did not regard this bit of news in such an apparently light vein. He crowded through a priority dispatch to the Commander in Chief, Atlantic Fleet, that should have brought tears to Admiral Ingersoll's eyes. It painted a mournful picture of three ships about to be destroyed by ice unless relief reached them in time. Of course the *Storis* and *Evergreen* would be withdrawn from vital escort work and ordered to proceed to northeast- Greenland. But they were not so iceworthy as the ships of our task unit and could hardly be relied on to do us any good. Heavy icebreakers were the only answer. The admiral concluded his dispatch by requesting that construction of four icebreakers be expedited.

Rumors often pierced wartime secrecy and eventually made their way to remote Greenland. One of these had mentioned the construction of four new heavy icebreakers on the west coast of the United States. We felt, however, that since we were at the end of the line, all this grapevine information reached us in a highly exaggerated form. For example, by the time this icebreaker rumor arrived in Greenland someone along the line had added bow propellers. "Positively fantastic!" we all agreed. Everyone who had bucked *storis* knew a propeller which stuck out in the bow would be smashed to smithereens within a few minutes. But the report brought some good laughs, even if it failed to make sense.

"Seriously, Captain," I asked V.P., "do you think the icebreakers will be available in time to do *us* any good?"

"Of course not," he replied. "Admiral Smith, for one, knows they won't. But he's using this opportunity to make a dramatic appeal to the uninitiated ones in order to get building priorities boosted. He wants the ships for next summer's operation."

I decided to prepare for the worst and set out to exercise the crew at abandon-ship drill, "condition ice." "Condition ice" was similar to "abandon ship" at sea except that in the ice we could load the boats to the gunwales with supplies. All hands would then line the gunwales and push them over the ice.

Among the more important things each man must provide for himself was a shaving razor. No experienced Arctic traveler wears a beard, because, as Stefansson puts it, the moisture of the breath congeals on the beard. If the face begins to freeze beneath this ice mask, you cannot thaw it with the palm of the hand as one ordinarily does—that is, without first freezing the fingers.

Beal, the chief gunner's mate, was out on the ice instructing the crew how to build an ice house. A year among Eskimos at Scoresby Sound had qualified him well for this sort of thing. I looked on from the bulwarks and, over the heads of the ship's company, saw Beal's house take shape.

But there was something decidedly incongruous about the scene.

One man who stood apart from the rest carried a suitcase. That was it—the suitcase! I wondered who would have the temerity to think of crossing trackless Greenlandic wastes with such fancy luggage. I sent for the man. He came on deck and saluted smartly, still gripping his suitcase with the left hand.

I might have known! It was Lieutenant von Rosenvinge.

"Captain, sir," Von began to explain, "Mr. Butcher made a dreadful mistake when he prepared the abandon-ship bill. I hate to say it, sir, but he made no provision for toothpicks!"

Von Rosenvinge patted his bag and continued, "In here, sir, I have Captain Von Paulsen's priceless collection of Eskimo toothpicks,

which are made of durable seal bone and can serve their purpose
repeatedly without being discarded. Why, what a pickle we'd be in,
trying to get along in northeast Greenland without toothpicks! Remember, Captain, the only trees in this part of the country are very
petrified.

"By the way, Captain," the lieutenant added, "there is something
else in here." He looked furtively about him, then pried the bag
open a trifle. It contained the ship's secret codes and papers. This,
strangely enough, made sense.

It was midday on September 11 when the ice pressure was greatest.
Four hours later we were drifting clear of Cape Broer Ruys on Hold
With Hope. The ice relaxed its grip. From this point we could see
into MacKenzie Bay, which lies near the entrance of Franz Joseph
Fiord—the longest fiord in the world.

In 1607 Henry Hudson, seeking the Northwest Passage, had
sailed his *Hopewell* into Franz Joseph Fiord. Whether or not 1607
was a good ice year we unfortunately have no record. There must have
been ice, though, and the risk the famed navigator ran in an effort to
seek a short route to Cathay was ample evidence of his courage and
skill as an ice pilot.

By 8:00 P.M. our propeller and rudder were no longer fouled by
ice. It was quite plain there would be no better opportunity for
maneuver. We were in the main sweep of the current, and the back
pressure of ice piled on the Liverpool Coast would be felt long before
we drew near it. Yet the ice was so closely packed that I knew we
would have little chance of making material progress. Again I sent
for my mentor and asked him what he would do.

His answer came in one word: "Blast."

I should have expected this advice because it was said that Captain
Von Paulsen had a mania for blasting. It was he who had been
responsible for the *Northland's* initial supply of 200 fifty-four-pound
wrecking mines.

So on the first watch we began to blast. This is done by nosing the
ship into the floe which blocks her. A rigid ladder is dropped, and
two men rush to the distal edge of the floe with a "ready" mine. Then
the mine is lowered through a crack of the brash-filled crevasse which
separates it from the floe beyond. It is dropped to a depth of six feet

below the *lower* surface of the ice. This done, the men retreat to the
ship. The ladder is raised, the circuit plugged in and the mine exploded. Invariably a crack will open up through which a ship can
pry her way.

With a well-drilled wrecking-mine team a floe can be cracked three
minutes after the ship noses into it. For forty-five hours we blasted.
At 6:00 P.M., September 13, the ship burst into a lead. In the meantime important developments had taken place.

On September 12 the *Polar Bjorn* had reported she had maneuvered
into a lead and was about to clear the pack. V.P. had ordered her to
proceed to Reykjavik.

Shortly afterward the *North Star* had advised the task-unit commander that she was in the clear and requested instructions. V.P.
ordered her to proceed to the intersection of the edge of the ice pack
with Latitude 73°30′ North. His purpose was to have help at hand
in case the *Northland* failed to escape. On the other hand, if we
succeeded in breaking through, the two ships could support each other
while proceeding south.

Now, with the *Northland* in a lead which was fairly wide and free
of ice, we began to grope our way eastward through the early darkness.

Harmon took two star sights, which showed we had made good a
distance of twelve miles in a *southeasterly* direction. The price of
this distance was twenty-one miles. During this forty-six hours we totaled revolutions for 300 miles and steered a *northeasterly* course.

Before midnight the unseamanlike clatter of loose gear brought a
realization that we were no longer in quiet water. I was aware of an
exhilarating sensation—the gentle rise and fall of the vessel to wave
action. We could not be far from the open sea!

Three months in ice had spoiled us. From now on everything
must be secured; we must be alert for enemy submarines. Wartime
sea routine must be resumed.

Soon floes about us were dipping into the trough of each wave,
singing *squosh! squosh!* and spilling water in roaring cascades as they
rose to the crest. For many crew members there would be seasick-
ness—but even this was preferable to the drab monotony of endless
ice fields.

Dawn, breaking through a cold drizzle, found the *Northland*

laboring in an ugly northeast sea. In late afternoon we made rendezvous with the *North Star*. Signalmen stationed themselves at the
halyards and prepared to "toss bunting."

At a signal from V.P. streams of code flags jumped to the yardarms,
instructing the *North Star* to follow our movements on course one-
eight-zero (south) at six and one-half knots.

"Execute!" V.P. snapped. The flags came down on the run.

Dorris Bell jerked the engine room telegraph to standard-speed-
ahead. The ship limped onto her course, and the *North Star*, steered
by her jury rudder, fell in awkwardly behind. The lame was leading
the blind.

A wild "Hurrah!" from the berth deck told us that the galley
grapevine was working normally. Already all hands knew we were
bound for Iceland.

*Part Two*

THE JAN MAYEN EXPEDITION

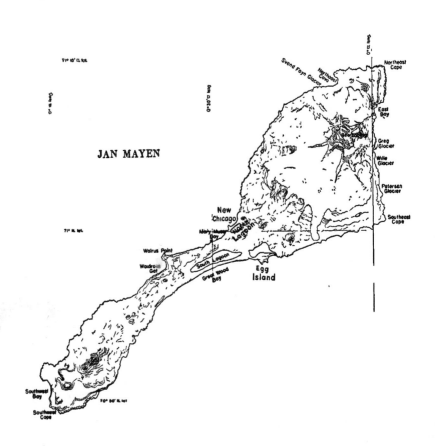

JAN MAYEN

Northeast
Cape

East
Bay

Greg
Glacier

Wille
Glacier

Petersen
Glacier

Southeast
Cape

Svend Foyn Glacier

Northeast
Cove

New
Chicago

North
Lagoon

Mary Muss
Bay

Walrus Point

South Lagoon

Egg
Island

Waldros
Gat

Greenwood
Bay

Southwest
Bay

Southwest
Cape

71° 10' CL tat.

0° 10' Long.

0° 10' Long.

0° 12' Long.

71° N. lat.

70° 50' N. lat.

# Chapter 11

## *ADMIRAL SMITH'S SECRET*

On April 15, 1912, headlines the world over screamed: EXTRA! EXTRA! TITANIC SUNK BY ICEBERG! The largest ship ever built by man, the White Star Line's challenge to transatlantic passenger carriers, the unsinkable *Titanic,* lay somewhere on the bottom of the North Atlantic. A world-shaking tragic end to her maiden voyage.

Crowding safety on a great circle course, the mammoth liner had dipped well into the area of icebergs and struck one—a small one—in the dead of night. The disaster took a toll of 1,513 souls out of 2,224 on board!

It was not until January 20, 1914, that statesmen representing nine major world powers convened to devise ways and means of preventing a recurrence of such a calamity. Legislators and monarchs hastened to ratify the convention which established an International Ice Patrol. To the United States—to its Coast Guard—fell the task of patrolling the northern sea lanes, of tracking down bergs, of predicting their drift and of warning shipping. Thus the science of oceanography achieved a new and practical importance.

One day a young ensign, the junior watch officer on a Coast Guard cutter assigned to the International Ice Patrol, reached port and purchased a one-way ticket to Cambridge, Massachusetts. Ensign Edward Hanson Smith's extraordinary interest and aptitude for ice observation had attracted the attention of his superior officers. Now he was

111

on his way to Harvard University to commence a grooming for the responsibilities of Chief International Ice Observer.

America's entry into World War I interrupted the training of this brilliant young officer. He was ordered overseas for duty afloat. But in 1920 Lieutenant (j.g.) Smith returned to Harvard, thence went on to Bergen, Norway, where he received his finishing touch at the oceanographic center of the world. On his return to duty with the International Ice Patrol, Lieutenant Smith, Chief Observer, scorned relief; he kept to sea, transferred from cutter to cutter in the ice area. Constantly he sought to eliminate the element of guesswork from his forecasts. He would be satisfied with nothing less than perfection. In 1928 Lieutenant Commander Smith led an expedition up the west coast of Greenland to Melville Bay for a study of the principal source of his icebergs. Afterward he returned to Harvard University with his field notes and compiled a thesis which earned for him the coveted Ph.D. in Oceanography.

In 1931 the Reich invited the United States to send a scientist to join Dr. Hugo Eckener, who took his *Graf Zeppelin* to study ice conditions at the North Pole. Lieutenant Commander "Iceberg" Smith was selected, with Lincoln Ellsworth, to represent this country. This experience was destined to prove invaluable when within a decade the Nazi tide surged over Europe and threatened to leap the Atlantic.

Almost overnight in the dark days of the summer of 1940 Greenland became of paramount strategic importance. A naval patrol was needed—at once!—to survey the poorly charted coasts of the world's largest island. It must spot the location of future airdromes and naval bases; mark, in some measure, the countless reefs and shoals; make a further study of ice conditions. A qualified leader, someone who understood ice, someone who knew Greenland, would be required.

Commander "Iceberg" Smith was the man for the job. He got it!

"Iceberg" Smith, one of the world's foremost authorities on Arctic ice, now became a diplomat. With American and Danish statesmen he aided in drafting the "Greenland Agreement," the pact under which the United States was granted base rights in Greenland "for the defense of the Western Hemisphere."

After the President's "shoot on sight" directive Greenland became a beehive of industry. United States bases and weather stations were built with feverish speed, and troops poured into the country.

In addition to the naval defense of the island Commander Smith was obliged to provide escort ships for insuring the safe and timely arrival of these materials and men. His forces were expanded. Armament was heaped upon a heterogeneity of vessels pressed into what was known as the Greenland Patrol. Commander Smith had to be satisfied with anything he could lay his hands on. There were Coast Guard cutters of ancient vintage, Navy gunboats, an assortment of patrol craft, tenders and converted trawlers—not to mention Commander D. B. MacMillan and his schooner *Bowdoin*.

Despite the makeshift character of the Greenland Patrol force, the *esprit de corps* was high. There was not an officer or man who was not proud to be a member of "Iceberg" Smith's navy.

# Chapter 12

# THE NORTHLAND GETS
# TOP-SECRET ORDERS

ON OCTOBER 25, 1943, the *Northland* docked at Narsarssuak, headquarters of the Greenland Patrol. It was here that Admiral Smith flew his flag and kept in touch with the diversified activities of the patrol through a powerful naval radio station at the base.

We had not come directly to Narsarssuak from Iceland after completing the northeast Greenland expedition. This had been an expectation of course. That is, we had more or less expected to depart Iceland immediately after replacing our damaged propeller with a new one which we had requested for delivery at Reykjavik. But as is so often the case with replacement parts, especially in wartime, our new propeller was delayed in transit.

As luck would have it several jobs requiring the *Northland's* services cropped up while we waited for the new propeller. Consequently when the "prop" arrived and was fitted to the ship we were ordered to sea on these unexpected assignments.

The last of our emergency tasks was the evacuation of some forty-odd civilian workers icebound at Cape Adelear on the southeast coast of Greenland, and when we arrived at Narsarssuak we had the evacuees with us.

I was standing on the bridge, watching our passengers disembark and chuckling at Mr. Butcher, who still smarted from what he considered an affront he had received a couple of hours earlier.

Butcher had been handling the ship and trying to push her through about six inches of ice carpeting the fiord leading to Narsarssuak. The *Northland,* never an icebreaker, was finding the going tough. But Butcher, inordinately proud of the ship and her capabilities, was determined she would make it.

We were slugging it out with the ice when a small Coast Guard tug—a sturdy little ship designed and built as a breaker—stood in from seaward. Her commanding officer, observing our bogged-down progress, generously ran ahead of the *Northland* and started opening a track for us. He then leaned out of his pilothouse door, better to see what was going on.

Butcher scooped up a megaphone and darted to the bridge-wing. "You can't do that to us!" he shouted at the tug. "Who said you could pass? We're the senior ship, and you know it. Come back here!"

The tugboat skipper cupped his hands to his mouth. "Pipe down, Butch!" he yelled. "That old ark of yours would get stuck on a piece of flypaper. Haw! Haw! Haw!" He gave his little ship more power, and she leaped ahead.

"That goddam ice-happy sea toad! I'll break my own track! He can't get away with that, can he, Captain?"

I was laughing too heartily to reply at once and finally managed to gasp, "Follow him, Mr. Butcher."

It was the only time I ever heard Butcher raise his voice, and I was still chuckling a couple of hours later when a command car came to a stop on the dock and an aide stepped out. This young officer boarded the *Northland,* introduced himself and told me, "Sir, the admiral wants to see you."

I immediately changed into my finery—that is, my neatest and best-pressed blue uniform—and the aide chauffeured me to the flag office, a lonesome shack about two miles from the head of the fiord. There I was hustled into the cubbyhole from which Admiral Smith operated the Greenland Patrol.

The admiral was seated behind a homemade desk when I entered. He rose, extended a hand in greeting and motioned with his free hand for me to sit down in the only spare chair his office was large enough to accommodate.

As we exchanged the usual cordialities I studied the admiral's physical appearance. In the score of years I had known him time had wrought little change. He was as handsome a man in a masculine way as when I had first seen him. Of average height, his body was compact, lithe and energetic, with quiet, brisk movements that were almost catlike. Despite their piercing intensity, his jet eyes were kindly, reflecting a magnetic personality.

The admiral smiled and plunged into the subject. "It's Jan Mayen," he said. That name brought to my mind a vague recollection of a little volcanic island in the lower reaches of the Greenland Sea. It lay roughly midway between Iceland and Spitzbergen. I had never been there, but I had seen it on the charts. "How soon can you get under way?" the admiral asked.

"In ten minutes, if you give me a ride to the ship, sir," I replied confidently. "Otherwise, in half an hour."

Admiral Smith laughed. "Well, it isn't that urgent. We'll need until midnight to grind out your operation order. Make it daybreak tomorrow."

"Yes, sir," I answered.

"What I have to tell you," the admiral went on, "is top secret. I've been plugging for some time for a high-frequency direction-finder station on Jan Mayen. The commander in chief has finally given me the green light." He rose from his chair and pointed to a speck of an island on a chart behind him. "I want to locate this direction finder where it can be beamed on northeast Greenland and on Norway too, if possible."

The admiral went on to express a belief that the withdrawal of the German Sabine Island force would not end the enemy's attempt to establish a weather-reporting station on northeast Greenland. Sooner or later, he said, the Germans would send out another expedition, set up a weather station and commence radio transmissions to the high command. A high-frequency direction finder on Jan Mayen Island should be able to intercept those transmissions and reveal the location of the enemy. Then, with his whereabouts definitely known, we could move in with certainty and destroy him.

This was to be our first consideration in choosing a site for the direction finder. We must above all be certain of beaming on northeast Greenland. However it was entirely possible that we could find a spot which also would permit beaming on Norway. If this were the case, the direction-finder station probably could keep tab on the enemy battleships *Von Tirpitz* and *Scharnhorst*, which were known to be in Norwegian ports. It would be of extreme value to the Allied forces to have knowledge of their movements.

Since V.P. had gone to the Pacific, I was to take command of the task unit. My job, the admiral explained, would consist of locating a site for the direction finder, landing the material and equipment, erecting the station and seeing to it that everything operated satisfactorily.

The station complement, which we would carry to Jan Mayen as passengers, would consist of approximately eight radiomen and a cook, under Lieutenant Arnold Peterson, with Chief Gunner's Mate Ira A. Beal second in command. I remembered that Peterson and Beal had wintered together in northeast Greenland during 1941-1942. They would make an ideal team for a place like Jan Mayen.

The expedition would have to be solely a *Northland* project, the admiral said. "I would like to give you a second ship—a cargo carrier—but there's nothing available. So you'll have to go it alone. Proceed to Iceland, pick up the cargo and the station crew and then get on about your business as soon as possible."

The admiral reminded me that it was late in the season and that I might expect the ice pack to drift down and spread about Jan Mayen in late November or December. In such an event I would be forced to abandon the job. He called my attention to other hazards: wind, sea, surf, darkness, cold, and finally to what the enemy would likely do when he gained intelligence of our operations.

"I want you to know," my superior officer said, "that it's a gamble and therefore you will not be blamed if you should fail." He paused. "There is very little published information about Jan Mayen, so I suggest you call on Captain Østrup, senior Norwegian naval officer in Iceland. He knows the island as well as anybody. Commodore Wentworth, commandant of the naval operating base, will help you all he can, so will Rear Admiral Watson of the British Icelandic Naval Command. All of them are in on the secret."

Admiral Smith went on to point out that I was on my own and

must make all decisions. There would be many snags which he trusted me to overcome. Moreover I was to bring back as much information as I could collect about Jan Mayen, its hydrography and topography.

"Do nothing to offend the Norwegians," the admiral cautioned. "Remember, Jan Mayen is their island. We must, without fail, subordinate ourselves to them in all matters concerning its defense. At the end of each week make a secret report of your progress to all your superiors in the chain of command. Admiral King will follow you with a great deal of personal interest, and you know how I feel about the project. I wish you all kinds of luck."

The idea of being under the personal scrutiny of the commander in chief himself rather knocked me off my perch. "Thank you, sir. I will do my best," I stammered, feeling like a schoolboy.

The admiral's face relaxed and spread into a smile. "Now tell me what you've been doing since your return from northeast Greenland. I've followed your reports, but they are necessarily impersonal."

I related events as they popped into my mind.

Angmagssalik . . . Kaj Jensen, the colony manager, had entertained us in a manner befitting a king. The handful of Danes were in tuxedos, their ladies in long dresses. Could we help them in any way? Yes! The hospital needed alcohol. We sent in five gallons. Our return party was never given. The ship was called out to answer an SOS.

"Danish governing officials always dress that way," the admiral interposed. "Keeps them from going native and elevates them in the eyes of the Greenlanders. Kaj! That old rascal! He wanted the alcohol to make aquavit! Glad you helped him."

The trip down the east coast and around Cape Farewell with a convoy . . . One morning I was roused with a message from the OOD. The S. S. *Liberty Glow* was lagging behind her station.

"Tell him, for Christ's sake, close up!" I grumbled, and went back to sleep.

After we had delivered the convoy to Kuniat on the west coast I glanced at the signal log. An entry caught my eye. It was a recorded message to the *Liberty Glow*. It read: "For Christ's sake, close up!" Well, it had produced the desired effect.

The mission at Cape Adelear . . . Couldn't tell where the harbor was until we were virtually on top of it. No wonder it was not charted. Return via Prince Christian Sound. Beautiful spot! A vast rock-walled ditch carved through the ice cap. It was so deep that we simply put the *Northland* alongside a cliff face to water ship. Water almost fell into our tanks. No, there was no ice south of Cape Dan, near Angmagssalik.

The *Polar Bjorn?* Yes, she had entered Cape Adelear just as we were leaving. No, I hadn't heard of her rescue of the Canadian bomber crew! The night following her arrival at Cape Adelear the doughty little *Polar Bjorn* sailed, following a course up the coast toward Angmagssalik. As she was passing one of thousands of barren islands which dot that stretch of coast her captain saw, or thought he saw, a light—a feeble glow on a bleak shore where no light ought to be. Captain Marø decided he had better investigate, just in case. The *Polar Bjorn* turned sharply to the westward and ran in toward the coast. Now the light was brighter, flared up at intervals. A signal!

The boat was launched, pulled by sturdy Norwegians. They felt their way among the bergs and growlers, into the rocky shore. There they beached their craft and climbed the slippery island wall, guided by the flame. The sight that greeted them as they walked into the eerie glare of the gasoline-fed beacon told, without words, a saga of privation: the shattered wreck of a bomber, six half-starved men huddled near the fire, two frosty bodies on the frozen snow beyond.

The frostbitten survivors, more dead than alive, were lowered tenderly to the waiting boat and taken to the *Polar Bjorn*. Luckily an Army doctor was on board. When the ship reached the air base at Ikateq the men were well on their way to recovery. . . .

The admiral wound up the conference with an invitation to dinner. It was pleasant to enjoy the company of others during a meal. The flag mess is generally shared by principal staff officers and the admiral's aides. In larger vessels of the Coast Guard and Navy the captain must dine alone. This is traditional—probably because through the years the captain has generally been such a mean old bastard nobody can get along with him! Hence the ostracism.

Tonight I was anxious to get back to my ship. I must read up on Jan Mayen, find out what we were up against and seek information on which to base an expeditionary plan. We would require much material and equipment over and above that projected for the station. I must know what to look for when we arrived in Iceland. It was nearly midnight when I marched over the gangway and sent the navigator to the ship's library for the required reading.

By the time the boatswain's pipe sent all hands to their station for getting under way at 5:00 A.M. I had completed a digest of all the information on board. It resolved into something like this:

Jan Mayen, an Arctic island between Greenland and the north of Norway, about seventy-one degrees north latitude, eight degrees west longitude (position doubtful). It is an island which originated entirely by volcanic processes, about thirty miles long in a southwesterly-northeasterly direction. Its narrowest part, in the central region, is less than two miles wide. The island is divided into three distinct portions.

The southern portion consists of a mass of irregularly placed peaks and volcanic craters of rugged outline, rising to nearly 3,000 feet. In most places it falls steeply into the sea. Here as throughout the island frequent falls of volcanic rock from the cliffs make travel unsafe.

The low central region consists of many large lava flows and volcanic sand deserts with practically no vegetation. There are several beaches of dark volcanic sand, mixed with shiny olive-green crystals and volcanic rock. These beaches are strewed with driftwood from the great rivers of northern Siberia. In the northeastern part of this central region are two lagoons, one on each side, separated from the sea by narrow sand bars.

The northern portion of Jan Mayen is, except for a small shelf of land at the northeastern extremity, entirely occupied by Mount Beerenberg. Its ice field and glaciers discharge into the sea. The impressive Beerenberg is about 8,000 feet elevation. It dominates the view from practically every part of the island on the few days when it can be seen. The most remarkable characteristic of Beerenberg is its ice-filled crater, which is more than one mile in diameter.

Henry Hudson discovered the island in 1607 and called it *Hudson's Tutches*. A few years later the Dutch, driven from Spitzenbergen by the British and Danes, established a whaling factory at Walrus Gat on the northwest side. It was raided and destroyed by the Basques, who held a grudge against the Dutch. But the latter re-established themselves and determined to hold their new factory through the winter months. A group of seven men was left on the island when the summer closed, as a token occupation force. All of them succumbed to the rigors of winter.

The jurisdictional status of the island remained in dispute until 1921, when it was awarded to Norway under a League of Nations convention.

Almost continuous fog, broken by fierce gales and heavy rain, characterizes the Jan Mayen summers. In winter the island is lashed by frequent violent storms of hurricane force. During the winter season a surf runs at all times on all parts of the island except when drift ice is present. Throughout this season landings are difficult and hazardous.

Save for a generalized location of the 100-fathom curve, there is no hydrographic information. A sketch chart existed, on which the Austrian survey of 1879 had plotted the topography in detail. But only a few sporadic soundings were noted—these at a considerable distance offshore.

I could see now that our trip to Jan Mayen would be no junket.

Usually I called my officers together immediately after sailing to acquaint them with the ship's mission. Thence they would report to their divisions and inform their men of the plans. This was the American way of doing things. It encouraged teamwork; men were not obliged to follow orders blindly.

This time, because of top secrecy, the flow of information stopped with the officers. The crew would not know what the ship was up to until she sailed from Iceland bound for Jan Mayen. Silence gave way to rumors, which flew from all recesses of the berth deck to the galley, the traditional center of ship's grapevine. There the cooks digested the gossip, philosophized and evolved the "official rumor." This one reached the wardroom and leaked into the cabin. It was like this: The admiral was "sore as hell" because the ship had failed to fetch a stool along with the piano she had brought from Iceland. He was sending the *Northland* back to Iceland for the piano stool. That was the reason for all the "hush-hush!"

# Chapter 13

# ICELANDIC OBSTACLES

A SIXTY-MILE gale shrieked across Reykjavik harbor. Huge seas pounded the mole, spread sheets of spray over the inner harbor. Inside the breakwater wavelets seethed angrily, grew to waves which crashed against the *Northland's* side. Exposed to the full sweep of the wind, she was pinioned fast against her berth. Pellets of fine snow whipped around my parka hood, bit into the exposed side of my face. I edged my way against the wind, holding with cocked head and squinted eyes for the *Northland's* gangway. Butcher, waiting on deck, could read unconcealed disappointment as I climbed the ladder.

Many obstacles had been dumped in the path of the expedition since the ship's arrival at Iceland almost a week before. Another had just been added. The first of these obstacles had greeted us on the day of our arrival; the rest followed in rapid succession.

"It is too late in the season!" said the Norwegians. "Jan Mayen is the wind factory of the Atlantic. North Lagoon is the only place you can get in. Everywhere else about the island are uncharted submarine pinnacles. They spring up and disappear sporadically due to volcanic action. Two steamers have been wrecked on them in the past few years. Last year the British tried to build a station. All their boats were smashed, and they had to give up."

Only Captain Østrup, the senior Norwegian naval officer present, offered encouragement. "It is a hazardous undertaking. People will tell you it is impossible. But neither can a bee fly. Somehow I think

122

you Americans will succeed. Our gunboat, the *Honningsvaad,* is due there with the winter relief force for the garrison about December first. She will lend a hand if you wish."

"Thank you, sir," I replied. "I expect to be finished by that time."

"Hmm!"

"It's jolly well late in the season," echoed the British. "But you Yanks can work wonders!"

There was a Lieutenant Commander Goodwin L. Dossland in charge of U. S. Naval Communication at Iceland. He wanted to join us. I wanted to have him. Dossland had been a college professor of radio engineering before the war. His knowledge of high-frequency direction finders would be a welcome asset to the expedition. I had a feeling that Lieutenant Peterson and his men would come to us with a knowledge of HF/DF operation. Installing the delicate equipment called for an expert.

A company of Seabees was completing work on a naval tank farm at Hvalfjordur, thirty-five miles from Reykjavik. The Seabees had already gained a reputation the world over for efficient construction in the face of difficulties. I would give a lot for only a squad of them.

I delivered a carefully rehearsed plea to the assistant commandant of the naval operating base for the services of Commander Dossland and eight Seabees. The answer was "No."

The next day I received a phone call from the naval base. The conversation went like this: "This is the supply officer speaking. The Army has no sacks for your coal."

"Put it in the sand bags we ordered."

"But they can't spare the men to bag it."

"We'll do it ourselves."

Another day, another phone call: "This is the supply officer speaking, Commander. The Army can't give you the tractor, jeep and stoves you ordered."

I dropped the telephone and rushed to the Army supply depot.

"I'm sorry, sir," a young major told me, "but we have no authority to issue any equipment other than that included in the list we received from Washington."

Without taking time to argue, I hurried to GHQ. There I was informed that the chief of staff was not in, but perhaps I would like to see Colonel Knight, assistant chief of staff for supply. Naturally I would like to see Colonel Knight, and I was hustled into the office.

Colonel Knight listened quietly to my complaint, then without making any reply picked up the phone and called a number. "Colonel Knight talking! How come you have no authority to issue expeditionary equipment to the *Northland?*" he demanded gruffly. The colonel started to listen, then interrupted the officer on the other end of the line. "Now get this straight! Have a tractor, jeep, trailer and three number-twenty stoves at the dock where the ship is moored by noon today! . . . What? . . . To hell with the papers! You people couldn't put a button on a henhouse door without a bunch of fool papers!" He slammed the field set back on the hook with a bang.

The equipment arrived well before the appointed time.

Two days slipped by. The ship was nearly ready to sail. Peterson and his crew had not shown up. Neither had we received a radio-transmitting set being flown to Iceland from Presque Isle. I was restless. Every day pushed deeper into the Arctic winter. Every hour was bringing the ice pack closer to Jan Mayen. Every minute was becoming priceless.

I was called on the carpet by the assistant commandant. An Icelander had complained that two of my men had threatened him with rifles. If so, the *Northland* was doing nothing to maintain friendly relations with the Icelandic government. I investigated. Two of my signalmen had been practicing on the dock with blinker guns. The Icelander had strolled between them and failed to see that these guns fired only stabs of light in dots and dashes. That was all.

The fifth day brought Arnold Peterson and his men. Still no radio transmitter. This was the only thing holding us up.

But now a doubt assailed me. We had not anticipated that so much material would be heaped on the ship. We had counted on carrying a two-story frame structure which would satisfy all housing requirements on Jan Mayen. Now we learned this was for the direction finder only. There would also be a Quonset hut for messing, one for quartering and a frame building to contain two large Diesel generators.

All this additional weight on deck caused the *Northland* to roll lazily on the slightest pretext—even at the dock! As I felt this roll I vaguely recalled having seen a letter bearing on the ship's stability. I remembered her reputation for top-heaviness and the concrete ballast in her bilges. I fanned through the files, found the letter. It read: "Under no circumstances shall the *Northland* be so loaded that the GM is reduced below a figure of 1.25 feet." The GM I knew to be a measure of stability. This directive was addressed to the commanding officer. It was signed by an admiral, my immediate superior, for logistics.

I asked the commodore commanding the naval operating base to have an "inclining experiment"* made. It was done—promptly. The result stunned me! The GM was .86 feet—far below the minimum 1.25.

"Protest your orders!" some of the commodore's staff officers advised me. "You had no way of knowing your ship would be so heavily loaded. No one will blame you if the expedition doesn't sail. But if you get into any kind of a sea and the *Northland* capsizes, you'll lose everything. And it will be in direct disobedience to orders. You won't have a leg to stand on."

But I did have to live with myself, so I ordered Mr. Murphy to stow all the coal in the shaft alley and spread the lumber over the wardroom country and berth deck. I calculated that this would increase our stability maybe a tenth of a foot.

We had banked heavily on picking up some lightering equipment in Iceland. I think we looked over every raft, scow and landing craft on the island. None was suitable for use as lightering equipment. We would have to use our own boats and perhaps the two large life rafts the vessel carried.         ·

On November 2 Lieutenant Commander Dossland rushed to the ship with bad news. A mistake had been made—a serious mistake. The radio transmitter intended for installation on Jan Mayen had been flown to the U. S. Naval Operating Base, *Ireland*. It would, of course, be flown on to Iceland at the earliest opportunity, but such a flight must depend on availability of transport aircraft and flying conditions. It might be a day, a week, or even longer before we received it.

---

* An inclining experiment is made by shifting weight of known mass a given distance across the main deck. A pendulum records the angle of heel incident to measured shifting. From these values the GM or stability is computed.

Dossland volunteered a solution. "We have a worn-out transmitter of the same type somewhere in the storeroom," he told me. "It will have to be partially rebuilt, but I can scrape up the parts and have it as good as new inside twenty-four hours. We'll get right to work on it."

"Good boy!" I exclaimed. "Every hour counts now!"

This incident convinced me that I must have Dossland with us on the expedition at all costs. I decided to make another bid for his services. This time I would use the honey-and-oil approach. I promptly invited Commodore R. S. Wentworth and his assistant commandant to dinner and included Captain Østrup and Von Rosenvinge in my party.

The evening was an outstanding success—in more ways than one. After the party the commodore paused at the gangway as he was about to leave. He turned to me and said, "Mr. Dossland will report on board in the morning for duty with your Jan Mayen task unit." Then the commodore smiled knowingly and added, "And four Seabees will come with him."

I followed Commodore Wentworth all the way to his car in an attempt to voice my thanks adequately.

Dossland did not wait for morning to pack his belongings and move on board. "Just in case the commodore should change his mind!" Dossland explained to me when his personal effects arrived at midnight.

The Seabees reported on board at noon and the substitute radio was delivered that afternoon. I immediately sent a sailing telegram giving our time of departure as 7:00 A.M. the following morning.

A furious gale broke that night. I was up and about early the next morning, anxiously awaiting a pilot. None showed up. I put on my parka and let the wind virtually push me across the street from where we were moored to the port director's office. There I learned from the duty officer that no pilot would risk taking the ship out in such a storm. The port director could not, therefore, accept responsibility for damage to my ship or other vessels lying inside the breakwater. If I sailed without a pilot under such conditions, I must shoulder all blame for casualties—and casualties appeared inevitable.

Fighting my way back to the ship against the wind, I thought of the consequences of further delay. I made a quick mental calculation.

My ship cost the government about $2,000 a day in operating expenses. On the threshold of departure her over-all value greatly exceeded that figure. I reasoned I could inflict considerable damage of a minor nature without plunging the taxpayers' equity in my ship into the red.

Mr. Butcher's countenance reflected my disappointment as I pulled myself up the gangway in that sixty-mile gale that morning. He stood immobile, awaiting my pleasure, oblivious to the little piles of swirling snow about his feet.

"Call all hands, if you please, Mr. Butcher," I said as nonchalantly as possible. "We will get under way at once, and you may take her out."

A grin spread across Butcher's ruddy features. He was happiest when he was handling a vessel under adverse conditions, when he could pit his skill against the elements.

"Aye, aye, sir!" Butcher saluted and started for the bridge.

"Wait!" I shouted after him. "Have Murphy, Von Rosenvinge and Harmon stand by near the gangway as a survey board—just in case."

"I won't give them any work, Captain," Butcher replied confidently.

# Chapter 14

# NEW CHICAGO

IT HAD been my intention to sail along the Icelandic coast to Langenes and await ideal weather conditions before making a dash for Jan Mayen. Good weather was the exception rather than the rule at this time of year, and I had a heavily laden top-heavy ship to keep on even keel. If a storm broke before we reached Langenes, there would always be shelter close at hand in one of many fiords along the north coast.

The day after our departure from Reykjavik we rounded the Icelandic Claw. The weather was fair, so I sent for Travers and asked for a forecast. Our weather prophet had the answer at his finger tips. "The weather will hold good for twenty-four hours," Travers declared confidently. That settled it. I decided to sail directly for Jan Mayen.

The weather held good for twenty-four hours—and a trifle longer. Then a southerly wind began making up. But this was a fair wind. Moreover when we sailed along the north coast of Jan Mayen two days after leaving the "Claw" we had a good lee.

On November 7 we were approaching our anchorage off North Lagoon, at the funnellike midsection of the island. It was 8:00 A.M., but still dark. Visibility was reduced to a mere hundred yards by the darkness and blanketing snow. "One mile to go!" The sound of rattling windows, of swishing seas and moaning wind all but dampened the report from the radar room.

"Signals!" the navigator shouted. "Send the recognition signal."

At 10 P.M. father and son bask in the August sunshine beside their sod house, near Thule, Greenland.

Chief Machinist's Mate Carl
(Snoose) Jensen, veteran of
Alaska, North Greenland and
Antarctica.

Lieut. Russell with "George." No canine
has ever traveled through as many degrees
of latitude.

Captain Carl C. Von Paulsen.

Rear Admiral Edward H. Smith.

On the flying bridge the signal searchlight stabbed out the letters "USA . . . USA . . . USA." Those were the letters agreed on with the Norwegian naval command. Ahead of the ship a faint light flared briefly, then faded. I knew our presence was acknowledged from shore.

The anchor plunged to the bottom a quarter-mile off the sand bar which completely captures the waters of North Lagoon. The wind whistled more furiously than before and sent biting snow swirling along our slippery decks, piling it behind bulwarks and other objects. But the anchorage was a cozy one.

Calling away the motor surfboat, I took Dossland, Hallencrutz, Murphy, Von Rosenvinge, Harmon and Peterson ashore with me to estimate the situation. The boat grounded through a mild surf with a single row of breakers and was instantly seized by a squad of husky men who steadied it while we sprang out. These were soldiers from the Norwegian garrison. As soon as the boat was secure one of them introduced himself. "I am Captain Spielhaug, the commandant here," he said in perfect English.

After presenting my officers I immediately made known our first task. Spielhaug was already familiar with the object of our mission. We now had to select a suitable location for our high-frequency direction-finder station. It would require an arc covering the Greenland Sea. It also would require good defensive qualities, lend itself to logistics and have available a year-round supply of fresh water.

Captain Spielhaug led us to a flat plot of snow-covered ground nestled at the foot of a steep hill near the beach. "I recommend this," he said. "Beneath the snow is a narrow-gauge railroad which runs all the way to the lagoon where our principal outpost hut is located. You could put your living quarters and power plant down there by our hut and use the railroad and push car for hauling your materials."

I turned to Dossland and asked, "What do you think?"

"You can't do much better," he answered. "This should give us coverage from Iceland clockwise to Trondheim and maybe farther."

"Then we will set up just as Captain Spielhaug suggests," I said. "You may commence operations immediately, Mr. Murphy."

Everything had been planned to the last detail, including the order in which supplies and materials were to be sent ashore and the organization for handling them. Lieutenant Murphy was to command the company of men on shore. His unit was divided into two platoons, with Hallencrutz in command of the construction platoon and Dorris Bell in command of the transportation platoon. Bell would unload the boats and transport the materials to wherever they were required. Hallencrutz, with his artificers, nonrated men and Seabees were to grade the land, erect the structures and install the equipment. In addition there was a headquarters unit which consisted of cooks, messmen, gunner's mates, a storekeeper and a signalman.

The most delicate task fell to Lieutenant Harmon, who had charge of the ship-to-shore movement. He was responsible for the boats and rafts. Beaching and launching these through the surf required skill of the highest order. It was the ideal job for Harmon, who had been brought up in the Coast Guard as a surfman and was happiest when handling boats. He had the pick of the crew to aid him. Among these was Travers.

The work of unloading the ship and loading the boats was placed under Butcher, aided by Lieutenant (j.g.) T. M. Krotky, the supply officer. The watches were made watch-and-watch in order to provide a maximum number of men for the project. Lieutenant H. B. Flippin and Ensign Morton Sills were on the sick list. This left O'Hara and Hershey in charge of the deck watches. The two ensigns, Maurice Rucker and Henry Rothauser, were turned to under Butcher. I even had a job for Von Rosenvinge—one which fitted him to perfection.

Terminal weather in Norway gave the Nazis a distinct advantage over American and British air forces for flight operations in the Greenland Sea. An air umbrella had been set up on paper to support the Jan Mayen expedition by British and American air coverage from Iceland. I had no illusions, however, and knew that the likelihood of our ever seeing an Allied plane was extremely remote. But there was something we could bank on. The moment the *Northland* opened up her radio transmitter she would be DF'd by the enemy and identified at once. Her presence at this time of year could mean only that an offensive operation was under way. Then Nazi bombers would be over us as thick as flies around a garbage wagon.

The German high command was well aware of the Norwegians' occupation of Jan Mayen. And he was just as aware as Captain Spielhaug that he could take the island with a well-supported battalion of troops. But the Norwegians' presence was defensive in character, hence there was nothing for the Germans to worry about.

It was imperative, therefore, that our operations remain undetected by the enemy and our ship's radio be kept silent at all costs. I decided on a departure from the communication instructions which had been given me by higher authority. And this was how Von Rosenvinge fitted into the picture.

With Captain Spielhaug's consent I arranged to billet Von Rosenvinge at Norwegian headquarters in the capacity of communications-and-liaison officer. It would be necessary, of course, for Von to encode and decode my traffic in Spielhaug's British cipher. It would be sent to the British through Norwegian radio. The British admiral commanding Iceland Command would pass it by hand to the U. S. naval operating base at Iceland, and thence it would "down the line" as a dispatch re-enciphered in American code. The reverse procedure would be followed with traffic addressed to me. Hence the *Northland* could maintain complete radio silence.

Returning to the beach, I was pleased to find the little railroad in operation with our jeep providing the motive power. A tent city was springing up, and heavy construction materials were being landed. After removing my parka and putting on boots, I pitched in and worked with the men unloading boats in the surf. This was the best way to supervise the first day's activity. Moreover it enabled me to determine how much my men could take. If I could stand it, they could!

Darkness fell in midafternoon. It brought clearing weather with increased cold. But by this time the tents were up, the cook shack completed and the cooks busy preparing supper. A pair of generators, weighing one ton each, had been brought ashore and were chugging away, illuminating the landing and railroad and lighting our tents and the Norwegian outpost.

This was the first time in history that an electric light on shore had cast its beam on the Greenland Sea. Our Norwegian allies were delighted, for Hallencrutz had run part of our circuit into their quarters while their outpost guard was helping us on the beach.

When the Norwegian guard knocked off at 5.00 P.M. it was further amazed to find an array of 20-mm. and .50-calibre machine guns set up in a quadrangle about the installation. Our allies promptly coined a name for the station: "New Chicago!" This name has stuck to the bar at North Lagoon to the present day.

Our men worked far into the night with only a pause for supper. I grew weary, my movements became mechanical. I was conscious of the occasional gleam of Harmon's slicker, wet with spray from the surf. This was when he shoved a surfboat or boxlike raft laden with gear through the breakers. We would wade into the cold water and steady the floating equipment while pushing it higher onto the rocky beach. Now and then we would be caught unawares by seas a bit heavier than their fellows and our boots would fill. For a few minutes our lower limbs would ache, but our body heat soon warmed the water sloshing in our boots, so no one minded it a great deal.

At times I silently obeyed the orders of petty officers who failed to recognize me in the darkness. Somehow I got a kick out of this. Once I was wrestling with a package a bit too heavy for me. Someone came to my aid. We carried it under a light, where I recognized Dr. Herbert E. Pedersen, the ship's surgeon.

Above the roar of the surf we heard the chugging of the jeep and the blows of hammers. Men already were setting up the Quonset huts. Around midnight it started to snow again. I wondered if Butcher's white collar were wilted. I was vaguely aware that the boating activity had paused. The men huddled wherever they could find a lee, smoking, talking, waiting for another boatload.

Suddenly the *Northland's* powerful searchlight cut through the darkness and focused on two objects bobbing in the sea off her starboard quarter. The motor cargo boat and a life raft were adrift, and the raw wind was sweeping them rapidly to sea!

I watched anxiously, wondering if Butcher would get the ship under way to go after them. In a few minutes the two craft were out of range of the searchlight. My heart sank. Out where they were, the seas were higher. Because of peculiarities of electronics, wooden craft would not show on the radar scope against such a sea return.

Then through the falling snow I saw smoke from the *Northland's* exhaust and knew she was under way. Would she find Harmon and the boats?

The answer was quick in coming. Seemingly far at sea a yellow flame shot up and slowly faded to a dim light which danced up and down. I knew Harmon had ignited some gasoline in a bucket to make a beacon.

Everyone was dog-tired now. I ordered work to stop until 8:00 A.M.

The next day was one of those days when everything goes wrong. It started with the breakdown of the motor cargo boat and the *Northland* having to dash off to the rescue. Then shortly after daylight Hershey, who had the deck, reported that our radar showed an airplane approaching from the east.

I rushed on deck, heard the drone of several engines and concluded that it was an enemy plane. I called all hands to battle stations. The weather was good but cloudy. Momentarily we glimpsed a large plane wing bearing the familiar black cross. But it was swallowed instantly by a stratum of lower clouds. Moreover the big Nazi bomber was well out of effective range. As the roar of his motors faded slowly into the southwest I hoped he had not spotted the *Northland* or the activity on shore.

I went into the landing to talk it over with Captain Spielhaug. "No," the Norwegian commandant agreed, "I don't think he saw you. He would have circled for a closer look, had he done so. Perhaps I should have told you, every Tuesday at 10:00 A.M. promptly that plane or one like it passes Egg Island. He must use it for a landfall."

United States and British forces in Iceland knew him as the "Milk man" because of the regularity of his flights. It was well known, too, that his mission was primarily reconnaissance and that he sought Murmansk-bound convoys. The *Northland* had been introduced to him early in the summer while en route to northeast Greenland. From that introduction it was obvious he avoided armed resistance.

Egg Island conveyed no meaning to me at the time. Later I was to learn that it is a semicircular volcanic neck connected to the south shore of Jan Mayen Island by a peninsula of volcanic tuff.

The work of landing materials and piecing them together on shore continued without interruption until well after dark, when moderating weather brought a heavier surf. Perhaps I should have called a halt to ship-to-shore operations when this occurred, but I was anxious to get as much as possible ashore and put some stability in the ship by decreasing her load.

About 5:00 P.M. one of the twenty-six-foot Monomoy surfboats had just been loaded and was awaiting a tow to the beach. Suddenly painter and stern line parted, and the boat began to sink. Butcher calmly ordered grapnels hove at her in an effort to snag her.

At this moment a powerful blast of wind out of the northeast spun the *Northland* on her anchor chain and pushed her away from the sinking boat.

We realized this was the beginning of a sudden northeast gale so characteristic of Jan Mayen weather. The boat was expendable. And because there were plenty of spare parts in the ship we were not too concerned over losing her load until a minute or so later when Lieutenant Krotky yelled: "The counterpoise wire! All we've got is in that boat!"

Krotky's shout was devastating. The counterpoise was essential to the operation of the HF/DF, and it could not be replaced east of Boston!

It was now apparent that the boat had been holed on her last trip through the surf when she pounded on a rock, but in the dark no one had noticed the stove-in plank.

Butcher's white, starched collar flashed as he grabbed a megaphone. Men poured into the nineteen-foot Monomoy. The boat was lowered from the davits on the run. Someone tossed in a heavy grapnel with a long line.

Even as the nineteen-footer followed the snow-streaked searchlight beam over the hissing seas, I felt the ship quiver and knew we must be dragging anchor—onto a lee shore! I gave orders for getting under way immediately, recalled the boats and had the chain hove in. Maybe, I thought, the gale would fetch the sunken boat and its precious counterpoise wire onto the beach during the night. I decided to anchor in Walrus Gat a few miles down the coast and search after daybreak.

Dutch whaling ships had based in Walrus Gat three centuries ago. It should be a fair lee in northeasterly weather, and this was what I needed. With so much loose gear about the ship I could not risk putting to sea until everything was secure. When the *Northland* rounded the cape and dropped anchor Walrus Gat seemed snug and cozy.

I was awakened during the night by an unfamiliar motion. A disturbing jerkiness seemed to break the normally gentle rising and falling of the hull. I suddenly realized that the keel was rhythmically striking bottom.

Hurrying to the bridge, I collided with the messenger whom the officer of the deck had sent to call me. It at once became apparent that the wind had backed abruptly to north. With scant shelter to dampen them the seas were piling into the shallow cove. Swells were mounting higher and higher every minute. Happily the quartermasters were trained in the operation of the anchor windlass; there was no time to set the special sea detail. We soon were steaming out of Walrus Gat, meeting the impact of the sea and wind.

I put the sea on our quarter after we got about a mile offshore and stood in a southwesterly direction around the end of Jan Mayen Island. Then, in its lee, the *Northland* stood along the weather or sheltered shore until we were opposite Egg Island.

Dawn broke and left no doubt that this was the prominent demivolcano which Captain Spielhaug said the Nazi plane we had seen the day before probably used as a landfall. It rose majestically out of the sea, a lone promontory among colorful coastal cliffs.

The weather was still overcast, but much clearer and bitterly cold. The white, regular slopes of Mount Beerenberg, a volcano which occupies virtually the entire northeast section of Jan Mayen, towered into the sky, its cone hidden by clouds. In the distance, to the southwestward, innumerable volcanoes were wholly exposed beneath the milky overhead.

But it was Egg Island which occupied our immediate attention. We easily understood why aircraft would use it as a natural beacon. There was no adjacent relief to produce downdrafts.

But ships? I knew there was a sound basis for the Norwegian's fear of submarine pinnacles in these waters, because volcanic necks are generally the origin of dikes which fan out in all directions.

To guard against striking such a rock formation I ordered the sonar men to echo-range ahead through an arc of forty-five degrees, had the chains manned and the ship's speed reduced to dead-slow. Thanks to this precaution, we located a shallow submarine ridge on the starboard hand but did not have to alter course to avoid it.

The ancient lava flow which connects Egg Island with the land forms a natural breakwater. This made a fine anchorage on the west side, sheltered from the surge pouring around the east end of Jan Mayen. The place was snug, with the surface ruffled only by racing white caps.

After anchoring I hurried ashore and crossed the island on foot, anxious to learn if the boat containing the counterpoise wire had been found. As I trudged into New Chicago I met Dossland. He was smiling smugly.

"So you found the surfboat!" I exclaimed, noting his delight.

"No, sir," Dossland replied. "It's better than that! When I heard the wire was lost I drilled down six feet and got a water ground. All I need now is some copper pipe. You have plenty on board."

I offered a silent prayer of thanks that we had Dossland with us.

# Chapter 15

## *JAN MAYEN BATHS— HOT AND COLD*

JAN MAYEN was an island with two governors. The onus of authority was vested in Captain Spielhaug as military governor—at the expense of the civil governor. All that remained to the civil governor was his title. He carried it with the dignity of a sovereign.

Mr. Øien, the civil governor, was a tall, sinewy man of perhaps fifty years of age. Fourteen of his years had been spent on Jan Mayen. The situation might have been difficult, had not Spielhaug and Øien enjoyed a mutual respect and been extremely tactful about showing it.

At any rate the presence of both governors on board the *Northland* was an education in protocol and diplomacy to my officers, my men and myself. It was not easy, we learned, to deal impartially with two important personages of exactly equal rank. This was particularly true when we became involved in such minute details as berthing and seating arrangements.

I solved the latter problem by placing Mr. Øien on my left, where the guest of honor customarily sits in Scandinavian countries. I explained privately to Captain Spielhaug that in the United States the guest of honor sits on the right of his host. Both were happy. That was on the night of November 12, when the two governors came to

dine with me at our anchorage off North Lagoon. At the time I had
not anticipated the berthing question.

On November 11, a sudden shift of wind to the south forced us
to vacate hurriedly our Egg Island anchorage. We cruised around the
east side of Jan Mayen Island and returned to New Chicago, where
there was again a lee, and resumed unloading cargo. Since the wind
continually blew with gale force, the seas remained sufficiently flat for
boating. But there was always a backlash from around the island
which produced a surf.

Conditions at North Lagoon were much the same as they had been
on our arrival at Jan Mayen, except that the hours of daylight were
shortening appreciably. It was some time during the darkness of late
afternoon on the twelfth that we holed the remaining twenty-six-foot
surfboat and also the motor surfboat. Luckily Harmon got both boats
under the davits before they sank. This left us only the motor cargo
boat and the two boxlike life rafts for moving cargo. Of course we
still had the two nineteen-foot Monomoy surfboats, but they were too
small for freight and could be used only on odd trips with men under
oars.

On the night of November 13, when Captain Spielhaug and Mr.
Øien came to dinner, it was with the expectation they would return to
shore after the movies. They stayed a fortnight.

Another abrupt shift of wind—to the north—made New Chicago
again a lee shore. There was barely enough time to hoist the motor
cargo boat and claw to windward. Our departure was so sudden that
we had to leave the two life rafts to pound on the beach. I again
determined to seek a lee on the south side of the island.

My two guests were delighted at being obliged to remain on board.
To them the *Northland* meant well-heated quarters, a night's sleep
between *sheets* and an opportunity to see the movies. The plan of the
day for tomorrow did not contemplate placing them on shore. Tomorrow would be November 14—Tuesday—"Milkman Day!"

I considered that my primary mission did not lend itself to seeking
combat with isolated planes and submarines. My duty was: First,
avoid contact with the Nazi bomber known as the "Milkman." Second, if he should sight us, shoot him down before he had a chance
to reveal our presence.

When the *Northland* reached her little haven behind Egg Island the stars hung bright and clear. And Egg Island was a natural ambuscade behind which the ship could crouch, unseen, until the German plane was directly overhead.

To carry out my plan I anchored the vessel close under the precipitous volcanic wall of Egg Island, buoyed the anchor and made ready for slipping the cable. As dawn broke at 9:45 A.M. the crew was sent to battle stations. The muzzles of all weapons were so elevated as to be ready for the "Milkman" the instant he passed over the ancient crater.

Actually I respected this German airman who dared all kinds of weather to make his rounds. But it was either him or us. If, however, he were to pass out of gunfire range, I doubted that he would observe the *Northland,* because her camouflage blended well with the snow and wind-swept outcrops of basalt lava.

"It's ten o'clock," Captain Spielhaug announced grimly. "He should be here any minute now." The Norwegian's jaw was set, his features drawn. There was no room in his heart for sentiment. To him a German was a German—one of a race to be exterminated. He hated all Germans with fervor.

The minutes sped by and spread into hours. Men at their weapons relaxed to sip the coffee served up to them from time to time. By 1:30 P.M. darkness had fallen over the island. The alert was secured. We knew the "Milkman" would not call that day. He did not call the following day, or the next. After that the weather became so bad he could not have sighted us.

I invited the two governors to remain on board and give us the benefit of their hydrographic knowledge. Neither Spielhaug nor Øien needed urging. Their answer was a ready "Yes!"

From November 15 to November 19 the wind shifted about so capriciously that the *Northland* was kept constantly on the move, seeking shelter. At times the anemometer needle climbed to ninety miles per hour. This was as far as it could move. At times the air was heavy with blasts of snow. At times, when the wind was from the north, the skies were swept clear of clouds—save for a billowy bundle that persisted about the summit of Beerenberg. And at times the air temperature plunged below zero.

By this time the only remaining piece of freight aboard the *North-land* was the high-frequency direction finder.

Considering all this, I resolved not to attempt landing this all-important piece of gear until we had the most favorable conditions. Truthfully, I was alarmed lest they never be good. The heavy surf persisted day after day. And each day brought closer the possibility of ice drifting in from the north.

On November 20 Beerenberg's summit was clear, save for a heavy white plume which tended sharply downwind from the crater. The crew was enthralled by the belief that it was witnessing the spectacle of an active volcano in eruption.

I was convinced that the supposed emission of steam was merely drifting snow. However I said nothing to dispel excitement. Sometimes it boosts morale to let men believe what they wish to believe.

On three sides Beerenberg pushed blue fingers of glacial ice down its steep sides to dip into the sea. These glaciers were so scored with crevasses that they completely isolated the northeast end to the foot traveler. Moreover heavy swells and a bold coast line made this part of Jan Mayen generally inaccessible to boating.

The mystery surrounding the hydrography of the island was being gradually and quietly dispelled. Each time the *Northland* shifted position the bottom topography of our chart was expanded. Where no recorded soundings had existed before, there were now three rows of them completely encircling the island. Most amazing to Spielhaug and Øien was the audacity of the Yanks in closing to within a half-mile of the coast, save where some wreck clinging to the rocks warned of outlying reefs.

On November 21 the wind steadied from the southeast to allow a landing at New Chicago. While the surf was too heavy to risk an attempt with the direction finder, we had an opportunity to replenish the rapidly depleting food supplies of our shore party.

Captain Spielhaug invited me to enjoy a Finnish bath at his headquarters. I accepted without hesitation. It would be a welcome respite from the salt-water baths I had been obliged to accept on shipboard.

I wondered what the Norwegians used for fuel to have a hot bath ready twenty-four hours a day. But I asked no questions. The answer came when we entered the bathhouse. The structure was built over a fumarole, a hole in the rocks from which natural steam constantly poured. I learned that there were several of these fumaroles on the midsector of Jan Mayen, though none was known to exist elsewhere on the island.

We saturated our bodies with steam and then dashed outside to roll in the snow. After this I was treated to a vigorous rubdown and a mug of hot rum punch. This was all so exhilarating I found it difficult to understand why our erstwhile guests enjoyed being battered about on board the *Northland*. But they did, and they wanted more of it. Both returned that night.

The frame structure which would house the direction finder was nearly completed and was now ready to receive the instrument. The sides of the building were heavily sandbagged up to the second story to keep it from blowing away. Most of the other heavy construction at New Chicago also was completed—except the job of getting two and one-half tons of direction finder ashore.

On November 22 the wind moderated, and the surf subsided a bit. Landing conditions were far from ideal, but I felt another such day might not present itself before the ice set in. I decided to send in the finder.

Our two life rafts were lashed together and brought alongside under the main boom. The heavy tackle creaked. The big package rose slowly from the deck, swung outboard and was gingerly lowered onto the waiting life rafts. There it was secured with heavy lines, and Harmon took over, towing the rafts and their precious cargo with the motor cargo boat.

The crew lined the rail to follow every move when Harmon began slowly towing the instrument shoreward. From the ship it looked like a floating grain elevator rolling precariously with every sea. I clutched the bridge railing tightly, thinking the rafts would surely capsize every time they dipped.

Travers, standing in the bow of the motor cargo boat with a line-throwing gun, looked anxiously at Harmon, who had the tiller. Just outside the row of breakers Harmon gave the word.

Travers fired. The thin, light messenger line arched shoreward, and Murphy and his men caught it and briskly hauled in. Then they took a strain on the heavier line which followed. In a few seconds the direction finder was ashore!

The comparative calm which enabled us to land the finder was short-lived. Again we were forced to move from place to place, seeking shelter where we could find it.

During the frequent movements of the *Northland* about Jan Mayen I had noticed a rather flat lava shelf lying along the northeast extremity of the island at the foot of Beerenberg. This apparently level place stretched four miles to the westward of Northeast Point. On its west end a stony beach bordered on a little cove which separated the shelf from the bold, glacier-scoured coast beyond.

I was anxious to get about the business of collecting information about Jan Mayen. The lava shelf intrigued me. So far as anyone in the Norwegian garrison knew, a landing never had been made on the northeast sector. It appeared that this place would be ideal for direction finding. It would be possible to take bearings through nearly a complete circle.

The cove was the only place where a landing could be made. I decided to make one. Spielhaug, Øien, Harmon and Hershey were selected to go with me. The landing was not difficult, and soon we were making our way over rocks of volcanic breccia which overlay the ancient lava bed.

After traveling a few hundred yards or so I was chagrined to stumble upon a log hut of indeterminate age. Wind had partially demolished the structure and erased any clue as to its origin. One of the Norwegians thought it might have been erected by the Louise Boyd expedition which had explored Jan Mayen a decade or more earlier.

East of the hut the breccia rocks became larger and more closely crowded. Had not a crust of snow lain in the interstices, travel would have been utterly impossible. We were so delayed by the difficult terrain that it was long after dark when we returned to the cove. Our clothing was torn and our hands lacerated by the sharp rocks.

Our first attempt at launching the eighteen-foot surfboat was sharply rebuffed by the seas which tossed it back onto the rocks. Using my flashlight I signaled the ship to turn the searchlight on the beach. This enabled us to see the seas, and the second launching was successful.

I took the steering oar. The others were large, powerful men, and the boat fairly leaped toward the ship until we were about halfway. Then it appeared to slacken speed to almost a standstill in spite of my companions' straining at their oars. I glanced around for the reason and found it. The boat was half full of water.

It flashed across my mind that the boat must have struck a sharp rock and stove in the planking during our first launching. I told the others what had occurred and asked Mr. Øien to bail. It was useless. The water rose rapidly to the thwarts. Our craft rolled lazily on its side and spilled us into the sea!

My first impression was that the water was warmer than I had expected. This, I knew, was because of my long-handled woolies. My concern was for our Norwegian friends. By American standards they were poorly clad. We all reached the upturned boat at about the same time and arranged ourselves on either side to cling to the bottom.

My hands quickly became numb because my torn mittens did little to keep out the cold. I wondered if we could all hold out until the other eighteen-foot surfboat reached us. I became conscious of a bitter chill creeping over my body and knew the others must be equally cold. No one uttered a sound. I suppose we all were too cold to talk.

Though it seemed like hours that we were in the water, no more than two minutes could have elapsed before the white-gray bows of a small surfboat shot into the circle of light in which we were centered. I resolved to risk no more Arctic duckings.

November 25, Thanksgiving Day, found the *Northland* at anchor near Egg Island, riding out a northerly gale. Our shore party had plenty of traditional food. I thought it would be a good idea to cement relations with our allies by supplying the Norwegian garrison with some roasted turkeys.

Harmon and I loaded our rucksacks with the turkey, landed and made our way to the main barracks, approximately midway between Egg Island and New Chicago. We delighted our allies with our contribution.

Afterward we continued over frozen North Lagoon and dropped in on New Chicago. Hallencrutz and his construction platoon were hard at work, but Bell's transportation platoon had little left to do and was observing a half holiday.

Lieutenant Murphy suggested we ride back to Egg Island in the jeep. The idea spread to Dossland, Hallencrutz, Peterson, Bell and Beal, who all piled into the five-passenger vehicle.

Hallencrutz drove slowly and cautiously along the eastern shore of the lagoon. It was well that he did. About a hundred yards from New Chicago the ice cracked, and the jeep plunged to the bottom with a roar. Fortunately the water was little more than waist deep. All hands came to the rescue, and we soon had the vehicle in water shallow enough for us to lift it out onto the ice. So ended the joy ride, and, despite my resolution, I had suffered another Arctic ducking.

The *Northland* returned to New Chicago on November 26. Harmon located some logs suitable for antenna poles and towed them to the HF/DF station. Landing the logs was more difficult than we had anticipated. An unusually large breaker swept onto the beach as Harmon started to back the motor cargo boat clear. The motor went dead. The breaker struck and spilled into the boat. As the crest caved she broached and capsized.

Harmon, Travers and the engineman jumped out and waded ashore. The boat was quickly salvaged and sent to the ship under oars. But the engine would require a complete overhaul, and the craft was useless for several days.

I wanted to explore the southwest end of Jan Mayen Island. We proceeded there the following day and anchored. Taking Harmon, Spielhaug, Øien and a photographer's mate with me, I left the ship in the only undamaged boat, an eighteen-foot Monomoy. We made a landing without difficulty, and the boat was drawn well clear of the seas. Then for two hours we scouted on foot without making any noteworthy observations.

In order to launch the Monomoy for our return to the *Northland* we arranged the oars athwartships on the gunwale. When the wash of a breaker floated the boat I gave the order to launch. At the proper instant we jumped in and took up the oars to pull into the next breaker. But the photographer's mate, in his haste to keep as dry as possible, sat down facing the wrong direction. That was enough. The breaker struck, the bows leaped skyward and violently swerved to port. Thrown into the trough, the craft capsized!

We struggled to our feet in the outwash and grabbed the oars as they drifted seaward. The cold, raw wind instantly frosted our outer garments, making us look more like snowmen than human beings. I danced about for a few seconds in an effort to stem the bitter aching that penetrated to the bone.

I would have signaled the *Northland* for another boat and left our surfboat to a salvage detail from the ship. But this was the only usable craft we had. The ship could not get to us, so *we* had to get to the ship! Either that—or perish. The thought was not voiced by anyone, but it lent wings to our efforts.

After several minutes of backbreaking work we had the boat righted, bailed and again made ready for launching. The exertion brought a warm glow to the body. We waited for a succession of heavy breakers to pass before launching. Next time we were successful.

I was forced to conclude it really made no difference whether I resolved to take chances or accept no risks. Duckings seemed inevitable.

# Chapter 16

# A MYSTERIOUS INTRUDER

"CAPTAIN!" Ensign Martin O'Hara's voice awakened me with a start. "Captain, I wish you would take a look at the SF radar scope."

I accompanied O'Hara to the radar room behind the pilothouse. We gazed at the green disk of the "P" scope and at the "A" scope with its changing pattern as Sloan deftly fingered a myriad of knobs.

"Range is ten miles now, Mr. O'Hara!" Sloan said.

"The pip doesn't look much like a ship," O'Hara commented. "But I don't know what else it could be."

"If it is a ship, she's a Kraut!" I added. I was conscious of my heart pounding fiercely.

Intelligence of any allied ship movements would have been communicated to us even though they might have been hundreds of miles from Jan Mayen. The Norwegian gunboat *Honningsvaad* had departed Iceland en route to Jan Mayen only yesterday. But she was not due for at least two days. Moreover her approach would be from southwest rather than northeast, the direction from which this intruder was advancing.

The *Von Tirpitz* had recently sallied out of her Trondheim base to raid Spitzbergen. Could she be bent on a similar mission to Jan Mayen?

It seemed logical enough. Such a raid, while devoid of practical results, would produce far-reaching political effects and also bolster the morale of the penned-up German Navy. With only the *Northland* and a handful of ill-equipped troops to oppose the capital ship her success was practically assured.

146

I gave orders to weigh anchor. The ship was quickly got under way and a message blinked to shore calling an alert.

"Do you think his radar will pick us up?" I asked O'Hara.

"Perhaps not, if you hug the coast closely, sir."

"Call all hands to battle stations!" I ordered. "Start a plot. We'll sneak along the coast to northeastward and have a peek."

I glanced at the clock. It was 6:00 A.M. This gave us another four hours of protective night. No use taking any other course. The visitor would surely pick us up when we rounded Walrus Point if we were to stand southwest. Our first task was to identify him.

I trained my binoculars in the direction of the target. The night was not very dark, but the air was heavy with moisture. An occasional dark cloud flew overhead and blended with the inky sea. Patches of haze danced like a fluttering curtain between the ship and an ill-defined line where sea met sky. Weird shapes appeared and vanished, conjuring any illusion the mind might select. Now it was a battleship, now something else, now again a battleship. But the vision never crystallized.

Everyone was tense and quiet. The conning officer gave soft-spoken orders to the quartermaster at the wheel. O'Hara's voice came through the speaking tube from the radar room: "Range, fourteen thousand. Bearing three-one-one, relative. Speed of advance, eighteen knots!"

This certainly seemed like a battleship! My mind had frequently rehearsed such an exigency. First we must establish the hostile nature and identity of the type of ship. Next we must get off a contact report. The minute we were brought under fire the radars and secret publications must be destroyed and the vessel run on the rocks. I wondered if I had enough nerve to go through with my plan.

The irregular line of white breakers on our starboard beam appeared to be drawing closer, and we heard the roar of the surf. "Deep six!" the leadsman called.

This was too close for comfort. I ordered the ship hauled out 300 yards and wondered if this added berth would make any difference in the ability of the enemy's radar to find us. The first inkling would be a salvo falling on or near us. Loss of life would be heavy. But I knew the British Home Fleet was laying for the *Von Tirpitz*, and timely intelligence might be worth many times the value of a tired old Coast Guard cutter.

"Range, eight thousand yards! Steering evasive courses. Corrected speed, twenty knots!" O'Hara reported.

Only four miles and closing rapidly! A diffused silhouette might break through the haze at any time.

The ship was pitching now, sending fine sheets of spray across the bows. The weather was cold and damp. I felt sorry for number-one gun crew out there on the forecastle head. But the men should not have long to wait.

"Range, five thousand yards," O'Hara broke in. "Target's fading rapidly, Captain!"

"A submarine submerging!" I exclaimed with considerable relief. "Bring her full left and run down the bearing." To O'Hara I added, "Start your QC, please."

For nearly two hours the *Northland* darted about, pinging wildly for the echo which would tell us we had located the submerged target. Then a nebulous idea crept into my mind. I brought the *Northland* back to New Chicago, but did not anchor her, because I might be wrong in my thinking. While she cruised about in wide circles I sent the battered surfboat ashore to fetch Dossland.

When the erstwhile professor of electronics came aboard O'Hara explained to him about the pip and its erratic behavior.

"What you had on your radar was likely a magnetic disturbance," Dossland remarked.

"I suppose it's something you can blame on sunspots," O'Hara commented dryly.

"Seriously, yes," Dossland replied. "We know that prominences, or flares, occur in the vicinity of active sunspots. They cause a marked increase in the radiation of powerful gamma rays. On reaching the earth's upper atmosphere, or ionosphere, ionization of molecules takes place, and ionized particles even penetrate the lower atmosphere. This phenomenon is also related to the aurora borealis in that the impact of ionized particles on the upper atmosphere causes the molecules to glow."

"Clear as mud!" I mumbled. "But anyway I gather it's safe to anchor. Set the anchor detail, if you please, Mr. Hershey."

On the morning of November 30 the *Honningsvaad* arrived. The Norwegians were justly proud of her.

Even as the Norwegian man-of-war anchored off New Chicago our men on shore were erecting a flagpole. Aside from this minor item, the U. S. Naval Direction Finder Station was complete. The direction finder had been checked and found accurate. Enough supplies were ashore to last Peterson and his twelve-man crew for a year. The *Northland* was free to sail.

We were anxious to return to Greenland and get on with our next task—whatever it might be. But I could not think of sailing without giving the *Honningsvaad* a hand in relieving the Norwegian garrison and unloading six months' stores for the troops who were to stay on Jan Mayen. Moreover our motor surfboat had just been repaired.

The captain of the *Honningsvaad* quickly accepted my offer of assistance, and our landing organization swung into action and worked 'round the clock.

Lieutenant von Rosenvinge was the last member of our party to leave Jan Mayen. The *Northland* was ready for getting under way, with her anchor at short stay, when I took a boat to fetch him and wish Lieutenant Arnold Peterson well.

It was now December 1. The morning had progressed to the late hour of 9:00 A.M., but day had not yet begun to break. Good-bys were hastily said under the glare of a cargo lamp. Peterson and his crew didn't look too happy at that moment. It would be summer before they could expect to see another friendly ship.

We waded into the wash of the surf, preparing to launch the boat. I turned to wave. The bright rays of the lamp fell on two signs I had not previously noticed. One read: NEW CHICAGO. The other was inscribed: LOS ANGELES CITY LIMITS.

Day was breaking when the *Northland* began her journey back to Iceland. The *Honningsvaad* had got off to a good start and was now hidden behind a smudge of smoke several miles ahead.

"Ice blink to northward!" shouted the starboard lookout.

I looked at the brightening horizon and confirmed his report. In a few days Jan Mayen would be enveloped in the ice! But there was no need to dwell on what might or might not have happened to us. The race was over and we had won!

# Chapter 17

# GOING DOWNHILL

THE tumultuous coast of Greenland has never ceased to fascinate me. Making an approach on a clear day, the voyager sees the orchid haze melt from the horizon to lay bare a ragged panorama. Sheer spires of granite and basalt push skyward to contain the great inland ice sheet. Through fathomless defiles, between natural ramparts, blue-tinted glaciers ooze slowly into the sea. Fronting them, the sparkling blue water is flaked with the white manes of mighty icebergs. As the traveler closes on the bergs the blink of pack ice casts its aura upward to warn him that he cannot, without effort, view at close range the beauty of the land.

Such was southeast Greenland on the afternoon of December 9, 1943, when the *Northland* sought to enter the Greenlandic coast at Prince Christian. It was my hope to navigate Prince Christian Sound, which slices through the south end of the island, in an effort to save time—to avoid cruising around the belt of pack ice which at that time of year stems southward of Cape Farewell for many miles.

To carry out our current orders we must organize and sail a naval convoy from Narsarssuak for St. Johns, Newfoundland, on December 11.

After leaving Iceland on December 4, the *Northland* had been battered by head winds during her entire passage across Denmark Strait. At times the storm had attained a velocity of ninety miles an hour and shoved the vessel farther from her destination. Now we were enjoying our first day of good weather.

I was extremely anxious to reach Narsarssuak on time. My concern sprang from reasons far more material than pride. The southbound trip from Greenland to Newfoundland was known throughout the Greenland Patrol as "going downhill." It meant a return to civilization, even though only as far as St. Johns. Moreover there was always the remote possibility of an escort force not being available at St. Johns to see the convoy beyond Newfoundland. In this event, instead of an immediate return to Greenland, there would be a trip to the U. S. I felt I simply must make that convoy!

In Iceland there had been news. Admiral Smith was promoted—moved up to the command of Task Force 24 of the Atlantic Fleet. He had been relieved as Commander Greenland Patrol by Commodore E. G. Rose, USCG. The turnover in staff officers had been nearly complete. Some had gone with Admiral Smith to his new command post at Argentia, Newfoundland. Others had gone to the South Pacific. Orders were in the mail for Von Rosenvinge to be Commodore Rose's flag secretary and aide.

And there was a rumor—to me a heartbreaking rumor—that I was to command the first new icebreaker, the *Eastwind!*

Prince Christian entrance was still thirty miles away when the *Northland* began worming her way through pack ice. She had penetrated no more than five miles when a northeast breeze made up, spreading dark, racing clouds overhead and cutting from view the gnarled land toward which we smashed. I did not like the look of this turn of weather and sent for Travers.

"You're in for a nor'easter, sir," the weather prophet reported.

I weighed our chances of reaching the sound before the full fury of the gale broke. It would not do for a low-powered vessel such as ours to be caught in a strong blow along this stretch of coast. There were too many scares (submarine pinnacles) against which we could be set. The risk was not reasonable. I decided to reach for open water, then claw up for sea room.

It was already dark when the *Northland* reached open water, and the storm was upon us. The moan of the wind through the rigging was broken by the angry wash of seas over the outer margin of pack ice and by the roar of water cascading from each floeberg as it rose with succeeding waves. The vessel buried her bows into the seas and struggled for distance to windward.

During the next three hours the mad northeaster stepped up its tempo, sent the anemometer needle rocketing to seventy, eighty and finally to ninety miles an hour, as high as it would register. The seas mounted higher and higher, spreading foam over crest and trough until the ocean about us was covered with a seething cloak of white.

Walls of water swept over the deck to break against the heavy glass windows of the pilothouse. At length one window caved in under the impact, and water poured in. I knew that our guns and possibly the entire bridge would go next.

I was not satisfied with the amount of sea room. Windward progress had been too slow. It would not be prudent to let the ship lay to in the trough. Her entire length would then be vulnerable to growlers and small bergs whose white mass could not be seen against the foam. Moreover her stability never had been too good. She might easily capsize.

There was only one thing to do: run before the sea. This, in such a storm, required full power to hold her heading and offset the *Northland's* inborn tendency to seek the wind.

I called the lookouts below, ordered the wheel put hard over and asked for full power. The radar could not possibly pick out any but large ice masses against such a heavy sea return. If we should strike ice—even a small growler—the ship would be sunk, just as the mighty *Titanic* had been lost. We could only hope for the best.

Mountainous combers lurched past the vessel as she careened to southwestward on her new course. The sensation was like alternately speeding on a surfboard and then slowing to a standstill, walled in by seas which towered above the trough. Heavy canvas covered the broken pilothouse window, yet water squeezed in with a steady stream and sloshed wildly about the bridge.

Midnight came. The storm increased in fury. Harmon relieved Bell of the deck. Bell would make his way below, down through the sick bay and laundry, then through the engine room to the officers' country. In his stateroom he would arrange his Dutch wives and sleep.

I wondered how anyone could sleep. Bell occupied the room next to Von Rosenvinge, and all of Von's junk must be crashing about from bulkhead to bulkhead.

A disklike something hurtled past the bridge and disappeared into the gloom ahead.

"That must be the crow's nest," Harmon remarked.

I was glad the watch was safely under hatches. Or was it really safe? Something large and white materialized out of the sea, very close aboard on the starboard bow. It slipped rapidly aft, and I felt a tightening of my scalp as I watched through the wing windows. Iceberg! Had we been fifty yards to the right, the vessel would have been smashed to bits!

About 2:00 A.M. Von Rosenvinge struggled to the bridge with a pot of coffee.

"What's the matter?" I asked. "Couldn't you sleep?"

"Captain, sir," he answered, "I gave up trying when Captain Von Paulsen's polar-bear skull bounced into bed with me. I do wish you would put the ship on a steadier course, sir. I can't tell where my room ends and the bulkheads begin."

"Pour the coffee," Harmon growled at Von Rosenvinge. "If we fetch up on an iceberg, at least *some* good will be done."

About an hour later we had a close call with another berg, not as large a berg as the first, but equally destructive.

Hershey relieved Harmon at 4:00 A.M. "Want to buy my J2F airplane?" he asked as he came onto the bridge.

"I'll bid thirty cents for it," I replied.

"No competition," Von Rosenvinge retorted.

The telephone buzzed. Hershey answered. "Hallencrutz says he thinks the ash cans* have carried away and are rolling about the fantail," Hershey reported when he hung up the phone.

I sent him with the messenger to investigate. A few minutes later he returned and said, "The ash cans are secure, Captain, but I'll take your thirty cents. The plane's gone and part of the cradle with it! When the wind blew it over the side it snapped the holding-down chains and carried away the starboard backstay to the mainmast!"

---

* Anti-submarine depth charges.

"Have Murphy put a relieving tackle on the mast before it goes too," I ordered.

The loss of our airplane marked the peak of the storm. The wind had abated considerably by 6:00 A.M., but there would still be danger until 8:00 A.M. when day broke. I instructed Von Rosenvinge to inform the Commander Greenland Patrol that we would be late for rendezvous.

I never welcomed dawn so gladly as I did that morning. There were several icebergs in sight, but they were well clear of us. No blink or pack ice appeared on the horizon. The sea had moderated appreciably. But in the pale light of morning it appeared more formidable than it had at its height. From time to time the ship perched on the crest of a mountainous wave, then raced forward to slide at length, with a sickening drop, into the trough.

I glanced aloft. Two searchlights and the upper part of the crow's nest were missing. But the after taffrail was intact, untouched by the plane in its flight over the side.

Lieutenant von Rosenvinge smoothed out two crumpled dispatches and handed them to me. The first one, addressed to the *Northland,* was a reply to ours. It canceled our convoy instructions. This was bad news. There would be no liberty in St. Johns.

The second dispatch unfolded a saga of the same storm we had just weathered. The U. S. Army transport *Nevada,* St Johns to Greenland, with troops aboard, had outdistanced her escort and foundered in the storm. The Coast Guard cutter *Comanche,* Lieutenant Langford Anderson, had found a boatload of thirty men and rescued them. Now the *Comanche* was searching for more survivors, but feared they were lost, because the *Nevada's* other lifeboat had been capsized in launching.

When the storm struck the *Nevada* it had been blowing sixty miles per hour. We calculated it must have required a 135-mile wind to carry our plane clear of the taffrail. Cape Farewell has a way of amplifying storms!

Harmon spent most of the morning with sextant and stop watch, hoping to shoot the sun's lower limb through the clouds. At last his patience was rewarded. From his line of position he estimated we had averaged fifteen knots since 8:00 P.M. Never in her life had the *Northland* made more than ten knots!

I judged it safe to take the seas on the starboard bow and ordered the ship put on a northerly course. Such a course was virtually a noncommittal one. I could either reach for Skov Fiord and Narsarssuak or be in position to intercept the St. Johns-bound convoy when it sailed.

Early the following morning we received the usual sailing telegrams dispatched by the escort commander. If I carried out my latest orders I would proceed to Narsarssuak. But I knew it had been the commodore's original intention to provide this convoy two escorts instead of the one it now had. I decided to act first and ask questions afterward.

"Mr. O'Hara," I said to the officer of the deck, "tell Mr. Harmon to lay an intercept course for convoy GS One Sixteen."

A broad smile crept over Martin O'Hara's face as he answered with enthusiasm, "Aye, aye, sir!" Soon I heard cheers rising from the crew's mess. I knew the galley grapevine was functioning smoothly.

About 2:00 P.M. we sighted the U. S. naval tanker *Laramie* escorted by the Coast Guard cutter *Tampa,* broad on our starboard bow. Harmon's computations had been amazingly accurate.

I blinked over a message that we would hitch-hike and sent a coded dispatch to the Commander, Greenland Patrol, informing him that we would carry out our original orders unless otherwise directed. In another message to the *Tampa* I inquired the speed of advance.

The answer flashed back: "Nine and a half knots."

This bothered me because our maximum sustained speed was nine knots. I sent for Mr. Hallencrutz. "Chief," I asked, "do you suppose you can coax more than nine knots out of your old coffee grinders? We need nine and a half."

Hallencrutz smiled. "Don't worry, Captain. We can make that much and maybe more. Remember, sir, we're going downhill."

*Part Three*

THE NORTHEAST GREENLAND OPERATION

*1944*

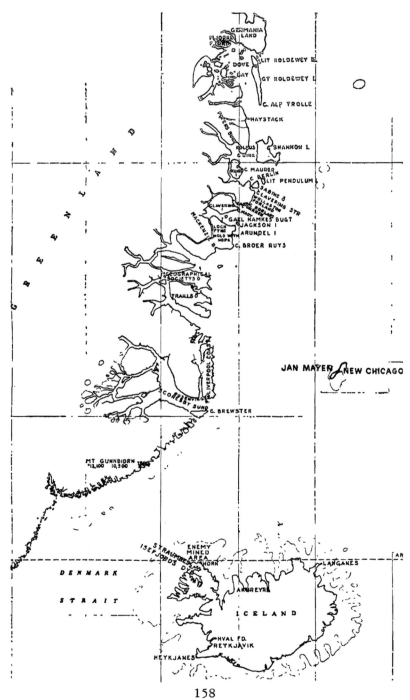

GERMANIA LAND

FLIORKA FIORD

DOVE BAY

LIT HOLDEWEY I

GT HOLDEWEY I

C. ALP TROLLE

HAYSTACK

DIPES BURG

KOLLAS C LINE

SHANNON I

KUHN I

C MAURER

C BERLIN

LIT PENDULUM

SABINE O

CLAVERING STR

HOLLAND

C BORLASE

CLAVERING ROSS

GAEL HAMKES BUGT

JACKSON I

ARUNDEL I

LOCH FYME

HOLD WITH HOPE

C. BROER RUYS

GREENLAND

MACKENZIE

GEOGRAPHICAL SOCIETY I

TRAILL I

LIVERPOOL COST

SCORESBY SUND

C. BREWSTER

JAN MAYEN NEW CHICAGO

MT GUNNBIORN 12,100 10,500

ENEMY MINED AREA

ISEFJORD'S D

STRAUMNES

C. HORN

LANGANES

AKUREYRI

DENMARK

STRAIT

ICELAND

HVAL FD.

REYKJAVIK

HEYKJANES

158

# Chapter 18

# A SHIP IS BORN

EVER since some anonymous paleolithic man straddled a log and paddled an unfordable stream, water-borne transportation has been the most economical conveyance for the human race and its effects.

As human ingenuity advanced, vast systems of inland waterways were utilized and developed by the peoples of northern Europe. But the economic advantage of these waterways was seasonally lost as a result of freezing. Each winter commerce went into hibernation. This periodic slackening of intercourse recurred for centuries—until the advent of *icebreaking* vessels.

And it was not only internal commerce that was affected by the weather. Terminal bases used by ships in foreign trade were annually locked in ice. In order to get vessels and their precious cargoes in and out of port recourse was often made to manpower.

Crews of men drilled holes through the ice. Then ten-man saws cut from hole to hole, hewing a channel through which ships could pass to and from the sea. Such a procedure, frequently requiring as many as 200 men to open up a terminal basin for a single ship, was slow and expensive.

Then came the screw propeller. With this new development in ship propulsion man found he could build a vessel designed especially for icebreaking. The first of these ships was constructed at Hamburg, Germany, in the middle of the nineteenth century.

Oddly enough the advent of the railroad age gave impetus to the

159

development of icebreakers. Railroad bridges were few. Construction of car-ferries mushroomed over northern Europe and on the Great Lakes. Ferry captains soon discovered that the icebreaking qualities of their vessels were improved when *backing* into a frozen slip, using the screw to *pull* rather than to push. Sucking the water from beneath the vessel created a vacuum under the ice. It helped the vessel's weight to crush ice. From this experience the idea of a bow propeller was conceived. Russia, greatly concerned with ocean icebreaking, adopted the idea.

It is easy to understand why Russia has led the world in the evolution of ocean icebreakers. Her maritime border, extending over a distance of 24,844 statute miles, is washed by the waters of many seas. Numerous ports on this vast coast line are not served by railroads. Periodic freezing disrupts the economic life not only of the ports but of adjacent areas as well.

Glance at a map of the Soviet Union and here is what you will see: a tremendous coast line on the Arctic Ocean and its tributaries, where every port, with the single exception of Murmansk, is frozen during the winter months. The southern coast line—bordering the Sea of Azov and the Black Sea—is in a sense even more frigid, for there is no "Murmansk" in these waters—no gulf stream to shoo the ice away. Along the eastern boundaries of the Soviet ice covers the northern part of the Sea of Japan and the coastal areas of the Okhotsk and Bering seas. Similarly in the west, in the Finnish Gulf of the Baltic Sea, ocean traffic is blocked by winter ice.

Russia's first ocean icebreaker, the *Yermak,* was designed in the latter part of the nineteenth century by Admiral Makarov. In building the *Yermak* the admiral overcame popular resistance to the bow propeller. He gave her three driving propellers and built her with a deep draft for added momentum and to minimize the risk of ice damage to her screws.

Admiral Makarov also employed the removable propeller blade, for it had been found that the bow propeller, while excellent in landlocked sea areas, was subject to damage in the Arctic pack.

Another device Admiral Makarov included in the *Yermak* was a system of heeling tanks by which the ship could be rocked when ballast water was pumped from wing to wing. This relieved pressure

Entering a field of shelf-ice floes.

Admiral's conference in *Northwind's* cabin. (Left to right) Capt. Moore, Capt. Cohn, Capt. Hourihan, Com. Isinghour, Capt. Thomas, Rear Adm. Cruzen. (Standing) Capt. Quackenbush.

Transferring freight from *Philippine Sea* to *Northwind*. Both ships worked around the clock.

Transfer of passengers at sea.

against the hull, permitting the vessel to heel her way through heavy ice.

The *Yermak* was the forerunner of a fleet of heavy Russian ice-breakers. Among the most notable Soviet ships which followed her down the ways were the *Joseph Stalin*, and *L. Kaganovich* and the *Krassin*. These steam-powered ships, about 325 feet long, with a sixty-five-foot beam and a thirty-foot draft, develop up to 10,100 horsepower. During World War II they were augmented by three American-built icebreakers awarded under Lend-Lease.

Russia has employed utility icebreakers which combine freight-carrying and icebreaking characteristics. It has been generally conceded, however, that utility icebreakers cannot be operated profitably. Fuel costs are prohibitive, and the space required for machinery drastically reduces the payload. Consequently the convoy system is in current use. By this method iceworthy carriers are escorted by powerful breakers.

In the United States prior to World War II icebreaking was limited largely to ports and rivers on the Great Lakes and on the Atlantic seaboard north of Cape Charles. The duty of keeping these waterways open devolved on the United States Coast Guard. It was not until World War II, however, that the Coast Guard began operating icebreaking vessels in the strict sense of the word.

During all these prewar years the Coast Guard felt the sore need of large icebreakers, particularly for duty on the Great Lakes, where the movement of iron-ore cargoes is of the utmost importance to the national economy.

Time was marching on, as the saying goes. And as time marched through the mid-thirties the Western democracies were gripped by a wave of isolationism. Yet many thinking men, including Rear Admiral Russell R. Waesche, Commandant of the Coast Guard, saw the handwriting on the wall.

Foreseeing the role Greenland would play in the strategic defense of the Western Hemisphere, Admiral Waesche realized the need for heavy ocean-going icebreakers capable of maintaining our supply lines in the Arctic. He also realized the necessity of extending the Great Lakes navigational season in order to increase the flow of iron ore to the great mideastern steel mills in the event of war.

Admiral Waesche ordered a promising young engineer officer, Lieutenant E. H. Thiele, USCG, to the Baltic states to study icebreakers and to try to devise improvements in the over-all design of this type of ship. After more than a year of intensive research abroad Lieutenant Thiele returned to the United States and worked with Lieutenant Commander Dale R. Simonson, USCG, a constructor, and with Gibbs & Cox, New York design agents. They eventually developed plans for icebreaking vessels that would be mightier, more powerful, more maneuverable and more self-sustaining than any yet built. These plans were filed away, for the temper of the American people was not ripe.

Time continued marching on. We moved into the year 1941 and the realization that war could not be averted. Congress hastened to authorize naval construction of all types, including ocean icebreakers. The United States Coast Guard—"Always Ready!"—was prepared with bids. These invitations called for four ocean icebreakers and one heavy Great Lakes icebreaker. The bow propeller was to be incorporated in all these ships.

Under this program the Great Lakes icebreaker, the *Mackinaw,* was built by the Toledo Shipbuilding Corporation. This company had built the *Storis,* a utility icebreaker of 1,700 tons and 230-foot length. Because of her large cargo space, machinery requirements in the *Storis* had to be reduced. She could not be depended on to handle ice more than three feet thick.

Launched on March 28, 1942, the *Storis* was rushed to Greenland immediately on her completion. When Congress authorized the *Mackinaw* its members made certain that the lakes would not be without an icebreaker. They gave her a 300-foot length and a seventy-five-foot beam, thus denying her transit through the St. Lawrence and Mississippi rivers.

The other four ships in the program, all ocean icebreakers, were known as the *Wind* class. Named *Eastwind, Southwind, Westwind* and *Northwind,* they were laid down and launched in this order.

When bids for the *Wind* type were opened only one firm submitted an estimate. This was the Western Pipe and Steel Company, a west-coast corporation. The all-welded, one and five-eighths-inch steel required for the icebreaker hulls presented an unprecedented problem with which shipbuilders were not prepared to cope. Mr. Slater, president of Western Pipe and Steel, was about to decline to bid when he had an inspiration. He thought of Monty Ward, a friend who had built iceworthy ships all his life. He sent for Monty.

"Monty," Slater asked, after the shipbuilder had digested the plans and specifications, "can you build these ships?"

For reply Monty removed his coat and went to work.

An icebreaker must withstand terrific pressures as well as deal shattering blows at the ice. Because of this, shell plating on the *Wind* ships varies in thickness between one and five-eighths inches and one and one-quarter inches from keel to sheer. Heavy frames are spaced at one-foot intervals below the main deck. Longitudinal stiffening is accomplished by large I-beams throughout the length of the hull. Further stiffening and efficient damage control are provided by both transverse and longitudinal watertight bulkheads which divide the hull into many compartments. At the bow, where the brunt of breaking ice is borne, the stiffening is even more extensive, particularly near the eighteen-inch-thick stem.

A portion of the forefoot is set approximately fifteen feet aft of the sheer of the stem. This permits the vessel to ride up on the ice and crush it with her weight as well as smash with the recessed portion of her bow. Moreover the recessing of the forefoot serves to protect the bow propeller.

*Wind* ship power is furnished by six double-acting, high-speed Fairbanks-Morse Diesel engines. Each engine is coupled to a 2,000-horsepower electric generator. These generators power any combination of three Westinghouse motors, two aft and one forward. When the entire generated current is directed to the two stern motors 12,000 horsepower is developed. When the bow motor is used one third of this power must be sent forward.

Steam for heating, cooking and evaporating a maximum of 10,000 gallons of water daily is supplied by two oil-burning boilers. Hot water is circulated through ice chests which are designed to keep the injection free of ice.

Heeling tanks on both sides of the *Wind* ships have a capacity of 150,000 gallons of ballast water or oil. The fluid can be completely shifted from port to starboard or vice versa in only ninety seconds. This produces a man-made roll of approximately fifteen degrees, which enables the vessel to "rock" through the ice.

Icebreaking and ice navigation require instant response to the will of the pilot. Two implements not usually found in vessels are used to obtain this all-important quick control of the *Wind* ships.

The first is a set of automatic bridge controls for all propellers. This eliminates the usual time lag where propellers are controlled from the engine room in response to bell signals from the bridge. The other is a selector switch at the steering position. When maneuvering a *Wind* ship in ice or in close quarters the helmsman throws the selector switch and steers with a lever. Rudder action is then instantaneous. Under any condition, or at any rudder angle, the ship requires seven and one-half seconds to answer her helm. It is essential, of course, for the conning officer to anticipate this time lag when giving orders to the wheel.

The wartime armament in these ships during World War II consisted of: Two turrets, each mounting five-inch, 38-caliber, director-controlled dual-purpose guns. Three director-controlled forty-mm. quadruple guns. Six twenty-mm. single guns. One Hedgehog. Six K-guns. Depth charges carried in depth-charge racks. One smoke generator.

A towing engine with 300 fathoms of two-inch wire rope is located in the after deckhouse. Auxiliary towing gear is provided by two smaller wing drums. The stern is notched at the center line to permit snubbing the bow of a towed vessel snugly to the ship. This is used only in ice in order to eliminate the danger of ice fouling the towed vessel.

Another towing engine is housed in the forward part of the ship. This is equipped with 300 fathoms of one and one-quarter-inch wire rope. It may also be used to make fast a deep-sea anchor where ground tackle is needed in water too deep for the bower cables. This was particularly useful for anchoring in deep Greenlandic fiords.

June 3, 1944. The *Eastwind* was finished. She lay at the delivery pier, resplendent in her fresh coat of white and a pastel shade of blue.

On shore, next to the dock, a sea of humanity stood in the noonday sun. Assembled there were the relatives, wives and sweethearts of crew members, the workers who had built the ship and a score or more public dignitaries. Stretched before a rostrum in three even rows were the rigid ranks of men in navy blue, standing like blue walls with white crests. The officers, with glittering brass buttons and gold stripes, stood apart, facing the men.

I, about to be in command of this ship, felt a surge of pride as I stood on the rostrum and looked at these officers and men. Nearly all of them—twenty-two officers and 336 men—had been hand-picked. They had been thoroughly trained as individuals and as a group, specializing in one of many complex teams. Tomorrow their training as a homogeneous unit would begin—a welding of many teams into a smart whole. It would impart to the ship a personality—my personality.

Most of the officers had come from the war theater in the Pacific. Most of the men had never been to sea. But I recognized among them the sunny countenance of Martin O'Hara, now a lieutenant (j.g.). With the chief petty officers I saw the sage features of James Sloan, who now wore the brass buttons of a radarman chief. Below me the executive officer, Lieutenant Commander Harold Land, barked an order: "Parade . . . rest!" The drone of voices melted into whispers.

Now all eyes centered on Lieutenant Rudy Vallee, his baton poised. It flashed downward. The band swung into a rollicking medley of songs of the sea.

The commissioning ceremonies were elaborate to an unprecedented degree for wartime. But I wanted to make the event impressive. I wanted my ship to have a good start. I knew, for instance, that if a crew member's sweetheart were to love the Eastwind, he would be likely to love her, too.

The band stopped playing. Lieutenant Commander William Jennings Bryan, Jr., USCGR, stood at the microphone. He was master of ceremonies and headed the list of speakers. Bill had aided me in the precommissioning detail. He would remain with the ship until she finished shakedown training. Now he started to speak. One became oblivious of the hot sun and of the crowd under the spell of his oratory. He spoke of things to come beyond World War II, of the Arctic, of the future of aviation and the air routes which must span the top of the world. He told of the role which the *Eastwind* must play in the world after the war had been fought and won.

Bryan's speech was a short one, but it might have been his illustrious sire speaking of free silver, of farm relief, of emancipation of labor before the turn of the century. The son had truly inherited his father's oratorical qualities and vision.

Other speeches followed. Commander E. H. Thiele, USCG, the ship's brain father, spoke. To him the occasion was the culmination of a dream, one materialized through years of hard work. The ceremony was climaxed by the setting of the watch, the measured pace of the guard of the day and watch standers marching to their posts. Then the ranks of blue dissolved, invaded by their friends and loved ones. Everyone marched on board to enjoy an informal luncheon prepared by a corps of cooks.

A ship was born.

# Chapter 19

## *SETTING THE NET*

THE *Eastwind* plowed a furrow up the east coast of Greenland, her massive, blunt stem throwing a huge bow wave which sent combers splashing on the wall of ice on her port hand. Since departing Boston more than a week before, the vessel had been enveloped in a dense fog. Normally such a foggy passage would have depressed the spirits of officers and men. But today, September 11, 1944, everyone was keyed to a high pitch. For on the morrow we would reach our destination and rendezvous off Cape Alf Trolle with the *Northland* and *Storis*.

In a way the fog had been kind. It had concealed the vessel from hostile periscopes. This enabled us to steer a straight course without any of the time-consuming zigzags almost always necessary to the safety of a ship in a war zone. And saving time had become all-important as we raced the brand-new *Eastwind* from her training grounds in the Pacific to this remote theater.

Rumors had trickled out of the Arctic and filtered into California as we shook down the *Eastwind*. These rumors told of a pitched battle in which the tiny Greenland Army had tangled with a powerful German expeditionary force. Hazy details snowballed into "facts" which approached the fantastic. I discounted these "facts." But I wondered how Captain Jensen and his handful of Danes had fared against the might of Hitler's machine.

Then a few days ago we had received relayed dispatches from

167

Butcher, in command of the *Northland*. Butcher's report, though couched in laconic phrases, unfolded the drama of a running engagement among floes of *storis* off Cape Trolle, north of Latitude 76 on the east coast of Greenland.

The slow *Northland* had encountered a fast German expeditionary vessel attempting to slip into Dove Bay. Butcher called for full speed and tried to close to gun range. The enemy refused action and began working offshore to escape. Butcher took up pursuit. Suddenly two explosions were heard on the *Northland's* quarter, and two columns of ice particles sprayed aloft from a large floe.

Butcher looked beyond the floe and saw nearly a mile of clearwater lead. He knew then that there was only one explanation for the explosion. *Torpedoes!*

Clearly an enemy submarine had navigated beneath the northeast Greenland ice pack. Her commander was charged with supporting the expeditionary vessel the *Northland* now pursued. He had done his job well. But he had misjudged the thickness of *storis*.

By employing his antisubmarine equipment Butcher might have located and destroyed the U-boat. But he decided, properly, to hold to his objective: the surface vessel with the enemy expeditionary force.

Although handicapped in speed, the *Northland* was more heavily armed than the vessel she pursued. But the greatest advantage the Coast Guard cutter enjoyed was one which Butcher was too modest to admit: his superior skill in ice navigation. After a chase of more than seven hours the *Northland* cornered and sank the enemy vessel, then saved everyone aboard her: a bag of forty prisoners.

During her engagement with the enemy surface vessel the *Northland* had severely damaged her rudder. Butcher improvised a jury rig and begged Lieutenant Commander Russell Thresher, USCG, the acting task-unit commander in the *Storis,* to allow the *Northland* to continue patrol operations.

With the *Eastwind* speeding to northeast Greenland, Thresher decided to screen the *Northland* with his *Storis* and refer the decision to me as soon as I relieved him as task-unit commander.

I already had begun an estimate of the entire situation. To a large extent, of course, this estimate was influenced by what I knew of the

*Eastwind's* capabilities. We had briefly tested her ice-navigating qualities by taking her into the pack off Scoresby Sound. This was her first taste of ice.

I soon concluded, as had the Russians before the turn of the century, that the bow propeller was useless in the Arctic pack. But there was no doubt in my mind that the *Eastwind* was a mighty icebreaker. She had plowed through ice that would have stymied the *Northland*— and at a speed of twelve knots made good! The *Eastwind* would not be at the mercy of the pack and forced to follow shore leads. She could aid other vessels through the ice, tow them if necessary. We could continue operations until late in the season.

So much for us. What of the enemy?

The Germans had been tenacious in their efforts to establish weather stations on east Greenland. There was good, sound military reasoning behind this tenacity, of course. D-Day had come for the Allies, and the invasion of Normandy and of Holland was on. German operations on this newly opened western front depended on weather information received from reporting stations far to the westward— in Greenland, where northern Europe's weather is born.

Moreover stations in Greenland served another vital purpose from the German viewpoint. They enabled the Nazi war machine to plan raids on Murmansk-bound convoys.

After pondering these two factors I concluded that Fritz would persist in his efforts on the east coast of Greenland. The annihilation of one expedition—accomplished by Butcher in the *Northland*— would not stop the enemy. We could be certain of further attempts. We could expect another attempt within a month.

Where would this new expedition land? And how could our three vessels—the *Eastwind, Northwind* and *Storis*—thwart this expedition? For thwarting it would require us to guard thousands of miles of coast line jigsawed with innumerable fiords and bays.

These were the questions in my mind when the *Eastwind,* bound west for rendezvous off Cape Alf Trolle, entered the pack at 10:00 P.M., September 12. The fog was gone. Stars peeked through a mild sky and cast a feeble light over the endless expanse of white.

The ice roared as the stem plunged in. Huge blocks popped

skyward, topped on edge and crashed with a resounding clangor onto the surface from which they had been rent, then scooted away as the onrushing beam violently brushed them aside.

O'Hara had extolled the virtues of the *Northland* as the best ice ship in the United States. Now he was forced to recant. Overawed by the ship's progress, he remarked: "It's a far cry from last year, Captain!"

"Yes," I agreed. It was like racing across a white desert.

By 4:00 A.M. the pack was behind us. Now the *Storis'* challenging searchlight stabbed through the night.

An hour later I broke out the broad command, relieved Lieutenant Commander Thresher and ordered a systematic reconnaissance of the coast by our three planes. The *Northland* and *Storis* needed fuel, water and supplies. These were transferred from the *Eastwind* while the flights were in progress. Meanwhile Thresher clarified the rumors we had heard while we were shaking down the *Eastwind* off the California coast.

During the previous March, Thresher told me, two Greenland Army patrolmen had found sledge tracks on Shannon Island. The men had hurried to Cape Rink and radioed their discovery to Captain Jensen at Deadman's Bay.

This intelligence tied in with bearings obtained by the high-frequency direction finder we had set up on Jan Mayen. Concluding that an enemy weather station had been established after the *Northland* departed the Greenland coast in 1943, Jensen radioed Greenland Base Command for troops and machine weapons. He suggested that these be sent by air and landed on Von Paulsen Field, Shannon Island, for rendezvous with the Greenland Army.

The United States Army concurred. But bad flying conditions delayed the operation. Jensen, huddling at Cape Rink with his five men, chafed with impatience and saw his supplies running low. He decided to attack the enemy station now known to be located on Cape Sussi.

The six men crept up on the station under cover of darkness. They studied its garrison for an hour or so and estimated its force at about thirty men. Jensen decided on an attack after midnight when most of the Germans would be asleep and when the new watch, recently aroused, would still be drowsy.

In preparation Jensen left his men and crawled to a rock within a stone's throw of the barracks structure. There, as he awaited the right moment for the attack, he was surprised by a German officer behind him.

The men faced each other with rifles poised. Jensen did not know who was the more surprised. The German fired first. Jensen shot him—dead.

The garrison was alerted. While Jensen retreated to his men the Nazis raced to their battle stations. Then all hell broke loose! The cold night was rent by the staccato of machine guns and the crackle of Mausers. The handful of Danes found themselves caught in a crossfire with well-trained infantrymen inching toward them in an enveloping movement.

Miraculously Jensen accomplished a masterly retreat and got his men off safely. But he was disappointed. He had failed to destroy the enemy. He would try again—after the arrival of American infantrymen.

When the *Northland*, in company with the *Storis*, nosed through the Arctic pack early in July she brought the long-awaited United States Army troops. The *Storis* set about her assigned task of moving Jensen's headquarters from Deadman's Bay to Sandotten and stocking his southern stations with food and fuel. Meanwhile the *Northland* fought to reach the enemy station at Cape Sussi.

Blocked by heavy ice, Butcher and the commander of the American soldiers, Captain Bruce M. Minnick, decided on an overland expedition composed of troops supported by bluejackets.

But moving a body of men across Shannon Island proved more difficult than anticipated. The weather turned bad. Rain, sleet and melting snow created innumerable morasses. On high ground ragged rocks made progress extremely slow, cut the men's hands and tore their clothing. Heavy packs, necessary to sustain them in the field, added to their difficulties.

Captain Minnick prudently decided to turn back and await more favorable conditions. On the return trip to the *Northland*, a flank scout found heavy tire tracks on Von Paulsen Field, the airstrip we had discovered in 1943. This indicated a strong possibility that the enemy had been evacuated by air.

Butcher made another attempt to reach Cape Sussi by sea when the landing force came aboard. This time he found a shore lead and battled his way to a point about two miles off the cape. Then midway between ship and shore he saw the crushed hulk of the German expeditionary vessel, the *Coburn*. It was held by the heavy shore-fast ice.

Viewing the shore with his glasses, Butcher could detect no hint of activity. Had the enemy marched to Von Paulsen Field, twenty-five miles away, and been evacuated by air? Or was he crouching in ambush? Butcher decided to send a reconnaissance patrol to find out.

Lieutenant Harmon took command of the patrol. He strung out his men, roped them together and set out across the ice which was already breaking up. At times the men plunged into crevasses concealed by a light layer of frozen snow. At times they ferried across open pools in an ice skiff, a combination boat and sledge.

Several hours of this put the patrol on the rocky shore, where it deployed to advance on the enemy station. But the enemy had gone. A German helmet perched on a cross which bore the inscription, "Lt. E. Zacher, 24.4.44," marked a rocky, wind-swept grave. This must be the officer Jensen had killed.

All this Thresher told me after I had taken command of the task unit. Continuing his summary, Thresher informed me that two Navy Catalina bombers in Iceland, under Lieutenant Commander Gilbert R. Evans, USCG, were at our disposal. Moreover the Coast Guard icebreaking buoy-tender *Evergreen* was now in Denmark Strait and bound north to augment our force.

When our three planes completed their reconnaissance I learned from them that ice conditions were very good over the entire area as far north as Isle de France in Latitude 78 North. With this information we could complete our estimate of the situation.

Allied bombers based on Iceland could conduct bombing missions only as far north as Sabine Island. The enemy surely knew this. Therefore he would not set up any stations south of Sabine Island unless he was forced to do so by adverse ice conditions. Or unless, in a show of bravado, he undertook an audacious attempt to run the gantlet.

For all practical purposes, however, we could count on Sabine Island marking the southernmost line of the enemy's area of operations. Where would the northern line fall?

The enemy probably could sustain himself in Greenland for only one year at a time. In order to resupply a station and relieve its garrison he would have to establish himself in a region that would not be icebound throughout the summer. How far north could he go and not be icebound throughout the summer?

After consulting the Ice Atlas I set Cape Bismark on the lower end of Germania Land as his northern limit. But this did not rule out the possibility of the Germans blundering into such a desolate place as Isle de France, well to the north of Cape Bismark.

But again, for all practical purposes, the area to be most closely guarded was the ninety miles of latitude between Cape Wynn, near Sabine Island on the south and Cape Bismark on the north.

What did we have to carry out this task of guarding ninety miles of east Greenland coast? How many miles would three radar-equipped ships be able to cover? O'Hara set up the problem on a maneuvering board. The answer came out *ninety miles:* just sufficient to span the vital area!

I then published an operation order. This established a station patrol and assigned each of our three vessels a sector of responsibility. At noon, September 13, the order became effective, and the vessels sped away to take up their stations.

We were now on guard in the vital area. But we did not overlook the possibility of the enemy making an end-run around us to the southward or to the northward.

To watch for a southern end-run Evans was ordered to conduct air reconnaissance of the coast between Scoresby Sound and Jackson Island. His Catalinas would fly from and to Iceland, of course. Bad weather would prevail. We would be fortunate if Evans' planes could make one flight a week.

I also sent a dispatch to Captain Jensen, requesting the Greenland Army to mover the gap between Jackson Island and Cape Wynn. Jensen readily agreed.

So much for the southern flank of the vital area. Patrol of the northern flank must wait until the *Evergreen* reported for duty in a few days. She would take over the *Eastwind's* station in the vital area while we scouted northward.

We could be reasonably sure the Germans would DF from Norway any signals they could pick up from my task unit. Therefore radio silence must be carefully observed. Transmissions were confined to urgent messages and short-range traffic, using low-power sets.

The net was now cast. We simply had to await developments. I still felt the enemy would show his hand around the end of the month—perhaps sooner.

# Chapter 20

## *THE BOW PROPELLER GETS A WORKOUT*

THE *Evergreen* reported on September 16. She required water, fuel and food, which we furnished from the *Eastwind*. Afterward she relieved the flagship and we hurried into Dove Bay.

Not far from Cape Alf Trolle, at the lower end of Great Koldewey Island and the southern entrance of Dove Bay, we sighted an island: Grouchs Snack. I expected the enemy would try to establish himself on such an island (typical of many in northeast Greenland) because it offered favorable communications and ease of defense. If we found him thus established, a swift assault at his rear under cover of darkness would be our surest way of taking him.

The *Eastwind's* landing force of bluejackets was highly trained in all phases of infantry tactics. But I felt the officers and men should have night rehearsals under conditions approximating those they would likely encounter in an after-dark assault.

Anchored off Grouchs Snack in the late afternoon, we exercised the landing force until almost 2:00 A.M., when we moved on to Watkins Falls near the entrance of Bessel Fiord in order to water ship.

While water was being pumped aboard I sent the plane to Sandotten with an invitation to Captain Jensen to return for a conference. It was with great joy that I saw Niels in the plane when it returned. He carried a tiny package which contained his toothbrush, a razor and

175

a change of underwear. This signified his intention to remain with us at least a week.

Jensen expressed a belief the enemy had retreated to the inner recesses of Dove Bay and was hiding out in one of the Greenland Army huts. If not this, Jensen said, the enemy might have gone to some nameless bay or inlet beyond the Greenland Army's patrol route. I could not share these views. But as I was anxious to explore the uncharted portions of the bay and test the bow propeller in fiord ice I agreed to a hasty reconnaissance.

The vessel got under way. It was afternoon when we entered one of the unnamed sounds which honeycomb the western side of Dove Bay. This waterway sliced between mountains spread with beautiful hues of varying strata. One particular mountain resembled a gigantic pipe organ. Frozen waterfalls sparkled like mother-of-pearl inlay between the lofty "pipes" of basalt. But other matters soon crowded the beauty of the surroundings from our minds.

The sound tapered into a mere channel after we had penetrated about a mile. It was sheltered from winds and narrow enough to be carpeted with a couple of feet of ice. I ordered the bow motor cut in, placed the ship on bridge control and started a performance record of the bow propeller. After a few miles of using the after and forward motors I switched all power to the two stern screws. The ship's speed did not appear to slacken, and I concluded that in relatively thin ice, such as we were breaking, a maximum of efficiency could be gained by making all electrical energy available to the stern motors rather than by splitting it up between the bow and stern.

After leaving this sound, which we named Østvendsund (Eastwind Sound) in honor of the first vessel to navigate it, we turned west. The ship soon entered the vast icy waste forming the inner, or western, side of Dove Bay. The nether light of dusk accented the ghostliness of the landscape and cast eerie shadows over specterlike bergs. In the distance a mighty glacier wall welded bay with the great inland sheet.

The entire region was desolate, devoid of life and sound. Nothing stirred, not a bird or a breeze—nothing save the soft wind, fanned by the ship's speed. The silence was almost overpowering, and the usual ship noises became thunderous. Ensign John Gira, officer of the deck at the time, summed up in one word the appearance of the country about us: "Haunted!"

"The Eskimos will agree with you," Jensen told Gira. "They would fear the 'Inland Dwellers' in a place like this. These creatures—these 'Inland Dwellers'—are supposed to be monsters, half human and half canine, who consort with evil spirits." He paused, then added, "I am sure this is the first ship ever to visit here."

Our charts showed the land areas in dotted lines, signifying them as unexplored. It was reasonable to assume Jensen correct in saying no other ship ever had entered this part of the bay.

That night the aurora borealis provided us with ample light. The display appeared suddenly. It lacked the resplendent coloring which characterizes it in southern Greenland. We were too far from the *magnetic* pole for anything but its brilliantly yellow light. By midnight we had the ship in charted waters once more and were heading southward.

The day following our departure from Dove Bay was a wretched Sunday. A blizzard howled down from the north, driving new fields of compact ice before it. Below, on the mess deck, divine services had begun. The voluntary response would have pleased any clergyman.

The *Eastwind's* complement did not include a chaplain, but there was no dearth of lay readers among the ship's company. This day Lieutenant Curtis Howard, the navigator, held forth in the pulpit and was having trouble in more ways than one.

First, Howard had chosen a difficult topic: one purposing to show that God was present even in northeast Greenland. Notwithstanding his civilian-life capabilities as an advertising man, he would have to use plenty of high-pressure sales talk to convince his congregation of *this*.

Secondly, the noise of six high-speed Diesel engines was an added obstacle to the point of Howard's sermon. The engines were slowly pushing us through an enormous ice field which we must work before reaching Gael Hamke's Bay and Sandotten. I felt sorry for Howard. Finally I asked him to declare a recess and climbed to the bridge.

When I reached the bridge I saw a whitish glow of a big berg looming ahead. Lieutenant John T. Young, the antisubmarine officer, had the deck and had just ordered the wheel put over to work clear of the berg. An idea struck me. I ordered Young to head for the berg and have an ice anchor coupled to the deep-sea anchor cable. He looked perplexed for a second. Then his eyes sparkled knowingly. "Aye, aye, sir!"

Young eased the ship's bow close up under the lee of the berg so that the bullnose touched. He held her there with the engines. Men armed with picks clambered onto the berg, roused out the anchor and quickly buried the fluke. When they were back aboard the cable was slacked a trifle and the *Eastwind* was in tow. I then ordered the engines shut down and had church call sounded again.

Lieutenant Howard resumed his sermon. Only the soft grinding of our improvised ice plow making its way through sea ice and the moan of the wind in the ventilators reached our little church. Maybe it would be easy to convince the men that God was bearing us toward our destination at a speed of three knots.

The number of buildings at Sandotten had doubled during the year. We counted *two!* The old patrol station had been augmented by a new headquarters building, the only building in northeast Greenland with electric lights and running water. Jensen was modernizing the Greenland Army!

On one side of the main structure a jeep was chugging. On the other side eight dog teams were tethered. A forty-five-foot launch, which the *Storis* had delivered in July, should have filled the skidway. But the craft was gone.

As soon as we stepped out of the *Eastwind's* boat Jensen read in the faces of his men that something was wrong. "Where is the launch?" he asked.

The senior of the two officers who met us reported that the boat was more than twenty-four hours overdue from a patrol of Gael Hamke's entrance. Attempts to communicate with her by radio were fruitless. Obviously she was in trouble.

Recalling the drift of the *Northland* last year, I could pretty well reconstruct what had happened. The launch unquestionably had been trapped in the ice and swept southward along the same line of drift. If she hadn't been crushed, we could probably find her somewhere between Jackson and Arundel islands. Jensen agreed. We hastened to the *Eastwind,* got under way and sped out of Young's Sound.

Surveying the ice before us—ice we must enter if we were to rescue Jensen's patrol craft—I wondered how long the bow propeller would last. More than once during these last few days I had silently cursed that propeller and fervently wished headquarters had supported my request that it be removed prior to sailing to Greenland. The blades were extremely vulnerable in close-packed *storis,* and we had been compelled to maneuver through detached fields with a great deal of caution.

I was not happy with the bow propeller. It was on my mind as I surveyed the pack we must enter to search for Jensen's launch and her men. By "nursing" the propeller, we might preserve it from damage. But this was an emergency, a matter of life or death. Moreover we were about to enter a field so closely packed that no amount of bow-propeller thrust would budge any of the floes. Something would have to give. I felt sure it would not be the ice.

The control levers moved down to standard-power, and the vessel leaped forward, crashing into the ice. Her stem reared. The pack yielded. Each floe groaned as it ground into its neighbor and threw up pressure ridges at the impact. Scooped-up water poured off up-ended cakes in roaring cataracts. This was the *Eastwind's* first real test in heavy, polar-packed floes. The speed with which she chewed her way through fascinated me.

Then I heard the urgent ringing of a phone. The junior OOD answered it. "Sir," he reported, "Commander Montrello wishes to speak with you."

Lieutenant Commander John Montrello, chief engineer, had learned his science at Massachusetts Institute of Technology subsequent to his graduation from the Coast Guard Academy. Although Monty never raised his voice, there was no doubt among any of his force, including the old-timers, that he was master of his department.

Speaking to me in his usual matter-of-fact voice, the young chief engineer reported that ice had pushed the rotor aft—only a fraction of an inch, but enough to unseat the brushes. This meant the bow motor was denied us for the remainder of the campaign. In a way I was happy. Henceforth we could treat the vessel as roughly as we needed.

Within two hours after entering the pack we sighted the Greenland

Army's patrol boat. She was marooned in an ice lake. The launch had been obliged to move about in circles to escape being frozen in! Only one hour's supply of fuel remained in her tanks. The chances of her crew—a lieutenant and a private—surviving would have been slight.

# Chapter 21

# INTO THE FAR NORTH

THE south flank of our patrol line was well covered. Lieutenant Commander Gilbert Evans' two Catalinas kept the coast between Scoresby Sound and Jackson Island under close surveillance, even when flying conditions were difficult. His flights were attended by further handicaps: he had no alternate air bases available; he *had* to take off from and return to Iceland. Moreover Jackson Island stretched his cruising radius to the limit.

Whenever possible, we also made air reconnaissance of our north flank, using the *Eastwind's* plane. This flank was giving me cause for alarm. The expected advance of the main Arctic pack had not yet occurred. Isle de France was surrounded only by shore-fast ice and open water!

I credited the enemy with more intelligence than to try to establish himself north of Cape Bismark. However the German staff was not devoid of the element of human dumbness. He *might* settle on Isle de France so long as it was ice-free. I determined to push north and be in a better position to intercept such a move. Moreover a dispatch from the *Northland,* our northermost patrol vessel, informed me she was running low on water. In order to save fuel I must stop at Watkins Falls and obtain a supply of fresh water to pour into the *Northland's* tanks.

Watkins Falls were already partially frozen when we arrived there on September 22. However a little stream bubbled into the fiord beneath a canopy of ice. I planted the deep-sea anchor and sent a detail ashore with a stream anchor for warping in the vessel's stern. When the boat landed I noticed that the men seemed reluctant to pile out. I reached for my binoculars and soon discovered the reason.

A big musk-ox bull held the beachhead. When any of the men made a move to jump out of the boat he stomped and snorted in a musk ox's most menacing fashion. No wonder the men were cautious. None had ever seen a musk ox. I was unable to determine how the beast had found his way into the cul-de-sac about the falls. He was obviously trapped and faced death by starvation.

The situation called for a policeman. We had one in the *Eastwind*, our gunnery officer, Lieutenant (j.g.) Elmer List. After service in the Navy during World War I List had been on the Long Beach, California, police force and had risen to the rank of captain. When World War II broke out he had entered the Coast Guard. Promptly sent ashore, List dispatched the musk ox with one well-directed shot.

From this point the chief commissary steward and his cooks took over. Delicious musk-ox steaks appeared on the supper menu of the general mess that night. But American reluctance to sample a new dish made the steaks unpopular with the crew. When I learned this I instructed the commissary officer to serve the same steaks the following day, but to feature them as beefsteak. As I expected, the crew unanimously endorsed them as the best steaks ever served!

We arrived at Mjorke Fiord on the north shore of Dove Bay that day. This was a Greenland Army outpost manned by two lieutenants, Nordum and Nielsen. Now—should we take the ship north of Cape Bismark for a look-see? Only an air reconnaissance could answer this question. But I wondered about a take-off in the skim ice forming on the bay.

Ensign Joseph T. McCormick, USCG—"Little Mac"—was my flight officer. His daring and skill as a pilot more than made up for any lack of physical stature. McCormick did not possess normal nerves. Like most Coast Guard aviators, he had a reputation as a foul-weather flyer—an attribute necessary to the peacetime operation of the service. It was said he needed only to extend his arm horizontally prior to take-off. If he could see his finger tips he gave the order to "let 'er roll!"

Our flight plan was laid to take us across Germania Land Peninsula to Skjear Fiord, then north to Isle de France. Fragments of ice striking the plane's metal hull as we sped for the take-off sounded like the staccato fire of a machine gun. My heart was in my mouth until we were air-borne.

We climbed a broad, barren valley separating towering formations of ancient rock. This valley marked a void in the great ice cap which set Germania Land aside like a huge, white table top. On either side glaciers tapered downward to end in a network of ribbonlike frozen streams. Here and there lakes that had been gouged out by retreating glaciers were silvery with ice.

Ascending to the level of the perpetual ice, we made out the crevasse-wrinkled fringes where marching ice met solid rock or spilled over in glacial form. We were about to dip downward onto the Skjear Fiord when something went wrong.

McCormick gunned the plane, and I felt us banking dizzily to reverse course. Through the intercom I heard him talk to the *Eastwind* in a matter-of-fact tone as though making a routine report. The plane was icing rapidly and losing altitude, he said. He would try for the fiord, but probably would have to pancake on one of the frozen lakes.

Then I heard O'Hara, who was on watch in the combat-information center: "Will send Jensen ashore with a rescue party at once."

We passed the last large lake and McCormick made his decision— to try for the fiord. The alternative was certain and instant death. I gripped the sides of my seat.

We sped down the valley. I looked at the wings, glistening with ice, then at the shore line. I wondered if we would make the fiord. I was scared. McCormick was giving his plane everything she had. Then we reached the beach, clearing it by a hundred feet which looked like so many inches!

We sat down on the skim ice with a clash that sounded like the breaking up of a restaurant full of dishes. McCormick dropped his wheels, and the plane came to a jolting, abrupt halt. He turned and gave me a grin. I was actually terrified speechless and did not find my voice until the plane was being hoisted aboard the *Eastwind*.

Clearly our scouting to the north had to be made by ship rather than by plane. But first I again wanted to exercise the landing force under conditions approaching those on such a place as Isle de France. I selected one of the little islands in the Olienterings Øerne group because it presented most of the obstacles likely to be encountered in an Arctic night amphibious operation.

Frankly I was proud of our landing force and glad we carried no soldiers. The presence of troops would have vested the Army with responsibility for shore operations. I had my own pet ideas of how an amphibious operation should be conducted in this part of the world. I knew the capabilities and limitations of my men and ships. Here a unified command—a naval one—was the only answer.

We broke off drill before dawn on September 24 and sailed out of Dove Bay via Koldewey Strait to contact the *Northland*. Despite his crippled steering gear, Butcher had shown more than ordinary tenacity in maintaining a tight patrol. I knew he would not have asked us for fresh water if he had been able to pump it from pools in the pack ice.

The *Northland's* tanks were nearly dry when we drew alongside. I learned from Butcher that when he had taken his station on September 14 he had found the fresh-water pools in the pack frozen solid.

Twelve hours after watering the *Northland* we made a landfall on desolate Isle de France. Save for tongues and a few detached fields of moderately packed polar ice, the *Eastwind* had sailed north in open water. I investigated the island. Isle de France was covered with snow and devoid of any visible flora and fauna, including man. Moreover a margin of newly formed ice clung to its uninviting shores.

I concluded that the enemy could not have established himself on those steep, bleak slopes without leaving some visible clue. So the *Eastwind* continued racing north. At five bells on the afternoon watch we sped over the south boundary of Belgica Bank. Here a few soundings had been recorded by the Belgica expedition, led by the Duc d'Orleans in 1902. The duke, pretender to the throne of France, had named the bank for his ship, the *Belgica*.

An hour later we were north of the Belgica expedition's soundings—in waters never before navigated by a ship. The news spread rapidly through the *Eastwind*. Officers and men now looked on themselves as polar explorers!

Niels Jensen, standing beside me in the pilothouse, voiced his enthusiasm. "Let's sail right into Danmark Fiord!"

Danmark Fiord is on the northern coast of Greenland and empties
into the Arctic Ocean. My own fervor for such a junket was on a par
with Jensen's, but we had more important fish to fry. I realized that
the Germans were not likely to go so far north as our own dreams and
excitement could have taken us that day.

Jensen's face clouded when I informed him of my decision to run
only as far as I considered the ice navigable for an enemy vessel. He
then asked me to run toward the coast and establish a depot on Lambert Land. This would extend the Greenland Army's patrol route,
whose nearest station was two hundred miles farther south. I could
see no particular advantage in a station so far north, but agreed to set
up a depot if we conveniently could.

The *Eastwind* encountered ice at 4:30 P.M. It was skim ice at first.
Then it gradually thickened to several inches. On our port quarter the
sun sank behind the great inland ice in a riot of color. Still the ship
hurried on, her stem singing as it cast up ice particles which swept
over the decks like flakes of hard snow. Floes of polar ice, scattered
about us, were becoming more numerous and more compactly welded
together.

By 7:00 P.M. the vessel was being slowed appreciably by new ice
at least two feet thick. She lurched repeatedly to impacts with heavy
detached floes which the watch could not see in the dark. There
could be little doubt that we had now reached the vanguard of the
main Arctic pack.

I had the ship put on a westerly course to close on Lambert Land
and noted our position: Latitude, 80° 03' North; Longitude, 15° 41'
West. Date: September 25, 1944.

We were less than six hundred miles from the North Pole—the
farthest north a ship had ever pushed under her own power! Moreover the *northeast* Greenland pack is the world's toughest. This was
indeed a historic occasion. But because of wartime secrecy it would
not receive acclaim.

We had fervent hopes of making a landfall on northeast Lambert
Land. But the configuration of the Arctic pack forced the vessel well

south of west during the night. At daybreak, September 26, the *Eastwind* was in sight of Cape Bourbon, about fifteen miles distant. South of the cape the François Archipelago stretched in clear relief against the background of icy mountains and glacial cliffs. The larger islands of this group had already been charted by the Duc d'Orleans.

Eight miles southeast of Cape Bourbon we met a barrier of heavy, shore-fast ice. While the *Eastwind* was capable of smashing through this, I was convinced that it denied our enemy access to the coast. The establishment of a depot for Jensen was unjustified, I felt. Therefore I set the ship on a southerly course to skirt the French Islands.

The daylight hours were devoted to filling in the topographic voids on our charts. By radar and sextant angles Howard and O'Hara plotted the hitherto unknown dimensions—elevations, lengths and breadths—of mighty glaciers and small islands. The dotted lines on our charts which indicated "unexplored" were erased and replaced with reliable data.

The wall of shore-fast ice persisted, giving us assurance that Nature was holding our northern flank secure for us. Viewing the crevasse-scarred inland ice recalled the epoch-making journey of Captain Ejnar Mikkelsen across Duc d'Orleans Land to explore Danmark Fiord. Many times this hardiest of explorers had plunged into crevasses while trudging ahead of his dog team. Many times he had dangled in his traces over a bottomless gulf, held back by the weight of his team, sledge and companions.

We named one of our newly charted islands Mikkelsen Island in honor of the explorer. Another was named Niels Jensen Island. I insisted that another be named after Dr. Frederick Cook, who, with Amundsen, saved the Belgica expedition to the Antarctic in 1897 and later became the first man to reach the North Pole (my personal view based upon oceanographic congruities).

As darkness fell I brought the ship onto an easterly course to reach well clear of the coast before heading south again. There was no doubt that winter was fast locking this portion of the Greenland Sea. And I felt confident that the enemy did not have a vessel capable of unlocking it. When we found him—if we did—he would be farther south.

# Chapter 22

# WE TRY TO FOOL THE ADMIRAL
# OF THE POLAR SEAS

MORNING of September 28 found the *Eastwind* well off Shannon Island and running southward before a whole northerly gale. She lurched heavily at times as mountainous seas caught her in a wide yaw. Fine particles of driving snow kept the decks white and slippery, making it difficult and somewhat dangerous to get about the laboring vessel.

I was on the bridge-wing, clinging tightly to the bulwark on the uproll, pressing heavily against it on the downroll. Suddenly the angry hissing of the sea and the wail of the wind were shattered by a crash.

I slid along the bulwark until I could look aft and see the deck. What I saw was not a happy sight. The hold-down chains securing our plane had snapped under the terrific wind pressure. The little aircraft was lying on its side with its port wing smashed against the deck. Lieutenant M. J. Cummings and his damage-control party were passing a six-inch hawser around the plane to keep it from being carried over the side. But even from where I stood it was evident that the J2F would never fly again.

This was a serious handicap. More than ever, now that the enemy might be approaching the area, we needed air reconnaissance. We would have to figure out something.

The figuring out did not take long. It was dictated by the weather.

187

Obviously winter was taking a hand and I soon would have to send the smaller ships to Iceland. The crippled *Northland* gave me particular concern. In spite of Butcher's capabilities, I did not relish having her meet the advancing polar pack with her jury steering rig.

Clearly it was time to re-estimate the situation. We had one new factor to take into consideration: the *Eastwind's* sister ship, the brand-new *Southwind*. The day our plane was damaged I received a dispatch saying the *Southwind* was departing Boston to join my task unit. But she could not reach northeast Greenland for at least a week. If weather and ice permitted, I wanted to keep the *Northland, Evergreen* and *Storis* in the area until the *Southwind* arrived.

What about a plane for the *Eastwind?* Well, since the *Storis* must soon depart, I would take her plane. And in view of weather conditions it would be wise to rendezvous as soon as possible. Then we could bring the *Storis'* plane aboard the *Eastwind* at the first favorable moment.

Consequently I sent a dispatch to Lieutenant Commander Thresher, ordering him to take the *Storis* to Freden Bay without delay. We also ran toward Freden Bay, working through some ten miles of ice before we came to anchor in the lee of Shannon Island near Cape Philip Broke.

When the *Storis* joined us the storm was raging even stronger. The two ships could not moor alongside each other to make the exchange of aircraft. Then around midnight the *Northland* broke radio silence. Butcher reported he was having "a little difficulty" due to his jury steering cable having parted. Heavy seas and floes of polar ice prevented him from making repairs.

A little difficulty! It was typical of the capable, self-reliant Butcher to imply he could get along without help. But I was convinced that we had better lend a hand.

Ordering the *Storis* to stand by at Freden Bay, we hove up our anchor and stood out of our snug haven. After nearly ten hours of battling the weather and crashing through a belt of heavy ice at the entrance of Hochstetter Bay we found the stricken *Northland*. She was drifting helplessly in the trough and in constant danger of being thrust against wicked *storis* and bergs.

There is little point in describing in detail the delicate maneuvers necessary to pass a line to the *Northland* in those heavily running seas and take her in tow. But I want to say that Chief Quartermaster Archie Brooks had the *Eastwind's* wheel and gave a demonstration of unusual judgment and skill in counteracting the wave motions which yawed us violently and tended to send our ponderous bulk crashing into the *Northland*.

We got her in tow and quickly worked up to twelve knots, giving her the fastest ride of her career—save, of course, for the night she was caught in the storm off Cape Farewell at the completion of our Jan Mayen job.

The *Storis* was now ordered out of Freden Bay to screen us against the possibility of submarine attack, while the *Evergreen* was called up to scout the pack for a lead to open water.

Once again that day we saw a demonstration of unusual judgment and skill. Lieutenant John E. Klang, USCG, skipper of the *Evergreen,* proved himself a worthy ice sailor. Without the aid of aircraft he readily located a lead into Pendulum Strait and took station outside to guide us in.

We had the *Northland* in relatively calm water by 5:00 P.M. Then we hove short the hawser and fitted her bow into our towing crotch. Thus coupled together, we proceeded like a two-car train.

The *Evergreen* now commenced an antisubmarine patrol around the *Northland, Eastwind* and *Storis,* which huddled together in Pendulum Strait while the *Northland* repaired her steering rig and the *Eastwind* and *Storis* exchanged planes.

Our experience with the *Northland* during these last twenty-four hours made me even more certain that I must get the three small ships away from northeast Greenland without delay. An air reconnaissance on September 30 added weight to this conviction. Using the plane we had taken from the *Storis,* Little Mac found the southern limit of the polar pack at Cape Bismark.

This intelligence of the rapid advance of the heavy ice was all I needed to make a final decision. From now on the three small ships would be subject to severe ice-and-storm damage. They would be getting stuck repeatedly. In need of assistance they would of necessity be forced to break radio silence and thus reveal to the enemy the location of each vessel.

Yes, it was high time the *Northland, Storis* and *Evergreen* returned to Iceland. But I hoped to turn their loss to advantage. I decided to try a little stratagem—a trick that might lure the enemy into a false sense of security.

Lieutenant Commander Thresher was placed in tactical command of the three vessels en route to Iceland. His orders directed him to make two weather transmissions daily to the naval weather center at Argentia. These transmissions were the hub of the stratagem. I knew that the enemy could DF our vessels. I hoped that when he picked up these frequent transmissions he would conclude that the Northeast Greenland Task Unit had suspended operations for the winter—and that he would not suspect the *Eastwind* was still in the area with the *Southwind* en route to join her.

If this bait were taken, the admiral of the Polar Seas—the German high-command officer charged with Arctic operations—could be expected to broadcast a signal to any enemy expeditionary vessel hovering between Greenland and Spitzbergen to proceed with her plan. To the enemy our frequent weather transmissions from the *Storis* might mean: "The coast is clear in northeast Greenland!"

The *Northland* had her jury rig repaired and was ready to sail at 8:00 P.M. on September 30. The *Evergreen* took her in tow and the *Storis* conducted an antisubmarine screen around them, while the *Eastwind* went ahead, smashing a trail through the ice. They all were safely through the pack by 2:00 A.M.

We exchanged parting whistle blasts, and the *Eastwind* turned back to the coast. The moon was high in a clear sky. Ahead of us the profiles of rugged mountains stood out in clear relief, their proximity exaggerated by the crisp, clear air. I was inwardly happy that we were not leaving this magnificent stronghold of Nature, happy that the *Eastwind* was master of the ice around us and of the Greenland Sea beyond.

# Chapter 23

## *CONTACT!*

WE KEPT the *Eastwind's* ready-gun crews on their toes by calling alert during every watch. If visibility was good, the OOD selected a target and ordered the turret crew to fire three rounds. The target chosen might be an iceberg, a floeberg or a rock. To exercise the heavy-machine-gun crews a weather balloon was released. We expected it to be shot down before it soared out of sight. All this created considerable healthy rivalry among the various gun crews. Those who failed to score a hit lost caste.

We sailed around Cape Borlase Warren on October 1 and smashed northward to Walrus Island. Here we paused for a shore-bombardment problem—training the turret crews in furnishing artillery support to our landing force.

The next day—October 2—we were off Cape David Gray, Shannon Island. The weather was fine and clear. Hochstetter Bay was largely ice-free, so I sent McCormick, with Lieutenant Commander Harold Land as observer, northward on an air reconnaissance. As soon as the plane was air-borne all hands were called to battle stations for target practice on an iceberg drifting near by.

The guns had no sooner begun hurling steel at the target when O'Hara called me on the battle telephone from his station in the combat operation center. "Captain," he reported, "the plane appears to be orbiting about ninety-eight miles north of here. It must be investigating something."

I gave orders to cease firing, secured from general quarters and instructed the control room to have the two idle engines made ready for cutting in.

Again O'Hara called on the phone. "Plane is returning, sir. It said something about a 'big ship,' but the message was garbled."

I ordered the *Eastwind* put on a northerly course and called for fourteen and one-half knots, full speed on four engines. In three quarters of an hour we sighted our plane coming toward us. Pausing only long enough to hoist it aboard, we roared ahead at full speed with six engines on the line.

Lieutenant Commander Land rushed to the bridge and made his report: "There's a big ship standing out to sea off North Little Koldewey. She's making about fourteen knots!"

I knew this was an enemy ship and that we must destroy her. But what type of ship were we up against? I pressed Land for details. But he could tell me little. Heavy machine-gun fire from the enemy ship had kept our plane at bay, preventing a close look. Pages of our identification book flew until we reached a silhouette of the German icebreaking plane-carrier *Østmark*. Land said the silhouette closely resembled the vessel he and Mac had sighted.

Several questions ran around in my mind at once. Had the *Østmark*—if this was the *Østmark*—planted an expeditionary force ashore? If so, where? What was she up to now? Would she hurry south to fight us? Would she steam north to hide herself in the pack? Would she attempt to escape to Norway? If she was headed for Norway, would her route take her via Spitzbergen or would she go direct? Was she supported by other warships?

We still were eighty-nine miles from her!

I made a mental estimate of the situation. The enemy vessel was our first and most important objective. Expeditionary forces ashore, if any, could be dealt with later. If the enemy ship intended engaging us, we would not have to worry about finding her. She would find us. If she intended hiding in the pack in an effort to escape, we could take our time in seeking her out.

For the present I must assume she would hurry off in the direction of either Spitzbergen or Norway. The ice pack would limit the courses available to her because Harold Land had observed the main pack to be following, roughly, the latitude of Cape Bismark.

The *Northwind* smacks the ice with everything she has, Bay of Whales.
Note turbulence at impact.

The going was tough for the *Sennet*.

The *Northwind* crushes out passages for the thin-hulled vessels. Note the
Ross Ice Barrier in the background.

I summoned all department heads and announced my plan. In order to launch our plane we must hug the coast of Shannon Island. The plane would take off at 4:00 P.M., one hour before dark. Lieutenant Commander Land and Little Mac must locate the enemy ship and orbit over her until we drew within radar range. By that time the plane would be nearing the limit of its cruising radius. If ice prevented Little Mac from landing near the *Eastwind* he must fly to Mjorke Fiord and land on the smooth ice. Nordum and Nielsen were still at the Greenland Army hut there. They could support Mac and Land until we picked them up.

At 4:00 P.M. the plane hung from our crane close to the water's edge. The vessel was stopped. After the plane was lowered into the crackling film of thin ice it took off and soared northward. The *Eastwind* resumed her wild pace.

In the combat operations center air plotters spread heavy black lines over the surface of the air-plot dial. Interpreting these, we would see that Land and McCormick were making a systematic search close to the coast. Then the plot lines stretched into Dove Bay and began running south. The plane was returning without having located its quarry!

It was now 7:30 P.M. The night would have been quite dark, were it not for a soft touch of moonlight. The plane arrived and circled the ship preparatory to landing. I signaled McCormick that we were plowing through several inches of slush ice and suggested he continue orbiting until we could break a strip for him.

But Little Mac chose not to wait. Several flares shot out of the plane and blazed brilliantly after settling on the ice. The aircraft came down for a landing among the avenue of flares. It touched gently and abruptly stopped. The ice was too dense to permit taxiing, so the plane stood fast while the *Eastwind* hove alongside. After hoisting it clear we resumed full speed.

Harold Land came to the bridge to report. The plane had searched the area between Great Koldewey Island and a point thirty miles offshore. At this point a heavy fog bank cloaked the sea area, preventing reconnaissance. The plane had returned to the ship via Dove Bay against the possibility of the enemy having doubled back. But the moonlight was too dull to make reconnaissance effective, Land said.

If the enemy ship were lurking in Dove Bay, we would have her pretty well bottled up. But I doubted the likelihood of this. It didn't seem possible the enemy would entrap himself.

My next consideration was this: To have cleared a distance of thirty miles offshore from Koldewey between the time she was first sighted and the time our plane returned the ship must be capable of making good at least ten knots. I was positive the Germans did not have a naval vessel capable of a speed of twelve knots through the frozen seas, especially at night and in a dense fog.

I therefore assumed the enemy ship's mean speed at ten knots and decided on a retiring search curve, or search from the flank to the eastward. Providing the speed was reasonably constant, our radar would pick her up, regardless of the course she steered.

The *Eastwind* swung onto her initial search course at fourteen knots. The ship's company was kept in an alert status, with half the battle stations manned while the other half of the crew was permitted to turn in, "boots and saddles." The galley watch busied itself with serving up hot coffee and doughnuts.

The night dragged on. The new ice became harder and thicker. With increasing frequency the ship jolted terrifically as she crashed into floebergs or floes of old ice. Sometimes I thought the hull must surely split. Targets appeared on the radar from time to time. Each time we thought: *This is surely it!* But the experienced men in the combat operations center interpreted the impressed impulses accurately. Without exception they turned out to be bergs. I grew less sure of my estimate of our enemy's speed.

Daylight came just as the solid, heavy wall of the main polar pack loomed across the northern horizon in an unbroken arc. It was now clear that Fritz either had made good his escape to Norway, was hiding in Dove Bay or had poked into the polar pack in an effort to conceal himself.

In the latter event Nature would hold him for us. So it remained for us to see if he had landed a force anywhere near North Little Koldewey Island—or to see if he was hiding out in some near-by fiord.

I wheeled the vessel onto a westerly course.

In the afternoon we reached a soft spot which had been an ice lake.

It was now carpeted with a surface film of thin ice. The *Eastwind* ran back and forth through this—into and before the wind—cutting a slick for our plane to make a take-off. McCormick's instructions were to investigate the Koldewey Islands and search for the enemy ship on the way. Lieutenant (j.g.) Alden Lewis, landing-force commander, went with Mac as observer. Lewis was instructed to chart offshore ice conditions and shore-fast ice which might serve as a beachhead.

The ice was a bit thicker here, and we all experienced a few anxious seconds before the plane was air-borne. But Little Mac displayed his usual skill and daring.

The plane returned two hours later and landed easily in a slick we prepared for her. Lewis reported on the bridge and led me to the chart table, where he unfolded a sketch.

"Here, Captain," he said, with the point of his pencil indicating an X inscribed on the southeast side of North Little Koldewey Island, "is a dump of what appears to be building materials. The right-hand crosshatchings over the contours represent snow. The left-hand cross-hatchings represent rock. You see, sir, there is very little clear area. Not many places where land mines can be planted. Koldewey Strait is clear except for drift ice. But the upper end near Storm Bay is frozen solid."

The pencil point moved offshore to a series of bold marks roughly paralleling the coast and extending south all the way to Cape Alf Trolle. Lewis explained these bold marks: "This is a tongue of the main pack. It is about twelve miles wide off the entrance to Koldewey Straits and Little Koldewey Island. The ice is *storis* floes. It is close-packed—about ninety-five-per-cent coverage. But I think the *Eastwind* can push through, sir."

"Course: two-six-five. Speed fourteen knots, Mr. List," I ordered the OOD. "Have the officers assemble in my cabin."

# Chapter 24

# NORTH LITTLE KOLDEWEY

I EXPLAINED my plan of action to the group of officers who crowded around Lewis' sketch map spread on my cabin table.

First, we must assume that the enemy was entrenched on the east side of Koldewey Island, prepared to defend his position. The reconnaissance just made had shown this island to be a natural fortress, and there was no telling how many men the Germans might have landed.

On the other hand, we had carefully rehearsed an attack on such a position by exercising our landing force night and day across similar terrain. Now at last were were up against the real thing. This called for a swift, surprise thrust at the enemy's rear at night.

I decided to push the *Eastwind* through the twelve miles of pack ice under cover of darkness. We would then enter Koldewey Strait and anchor inside South Little Koldewey Island, which is separated from its northern twin by a few hundred yards of shoal water. Four o'clock would be H-Hour. We would move up North Little Koldewey, put our landing force ashore at H-Hour, then stand by to furnish artillery support in case it was needed.

As the *Eastwind* drew near the belt of heavy ice which stretched along the Koldewey coast she plunged into a dense fog. It was now 6:00 P.M. and, knowing the ice might be tougher than reported from the plane, I determined not to wait for darkness before pushing in.

It was well after midnight before the ship had battered her way through to inside the pack. The radar ferreted out the narrow gash which separates South Little Koldewey and Great Koldewey islands. We entered canallike Koldewey Strait. Inside the strait we found ourslves bucking a swift current which flowed out of Dove Bay. Sweeping to the sea, it carried huge masses of icebergs, floebergs and large floes which popped out of the Stygian darkness like silent specters. It was clear there was too much ice flowing through the strait for us to think of anchoring. We must keep moving upstream into Dove Bay.

Now a fear assailed me. Could we get past North Little Koldewey without the noise level of the ship alerting the Germans? I had all machinery secured except the one motor needed to buck the current. Of course, running one Diesel engine at slow speed would throw sparks, but I relied on the fog to conceal them. We crept quietly up the strait.

At 3:45 A.M.—H minus fifteen—we were back again at North Little Koldewey, breaking ice for our boats to get ashore. Promptly at 4:00 A.M. Lewis, with his scouts and headquarters detail, hit the beach, or, more correctly, the ice footing. Ensign D. O. Ellis' infantry platoon, then Ensign John Gira's weapons platoon landed in rapid succession. The problem was now entirely in Lewis' hands. He began moving his company stealthily across the frozen island with the thermometer near zero. The darkness quickly swallowed our men, but these sailormen were well rehearsed in keeping contact with one another at night.

The battle of North Little Koldewey was over within an hour after H-Hour. There were no casualties on either side, and not one shot was fired. Again my estimate was fluky—I had sent a giant to do an infant's work. But, I told myself, had it not been for Lewis' tactical skill and the disciplined and co-ordinated soldiering of my men, the Germans might have defied a division—like Leonidas at Thermopylae!

Lewis' reconnaissance patrol ferreted out the German outpost guard and overpowered it before the alarm could be spread. Then it located the main body of Germans without being observed. Lewis deployed his force in an enveloping advance and had the enemy penned between sea and rocks before the interior guard was aware of what was taking place.

Lewis called on the force of twelve Germans to surrender. Everyone raised his arms—everyone, that is, except the commander of the garrison, Ober-Lieutenant Karl Schmid of the Naval Artillery. The intrepid leader realized at once he must destroy his secret documents and was willing to lay down his life in the attempt.

Thurman F. Chafin, a seaman, saw Lieutenant Schmid strike a match and attempt to light an oil-soaked bag which lay at his feet. Chafin rushed the unarmed commander with his rifle and knocked the burning match from his fingers. He then snatched up the bag and delivered it and Karl Schmid to his commanding officer.

Following this capture, Lewis dispatched Gira's platoon on a sweep of the island to round up any isolated elements. None was found.

In the meantime Ellis marched the prisoners of war across the island to the beachhead, whence they were brought, half frozen, to the ship. I believe these forlorn-looking souls fully expected to be shot. Dr. Goebbels' propaganda machine had done a thorough job. They certainly did not expect the humane treatment Americans customarily give their captured enemy.

First the prisoners were stripped, bathed and issued clean clothing. Next they were given a hot American breakfast. In the meantime their uniforms, immaculate as they were, would be sterilized before being re-issued to their owners.

Ober-Lieutenant Schmid had one request to make. Could his crew's mascot, who was also a prisoner, be allowed to remain with his men? This was a little black dog of doubtful ancestry named Zipper. I readily consented.

While our German friends were being properly disposed of, the *Eastwind* moved around the island to the station our men had just captured. There was a mass of equipment of all sorts—about 200 tons of it—which must be inventoried and brought on board. It included well-built housing, valuable radio and meteorological equipment, tons of food and munitions and countless miscellaneous items.

A few of these miscellaneous items nearly brought tears to many eyes. All that good German beer and rare French champagne was frozen solid by sub-zero temperatures before it could be brought from shore to ship. Still, there was an abundance of ardent spirits whose alcoholic content preserved them for Dr. Smith to add to his medical stores.

These low temperatures made our anchorage a precarious one. An endless parade of large floes marched through it on their journey from Dove Bay to join the main Arctic pack. This main pack was only a few miles offshore and, it was clear to us, would spread shoreward day by day. Our work, hampered as it was, would be a race against the inward movement of *storis*.

The important job of evaluating the documents which Lieutenant Schmid tried so valiantly to destroy was given to Lieutenant (j.g.) Harry Kelsey, my communications officer. Kelsey selected two crew members to assist him. These were Gerald Varrelman, yeoman, first class, and Werner Mueller, an electrician's mate. Kelsey and Varrelman had learned their German in college. Mueller had spoken it fluently on his parents' farm in Wisconsin.

At the end of the first day the translation detail had determined that our seizure was indeed a far-reaching one. It knew, for instance, that the following top-secret German documents were now in Allied hands—and uncompromised, as far as the German high command could tell:

(a)  The all-important German submarine-contact code.
(b)  Operations plan of the admiral of the Polar Seas.
(c)  Detailed hydrographic, meteorological and geographic information about Spitzbergen and Nova Zembla.
(d)  Land-mine plans for German stations in Greenland, Spitzbergen and Nova Zembla.
(e)  Naval operations charts of the Polar Sea regions.
(f)  Deployment of Arctic naval forces.
(g)  Weather and communications codes.

Further translation uncovered details of three German Arctic naval expeditions. Each bore a code name which suggested its leader. The one we had just captured, under Lieutenant Schmid, was called *Goldschmied*. The expedition which had run afoul the *Northland* was led by Ober-Lieutenant Weiss and named *Eidelweiss*. A third one, *Haudegen*, was ordered to Spitzbergen. It was commanded by Ober-

Lieutenant (Dr.) Dege, an eminent authority on the geology of the island.

Schmid's orders, we found, had originally been to establish a weather and radio-relay station on Nova Zembla. When the admiral of the Polar Seas learned of the destruction of *Eidelweiss* by the *Northland* he had diverted *Goldschmied* to northeast Greenland.

"Attempt to locate your station on Isle de France," read the admiral's orders to Lieutenant Schmid. "If ice prevents your getting in to Isle de France, select a suitable location. It is imperative, however, that you keep north of bombing range from Iceland."

A word of caution was added to Schmid's directive about the *Northland.* She was known to be operating in the Greenland Sea with some other vessel, possibly the *Storis.* However, both vessels were expected to leave the area prior to *Goldschmied's* arrival.

I was pleased to note here that there was no reference to the *Eastwind* in Schmid's orders. I attributed this to our having avoided a stop at Iceland en route to northeast Greenland. Had we called at Reykjavik, I believe the information would have leaked out.

The order written by the admiral of the Polar Seas went on to designate the naval transport *Externestiene* as *Goldschmied's* expeditionary vessel. She was to be provided with a destroyer and submarine escort.

It was the *Externestiene,* then, that Land and McCormick had sighted on the second of October! I was anxious to find out more about her.

In the meantime I dispatched a summary of documents seized to upper echelons of command and requested that the *Storis* be sent from Iceland to fetch them. Permission to use her as a courier vessel was granted me immediately.

Taking stock of the situation in the light of what we now knew, I concluded that the *Externestiene* was an iceworthy ship, but not an *icebreaker.* She might, therefore, still be lurking in northeast Greenland—possibly with her submarine escort. In such event it was plainly my duty to seek her out and destroy or capture her.

I turned over in my mind the idea of manning the German transmitter and sending fake weather in our captured codes. We might thereby lure the *Externestiene* into our hands and at the same time raise havoc with Nazi Western European weather prognoses. But there was too much danger of our transmissions being recognized by a clever enemy. He would then know his codes were compromised. I discarded the notion.

McCormick made several flights during the second day we were at North Little Koldewey in an effort to locate the *Externestiene*. None was successful. But we were closing the search area, and if she were hovering in the area, we would be sure to find her. The submarine, I believed, must have returned to open water after seeing the transport into the pack. But I was to have occasion to reconsider this supposition.

The darkness of midnight, October 5-6, was broken only by the white, snowy shore line of North Little Koldewey, whose wind-swept crest blended with the indefinable black sky somewhere beyond it. A silent procession of ghostly white floebergs flowed past the vessel, drawn toward Bismark Strait by the flood tide. The ship was in utter darkness. On shore the flicker of cargo lamps cast an eerie glow over the figures of men who were loading the boats with booty.

Suddenly the urgent *Bong! Bong! Bong!* of the general alarm split the cold, crisp air.

I rushed to the bridge, scooped up my glasses and trained them down the OOD's outstretched arm. No explanation was needed. Centered there in my line of sight was the unmistakable outline of a submarine—a German submarine!

The underseas craft was stealing in toward us, partially hidden among floebergs which seemed to travel with it. I judged its speed to be about three knots. I thought: *Her skipper is smart!*

"Propeller beats! Five zero r.p.m.," sounded constantly from the "Squawk Box" (the 21-MC intercom to combat operations center). That would be about right for the speed she was making. The sub was less than a quarter-mile away and should start maneuvering for firing position in a few seconds. This we must prevent.

I ordered a searchlight-illuminated forward-turret attack with heavy machine-gun support—the after turret being masked.

On the fire-control bridge List swung his director on the target and made certain the searchlight crew was "on." Young also had his director controlling two 40-mm. "quads" lined up.

At a word from List the violet beam of the searchlight flashed on and flooded the target. A split second later two tongues of flame licked out of the five-inch twins.

Even before two columns of ice particles and spray rose from the base of our target we knew we had been fooled. Young checked his heavy machine-gun fire. We had thrown steel at a floeberg.

I sought the explanation of the propeller beats reported from "combat." No one had paid the slightest attention to the motor sailer returning with a load from shore. It turned up fifty revolutions per minute.

"Good practice," I consoled, but my face was a trifle warmer than it should have been.

The following afternoon we received another scare.

The plane was launched, and McCormick made ready to take off on another recco flight. He had taxied no more than a hundred yards from the ship when the ice began moving into his take-off strip. He spun his aircraft about and made for the ship, taxiing downwind. As he passed under the crane Mac made a grab for the hook and caught it. The driving force of the wind was too much. The airman was yanked out of his cockpit and plunged into the icy water. McCormick bobbed up a few times, and then his helmeted head disappeared beneath a large floe of ice.

On the bridge Lieutenant Commander Land, with presence of mind, threw the control levers to half-speed-ahead. He figured the screw current would suck the flier out from under the floe. It did. Mac was fished out by the crash boat and rushed to the sick bay.

Dr. Robert H. Smith prescribed a generous portion of ardent spirits, which the pilot eagerly accepted. "Now get out of those wet clothes," the surgeon ordered.

"What wet clothes, Doc?" McCormick asked in feigned astonishment. "These flying clothes are watertight. Only my face got wet. But thanks just the same for the hooker on the house."

"Well, now, young fellow," the doctor said, grinning, "for being so clever you may have another one on the house." Dr. Smith retired to the pharmacy and returned with a second drink.

Mac sipped it suspiciously, then set it down and fled. Even 151-proof rum can't conceal a stiff dose of castor oil.

# Chapter 25

# LIEUTENANT KARL SCHMID, GERMAN NAVAL ARTILLERY

I READ the note a second time. It pleased me because I knew that the carefully penned words came from the writer's heart.

Dear Captain:
I am grateful to you for the kind treatment accorded my officers, my men and myself by the personnel of the *Eastwind*. It is unfortunate we have been associated in difficult circumstances.
To you and your fine *Eastwind* I wish—good luck.

Respectfully,
Karl Schmid

In the week since the *Eastwind's* landing force captured the enemy garrison I had come to know Karl Schmid fairly well, and I shared his feeling that it was unfortunate we could not have been associated in more favorable circumstances.

Some of my knowledge of the man had been gleaned by translating the enemy documents saved from destruction by Chafin. Some had been acquired by personal contact. But there was much more I would have liked to learn during that week. I believed that Karl Schmid undoubtedly had a good understanding of the enemy's Arctic plans.

A lieutenant of German Naval Artillery, Karl Schmid held a Ph.D.

earned at Stuttgart University. And he not only had been a student there; he had also served as a professor in the university's college of geography.

Prior to World War II the Reich needed mountain-wise geographers spotted here and there beyond the world's commercial frontiers. So Dr. Karl Schmid, who had spent his childhood in the Alps, was relieved of his university duties and given an assignment in the Andes. I do not believe he completed this particular job, for he was recalled to Stuttgart shortly after Munich.

The war came, and early in 1943 it was apparent to Hitler that Germany needed a polar weather empire. Africa had been invaded by the Allies. The German armies were bogged down on the eastern front. Hundreds of ships were getting through to Murmansk with war cargoes. And there were hints of an Allied invasion on the western front.

In brief, Hitler's operations were no longer unopposed. To meet the growing pressure on every front he vitally needed accurate weather data—data which could be acquired only by sending men to the Arctic regions.

The establishment of polar bases required leaders of an unusual caliber. The garrisons would be cut off from sea and surface support during most of the year. Consequently the officers in command must be capable of exercising an unusually high degree of initiative. Moreover they must be scientists. And of course they must have a certain amount of cold-weather experience.

Karl Schmid admirably met these requirements. And so once more the professor hung up his gown at Stuttgart University and replaced it with the uniform of the German Naval Artillery. After a suitable indoctrination in military tactics, meteorology and communications he was ordered to establish a weather station on Nova Zembla. A brand-new vessel—the *Externestiene*—was assigned to transport his men, materials and supplies. The expedition, it will be recalled, was assigned a code name: *Goldschmied*.

What, I wondered, would be the plan now that *Goldschmied* also had been captured? Would Expedition *Haudegen* be ordered from Spitzbergen to northeast Greenland? And what had happened to the *Externestiene*, Karl Schmid's expedition ship? Was she still in the vicinity? If so, where was she and what were her orders? So far our plane had failed to turn up an answer.

Karl Schmid undoubtedly knew the answers to these questions. But I knew he would shut up like a clam if I undertook an interrogration.

On one occasion I thought I saw an opportunity to pick up a hint or two. Schmid came to me and asked for permission to say a few words to his men. I wondered if perhaps he wanted to warn them to keep mum about any knowledge they had of the enemy plans. In issuing such a warning he might say something of value to us. I gave my permission, but sent Mueller to listen in.

"He told his men," Mueller reported to me, "that they are being treated with far greater courtesy than they ever expected and are much better fed than they ever were at home. He ordered them to render as full a measure as possible of co-operation with the ship's personnel."

While this was not what I had hoped to learn, it pleased me none-theless. And as time went on I was glad I habitually kept a smart ship with my men in blue uniform and my officers in complete dress with blouses and neckties except when their work required Arctic outer garments. This, I knew, elevated us in the eyes of the Teutons. Moreover we stacked up well with them as they carried out Schmid's order to the letter, conducting themselves in a thoroughly military manner, maintaining a neat personal appearance and keeping their quarters immaculate.

But I did not have the answers to the questions in my mind. So I decided to give a dinner party, inviting Karl Schmid and his officers, Lieutenants Hanns Pieker and Walter Sander, along with my executive officer and my chief engineer. Perhaps between the three of us we could gain some useful information. A careful question here and a few remarks there might be pieced together and tell us something about the *Externestiene* and about Expedition *Haudegen*.

My Negro steward, James Strather, had been a valet to a millionaire in civilian life. At his request I always pronounced his name with a very proper British inflection, calling him "Jymes."

When I told Jymes that the German officers had accepted my dinner invitation with pleasure and that the party would be formal his black face spread into an abundant grin. This was a long-awaited opportunity to display his artistry and knowledge of social ritual. Moreover perhaps he could now justify his insistence that the *Eastwind's* cabin mess required two pairs of silver candlesticks which, to humor him, I had purchased out of my own pocket before sailing from Boston.

With the cabin lighted by soft candlelight for the dinner party the contrast in uniforms was colorful: the Germans in well-tailored green and we Americans in service dress blue with black bow ties. Jymes was doing well.

I felt that cocktails would put my prisoner guests at ease and perhaps loosen tongues. And why not? We had an ample stock of the Germans' own liquor. It was of the very best, too. But Karl Schmid discreetly stopped with two cocktails. His officers, taking their cue from him, followed suit.

No, we did not obtain much information. Nevertheless the evening was delightful—so delightful, in fact, that we almost forgot the official status of our guests. So far as its purpose was concerned, that party was a failure. But later, at a second dinner and at a few teas, I gleaned enough to convince me that if Expedition *Haudegen* did try to get into Greenland it would not set up south of Jackson Island. But of the *Externestiene* I learned nothing.

My liking for Karl Schmid grew. I returned to him a manuscript which he had spent many years preparing and gave him every opportunity to continue his work in the interest of science. I knew his material would never fall into Nazi hands, and there was a possibility it might benefit the Allies.

One time at tea I asked Dr. Schmid how the masses of German people accepted Hitler and his Nazi party.

"You have a saying in English," Schmid replied, "that a drowning man will grasp at a straw. Before Hitler's rise to power the German people were beaten and starving. Hitler offered them employment and food. The answer is a natural one."

Dr. Schmid continued, "You Americans hate the Japs. I do not believe, now, that you hate us, their allies. At least we do not hate Americans. How could we? Most of us have relatives and friends in America. I have five nephews in your Army and Navy."

Schmid added heatedly: "But we do hate the Russians. Do you know, Captain, Germany is all that stands between Communism and the Western world? We will lose this war. Then *you* will have to fight the Russians."

I made no comment.

Yes, I warmed to the man. But nothing, I think, did more to enhance my liking for him than our Annual Northeast Greenland Pie-Eating Contest, which took place a few days after his capture.

Two teen-age brothers were the winners. When the "King of the Choppers" awards were pinned on their trouser seats they were asked if they had anything to say. One brother took the microphone, hesitated briefly and then asked in seriousness: "Please, sir, can I have another piece of pie?"

"This is America at play," I told Schmid.

"You will find, Captain," he said, "that many parts of Germany produce people who are equally human. You saw the Polar Bear certificates my men and I received." He then described the monkeyshines aboard the *Externestiene* when she crossed the Arctic Circle en route to Greenland. As I listened I recalled that Schmid and many of his group were from Wuttenberg in southern Germany, and it was impressed on me that some sections of our enemy country produced "a different breed of cats" than the Prussians.

A week passed while we awaited the arrival of the *Southwind* and the return of the *Storis* from Iceland. Meantime we had loaded our booty and resumed patrolling according to plan.

It had taken three days of hard work to dismantle the buildings and bring them aboard the *Eastwind,* along with the fuel, stores, ammunition and equipment which the Germans had landed on North Little Koldewey. We got it all except ten drums of Diesel fuel which had to be left ashore when large quantities of ice began moving down from Cape Bismark and put an end to boating.

Before we left the island, however, I ordered the place thoroughly policed. No doubt there were many unasked questions about that order. I imagine the shore party grumblingly wondered why we should clean up a place where man probably had never been before and might never be again.

I gave no explanation with my order and doubt that I can give one now. There was an intangible involved, an intangible which integrates into the types of discipline so necessary among men who must battle the Arctic elements. The keystone of that discipline is cleanliness.

We unloaded some of the captured foodstuffs at Mjorke Fiord, relieving Niels Jensen of the problem of stocking that northernmost outpost of the Greenland Army for at least two years. Nordum and Nielsen, the two lieutenants stationed at the hut, welcomed the German rations with broad grins. Hitler's European armies lived on a restricted diet, I am told. But he lavished food, with proper regard to fats and oils, on his Arctic forces.

It was now October 6. We stood down through Dove Bay in order to rendezvous with the inbound *Southwind*. On the way we kept a sharp surface watch for the *Externestiene*, thinking she might be so adroitly camouflaged that our plane could not spot her from aloft. By now we thought we had a vague idea of the type of ship we were hunting. This information had come to us unwittingly through Lieutenant Pieker, Karl Schmid's second in command and an accomplished artist.

Pieker had made a number of water colors, which I restored to him after concluding they had no military value. He subsequently offered me the collection as a personal gift in appreciation of the kindness shown him aboard the *Eastwind*. I had no desire to own the pictures, but in order not to injure his feelings, I had decided to accept one when I suddenly was struck by a scene which I thought might be of some use to us. It showed a vessel at anchor in a Norwegian fiord. The place was obviously Tromso. And it seemed likely that the vessel was the *Externestiene*.

I accepted the picture and turned it over to one of the *Eastwind's* amateur artists, who prepared silhouettes and plan views of the ship depicted by Pieker. At best, of course, these could be only an approximation of the *Externestiene*—if that ship *was* the *Externestiene*.

We met the *Southwind*, our sister ship, in Hochstetter Bay on October 9. Her skipper, Commander Richard M. Hoyle, USCG, reported on board the *Eastwind* to receive his patrol instructions. I was glad to have Dick Hoyle in command of the other icebreaker. He was one of the foremost oceanographers in the service of the United States. And northeast Greenland was virtually virgin territory for investigations in this branch of science.

The hundred-mile patrol area was divided into two sections, with the northern section assigned to the *Southwind*. I chose the southern section for the *Eastwind* in order to be in a better position to maintain liaison with Niels Jensen and his Greenland Army. After a negative air reconnaissance we each got under way for our respective stations.

The *Eastwind* proceeded around Pendulum Island into Young's Sound and hove to in the flat, smooth surface ice off Sandotten. Here once more we played Santa Claus to the Greenland Army, unloading captured building materials, food, stores, meteorological instruments, radio equipment and cases of spirits. For good measure I threw in some German ordnance equipment. But I held on to a stack of Mausers and an accompanying magazine of rifle grenades. I wanted these because repeated efforts to obtain U. S. grenades for our own rifles had failed. In addition the *Eastwind's* gunnery officer insisted that we retain several trench mortars with their ammunition.

Patrolling continued until the evening of October 11, when the *Storis* met us off Cape David Gray. We immediately began transferring our remaining booty, prisoners and captured documents.

It was after he boarded the *Storis* that Karl Schmid sent over his note of appreciation. I read it a second time as I watched the *Storis* depart for Iceland. Karl Schmid had been a pleasant guest—but not a helpful one. Where, I wondered, was the *Externestiene?* And what was cooking with Expedition *Haudegen?*

Chapter 26

*THE NET IS CLOSED*

WHILE there were many questions in my mind, there was one thing of which I was certain. The initiative clearly lay with the enemy—and it was our job to outguess him.

The best guess we could make was this: Unless Expedition *Haudegen* had already established itself on Spitzbergen, it now would be ordered to northeast Greenland in the absence of an "all's well" signal from Expedition *Goldschmied*.

If this happened, where would *Haudegen* attempt a landing? We did not have to guess. Ice conditions still permitted *Haudegen* to get ashore somewhere within our original hundred-mile patrol limits— between Cape Wynn to the south and Cape Bismark to the north. Later, though, the southward march of the main pack would limit this area. We could guess that the enemy must be aware of this. We also could guess that he knew he must act quickly if he intended acting at all.

I made one more guess: that the mid-October period was the most vital and that an attempt to land might be made immediately following a blow when winds would have opened up helpful leads through the ice.

We got such a blow—a two-day howler—on October 12 and 13. Air reconnaissance was out of the question in such heavy weather. But the ship could reconnoiter the surface. Consequently, in the belief that any enemy activity likely would be to the northward—and soon—

210

I sailed the *Eastwind* around Cape Philip Broke to exploit ice conditions.

We put in a busy two days charting leads. Then when October 14 dawned bright and clear I ordered both ships to make an air search. The *Southwind* was unable to comply with this order because of a lack of open water. But the *Eastwind* found a clear spot in Pendulum Strait, and Little Mac took off with Lieutenant Commander Land as observer.

Wanting to put the ship in a better position to support the plane, we began crashing northward through Pendulum Strait. It was 2:00 P.M. when we hove to in a pool south of Cape Philip Broke. The returning plane was sighted about an hour later, and McCormick soon taxied under the crane. Lieutenant Commander Land was standing in the rear cockpit, his hands funneled to his mouth, manifestly shouting something of importance. But the noise aboard the *Eastwind* prevented us from hearing.   ·

Watching Land and straining my ears to hear what he was shouting, I suddenly concluded he was trying to report a contact!   "

"Mr. Howard," I ordered, "shape a course for Cape Philip Broke with all possible speed on four engines. I'll have six engines on the line as soon as possible," I added.

The *Eastwind* leaped into a film of new ice glazing the sea. Land was soon beside me, panting after his hasty dash from the plane cradle to the bridge. "A ship, sir!" he exclaimed between breaths. "She's frozen solid in a consolidated field of polar ice about ten miles off Cape Borgen, Shannon Island. She's a big ship. About two hundred feet long. Painted white with black stripes."

I scribbled off a contact report which included instructions to both the *Southwind* and the *Eastwind* to "Go get 'em!" Our sister ship, I knew, must be somewhere in the vicinity of the target. But it was likely she was hemmed in by heavy ice the same as the enemy, and I was uncertain that she could hammer her way through. Luckily for us, we had used those two days of storm for charting leads. This information would be invaluable with the approach of darkness.

As soon as all six engines were delivering full power I called my senior officers to the cabin. As they huddled around a chart spread on the table I outlined a plan for taking the enemy vessel intact.

With a fine pencil I traced the leads we had exploited only yesterday. Because of freezing conditions and the lack of wind those leads must now be carpeted with fairly thick new ice. But the heavy ice through which they were etched must be static. As a result we should be able to make good speed through those frozen leads for at least twenty-three miles. This would put us seven miles from our objective.

At that point—seven miles from our objective—the ice was probably well consolidated and hard. We would find tough going then and could not expect to be within range much before 10:00 P.M. This was desirable, however, because the aurora display would not subside until between nine and ten o'clock. And if possible I wanted to take the enemy by surprise—under cover of darkness.

What about the enemy's radar picking us up? I didn't think we need concern ourselves about that. It was likely the enemy would not expect a night action. In all probability his radar would be secured to conserve precious energy.

The *Eastwind* would sneak in to a range of 4,000 yards, make a turn to the right, unmask her batteries, light the target with illuminating projectiles from one turret and pour out shot from the other. I had no stomach for taking life. Consequently no fire would be directed into the enemy unless he chose to fight it out.

"Our first salvo," I directed Lieutenant List, the gunnery officer, "must be a 'short.' The second must be an 'over.' On the third I want a 'near hit' planted directly to one side of the vessel." It was my hope that this third salvo, the "near hit," would scare Fritz into surrendering. My officers voiced their approval with enthusiasm and expressed the hope that the *Eastwind* would arrive and engage before the *Southwind*.

When we sped past Cape Philip Broke there still was a dash of sunset clinging to the mountaintops in the west. This light lasted long enough to guide us through leads past Cape Paunsch. Then when we wheeled abruptly to the eastward the yellow-crowned flares of the aurora burst across the heavens to guide us into the ice-coated channel leading offshore.

We soon found this channel filled with brash and small floes cemented together by new ice. A turn to the north sent us crashing against an unbroken sheet of young ice into which polar floes were frozen.

There was no great difficulty in shattering this sheet at first, but it became more obstinate as we roared north, for the polar floes were more and more predominant. When the brilliance of the aurora had spent itself we traveled in total darkness, and it was impossible to dodge the heavy floes and discern the soft spots.

Ice eventually squeezed around the ship so tightly that she was slowed to a stop. We backed cautiously and rammed ahead at top speed. This netted us a gain of a few fathoms. We backed and rammed once more, moving ahead another few fathoms. Over and over, after that, we backed and rammed, backed and rammed— bucking ice, as we called it.

Then I heard the long-awaited report from our combat operations center: "Target! Bearing three-five-zero! Range, seven miles!"

"Sure it isn't a berg?" I asked.

The answer came back from COC: "The radar doesn't lie, Captain! That target is steel!"

I recognized O'Hara's voice and chuckled as I recalled a time when he and Sloan had mistaken a convoy for an uncharted island. "Set Condition Able," I ordered.

The officer of the deck moved the general-alarm lever, and the *Bong! Bong! Bong!* burst out impatiently as the crew rushed quietly to battle stations.

We still had five miles to go to reach the point where the *Eastwind* would launch her attack. And those five miles were all ice miles— many times as arduous as sea miles, for the ice became heavier with each lunge. The vessel reared and slowed with the violent impact of each charge into the ice. At times I thought she must surely buckle some of the frames in her forepeak. But the forward damage-control party kept assuring me the hull was holding up under the terrific beating.

Still we crunched, lunged and bucked through the ice. Our heeling system was ready. I was loath to employ it, however Heeling would alternately depress one screw and elevate the other. Each time a screw elevated it would be vulnerable to ice damage. And this was no time for experiments.

"Stand to!" I ordered.

Had the enemy seen us? Would he open fire with a well-directed salvo? Would he scuttle ship and light out across the ice to lose himself among the rocks of Shannon Island? Was this ship the *Externestiene,* held tightly in the ice and camouflaged to prevent us from finding her? Or was this Expedition *Haudegen* seeking to take over *Goldschmied's* interrupted task? Those questions coursed through my mind as I put on my steel helmet and climbed to my battle station on the flying bridge.

After what seemed an eternity the intercom screeched, "Range: four thousand yards!"

"Unmask the batteries," I ordered.

"Roger from ship control!"

Curtis Howard began working the ship slowly astern to charge into a change of course. The engines roared when she jumped ahead. Then with a sickening jolt she careened dizzily to starboard.

Combat operations center reported: "Range: four-five-zero-zero!"

We had waited long for this.

I ordered: "Shift control to Combat and commence firing when ready." This meant that Lieutenant Commander Land, the combat-operations-center evaluator, would direct the immediate movements of the vessel and issue orders to Fire Control.

Two blinding flashes blazed from the after turret, and the still night air was rent by a frightful roar. Two projectiles zipped through the darkness, climbed skyward and burst into a brilliant pair of lights which commenced settling slowly. I looked intently through the eerie glow, seeking the Nazi ship. But all I could see was a white desert studded by shadowy, imprisoned bergs.

A second illuminating salvo burst from the after turret, and the heavens on our port hand again resembled a Fourth of July display. Anxiously looking again, I saw no sign of a ship, and my heart sank.

Then a salvo roared from the forward turret and zoomed toward what I took to be a berg. Two columns of shattered ice particles spurted skyward about 200 yards short of the target.

"You're wasting ammunition firing at an iceberg, Mr. List!" I shouted into my telephone.

"O'Hara says it's a steel target, Captain," the gunnery officer replied.

"Very well, you win," I conceded. "But I still think it's a berg!"

Another illuminating salvo split the air almost simultaneously with a second salvo from number-one turret. This time the target hid the impact, and I knew that our second "'business" shot must be an "over," as planned.

"New target bearing: zero-five. Range: five miles. Shows IFF!"*

This new target must be the *Southwind*. We were closer to the enemy than she. Moreover we were set up for action. So I would proceed with our plan. Now the *Southwind's* searchlight cut across the ice and rested on the berglike object at which we were directing our fire. The third discharge from No. 1 threw up twin columns of ice directly ahead of the target—and very close, as planned.

There was no doubt now. It *was* a ship! The target dropped immediately after the impact of the third salvo, and it was my impression that we had struck her with a freak ricochet and that she was sinking. I sent a message to this effect to the *Southwind*. But immediately I saw I had been mistaken, for the target abruptly stopped settling.

Then a series of quick flashes stabbed toward us. These were followed by a well-transmitted blinker message in plain English: "We give up."

To make myself clear I wrote a reply which I had Mueller translate into German before the signalman sent it. Our blinker then flashed in German: "Do not scuttle ship."

I purposely failed to add the words "or we will fire" because I knew I lacked the heart to open up our guns on defenseless men.

"Mr. Howard!" I barked into the intercom. "Close on the enemy ship now! Mr. Kelsey, tell the *Southwind* she may try closing."

---

* Interrogatory, Friend or Foe. An electronic system developed in 1943 to distinguish between enemy and friendly vessels and aircraft.

# Chapter 27

# WE CHRISTEN THE EASTBREEZE

HAD it not been for a small lake which we ran into, I doubt that we would ever have reached the surrendered enemy vessel. But this small lake gave us a chance to "freshen the nip," a point where we had relatively easy going in open water for a short distance and could build up momentum again for charging into the heavy ice immediately beyond.

Two hundred yards short of the enemy vessel I decided we had gone far enough for the night. The time was now 2:00 A.M. We had fired our first salvo shortly before 10:00 P.M. This meant we had consumed *four* hours in making good a little less than *two* miles. Yes, we were in some pretty tough ice. And that wasn't all. We had obviously damaged our starboard propeller somehow.

A platoon of our landing force crossed the remaining 200 yards to receive the vessel's surrender. Another party—a squad of technicians which included Mueller, who could serve as translator—was sent over to make a thorough survey of the ship. Lieutenant Commander Montrello, in charge of this party, had orders to keep the vessel's captain and chief engineer on board as hostages against booby traps and scuttling charges.

In about a half-hour the glare of our cargo lights picked out the gleaming white steel helmets of the landing force returning as it emerged in two files from behind huge hummocks of ice. Between those files of our men I saw a single file of green-clad figures. It was a startling scene. Captors and captives seemed to be appearing from behind the dunes of a fleecy-white desert. For a moment I found it hard to realize that we were more than ten miles at sea.

I felt a pang of sympathy for the prisoners as they mounted the ladder and reached our deck one by one. They looked cold, friendless and beaten. Yet they were lucky to be alive. Some other ship, perhaps, would have killed them all at the first salvo. Now they must be searched, bathed and given a change of underclothing and socks. Coffee and doughnuts would follow.

I looked for the *Southwind*. She was more than a mile away and apparently was having difficulty with the ice. There was nothing we could do to help her. And as I was beginning to get curious about our prize I decided to go over and have a look at her.

Prize! This was a misnomer. Surely we never would get the enemy ship out of the polar field in which she was imprisoned.

We already had learned from our prisoners that we had captured the long-sought *Externestiene*. As I made my way over the ice to her I reflected that our season's work was still unfinished. We could not consider our mission completed until Expedition *Haudegen* was in our hands or effectively barred from Greenland by Nature.

Montrello was questioning the captain and chief engineer in the *Externestiene's* wardroom when I went aboard. The captain, Lieutenant Luther Rother of the German Navy, was a giant of a man with a countenance which reflected an inherent good nature. His English bore only a trace of an accent, and I was prompted to compliment him on his mastery of our language and inquire where he had learned it.

"I sailed with the Standard Oil Company for several years, Captain," he replied. "It was a good company to work for. I wish right now, of course, I had stayed with them."

Lieutenant Rother and Chief Engineer Helmot Marks led us through the engine room and pointed out five mines which had been planted as scuttling charges. Although Lieutenant Rother apologized for the run-down condition of the machinery, I was impressed by the newness and general cleanliness of the vessel and her modern propulsion plant.

By questioning the two officers we learned that the *Externestiene* was commissioned on July 3, 1944, exactly one month to the day after the *Eastwind's* commissioning. Designed for work in ice, she displaced about 1,000 tons and was something over 180 feet in length. Her single screw was turned by a triple-expansion steam-reciprocating engine with a steam-turbine engine which could be coupled to the propeller shaft for economical cruising and for added speed.

The captain pointed to a pile of ashes on the floor plates of the oil-burning fireroom. "My classified publications," he explained. "I broadcast a contact report as soon as you opened fire."

We already knew about the contact report. Our radiomen had picked it up, and Kelsey, our communications officer, had handled the decoding and translation. I asked Lieutenant Rother if he had seen our plane the previous day.

"Yes, sir. We could have shot it down, but I refrained from doing so because I was certain nothing could reach us through the ice. I have spiked all our ordnance, but have not damaged the hull or machinery. But you probably will scuttle my ship, for you will never get her out of this ice."

Although I made no answer to this, I agreed in my own mind—and with a sinking feeling in my heart. But my ego was buoyed as Lieutenant Rother continued talking.

"We thought we were being attacked by huge tanks traveling over the ice," he said. "I had no idea any ship could ever break through. Your first two salvos straddled us. Your third one was so close that I thought the next would surely hit and perhaps kill some of my men. I did what any commander would have done when he found himself outgunned by such odds. I surrendered."

Meanwhile the *Southwind* had been smashing through the ice and was within a mile of the *Eastwind* when I returned aboard. A blinker message from Dick Hoyle read: "We have damaged our port screw."

"Aw, that's nothing," I blinked back. "I have damaged our starboard screw all by myself." I ended this message with a request to Dick Hoyle to come aboard the *Eastwind* and talk things over.

Day was breaking when Dick climbed our ladder, and we had our first view of the surrounding ice. His opening remark reflected my own sentiments: "How in hell did we get here?"

I had the impression of three vessels having been borne away from the earth by some supernatural force and dumped in the heart of some frozen badlands on a distant planet. Another question leaped into my mind, but I kept it to myself for fear of betraying a lack of confidence. That question was: *How in hell will we ever get out of here? Surely,* I thought, *Lieutenant Rother had not been exaggerating when he boasted that we would never use his ship.*

Dick told me that the *Southwind* had only the stub of one blade remaining on her port propeller. I felt certain our starboard screw had not been damaged so severely. Although the ice around us prevented a thorough examination, it was the opinion of Mr. Cummings, the *Eastwind's* first lieutenant, that we had lost only one blade.

Convinced that the *Southwind* was in worse shape than ourselves, I decided that Dick Hoyle should lose no time in attempting to get her out of the polar ice. But we would remain long enough to remove all booty of any value from the *Externestiene* and then perhaps finish her off with a scuttling charge. If the *Southwind* got into trouble, I told Dick Hoyle, we would try to help her out. He assured me he would do his best to see that we were not diverted from our work.

The *Southwind* got under way about 7:30 that morning, ramming with all her available power, leaping at the ice, backing, leaping and ramming again and again. Her progress was slow but steady, and I felt a little easier. Then I looked at the *Externestiene* embedded among the hummocks. Her plight looked hopeless. It would be best to scuttle her and have done.

But my officers and crew were effervescent with dreams of sailing their prize into Boston Harbor. I could not share their optimism, but it pleased me to see them so enthusiastic. And, frankly, I also was feeling somewhat elated.

I knew, as my officers and men also knew, that our action against the *Externestiene,* despite its one-sidedness, was something of a high-water mark in naval history. No sea engagement ever had been undertaken so far north. More than this, our capture of the *Externestiene* was the only capture at sea of any enemy surface war vessel made by a United States naval force during World War II.* In fact, it was the only such capture since the Spanish-American War, a half-century before.

Yes, I could understand the enthusiasm of the *Eastwind's* company and appreciate their desire to bring their prize into port. *Well, I* thought, *the least I can do is to show them the futility of a salvage attempt, even if the demonstration costs us additional damage.*

While the propellers turned ahead to wash out a track for backing I studied the ice carefully to select the soft spots. Several minutes of this propeller action gave us clear water astern, and the *Eastwind* was backed cautiously for half her length. Then I set my teeth and jammed down the controls to full-ahead.

The big icebreaker roared into a charge, mounting the ice and crushing forward for about a hundred feet before losing way.

"Let's try again!" I said.

Another ten minutes of churning cleared away enough debris to let us back nearly a full ship length. We moved astern slowly. Then; like a runner hearing the starter's pistol, we lunged from our mark as the controls again called for full ahead.

But we weren't making a runner's speed! Rather, we bucked, veered, swerved, jolted, trembled, lumbered ahead a few feet at a time. But after an hour we had almost closed those remaining 200 yards between us and the *Externestiene*. By 8:30 A.M. we were athwart her stem and so close that we could have spit on her forecastle.

The cheers of the men infected me with their enthusiasm. What had begun as a futile demonstration on my part now became an all-out effort to salvage a couple of million dollars' worth of valuable ship. And, truth to tell, I began to savor the sentimental aspect of the situation. Aside from the *Externestiene's* monetary value, delivering

---

* A diligent search of naval records reveals that the only other United States capture of a German naval war vessel at sea during World War II was accomplished by Captain Dan V Gallery, USN, in command of a task group composed of a small aircraft carrier, U.S.S. *Guadalcanal,* as flagship and the United States destroyers, *Chatelain, Pillsbury, Jenks, Pope* and *Flaherty.* On June 4, 1944, Captain Gallery and his group captured the German submarine U-505 in command of Oberleutenant zur See Harald Lange

to the United States a hard-earned prize of war would be a thrilling achievement!

We now moved across the *Externestiene's* bow with short jabs, per-sistent jabs, hitting the ice like a boxer relentlessly striking at one place to fell a giant. Luckily the weather was on our side. It was cold, yes, but it was also clear. Nothing buoys the spirits of men like a cloudless sky and a beaming sun.

Moreover the air was calm. This was particularly helpful, for a wind might have set us against Shannon Island ten miles away. As it was, the consolidated field in which we were working was con-trolled only by the ocean currents. And because these currents had a southern set, we were drifting southward at a velocity of about one knot. This drift could do us no harm. Rather, it might aid us in forcing a passage into Hochstetter Bay where I had ordered the *Southwind* to rendezvous if all went well with her.

As soon as we had plowed a track well past the *Externestiene's* bow our gunnery officer planted wrecking mines on each side of her stem. These shook her loose when they were detonated. But the responsi-bility of making her ready for sea fell to the chief engineer, Mon-trello.

I had set nightfall as the deadline. By then Montrello must ac-quaint himself with a labyrinth of pipes, correctly label valves and controls in English, renew a gasket here and a bearing there and lubricate the entire power plant. More than this, he must teach a gang of Diesel men how to set up steam and operate machinery of a type totally unfamiliar to them. In this Montrello had the assistance of Chief Machinist's Mate Bell, the only enlisted man aboard the *Eastwind* who had ever been shipmates with steam-driven machinery.

Montrello had his problems. But we also had ours aboard the ice-breaker. The ship now had to be worked in a semicircle to the *left*. Such a maneuver would not have been too complicated if we could have made full use of our *starboard* (right) propeller. But with one blade missing on that propeller the ship had a tendency to veer to the right.

We solved the problem by enlisting the aid of Nature even though some risk was involved. When we drove toward a hard hummock of old ice and struck it a glancing blow with the starboard bow our head naturally lurched to the left. Unfortunately, though, each time we hit a hummock in this fashion our stern swung to the right as our bow went to the left. This exposed the starboard screw to further damage from the ice.

An alert propeller watch combined with expert teamwork on the bridge resulted in such precise timing that we ultimately concluded the maneuver unscathed. It was midafternoon by then, and we were back in the ice lake through which we had sped the previous night.

So far, so good. The most difficult part of the operation was now completed. We began breathing easier, and I took time to look around.

Focusing my glasses on a black dot slowly moving on the horizon, I saw the *Southwind* inching her way toward Cape Philip Broke. Dick Hoyle was as good as his word. He had promised to take care of the *Southwind* and not divert us from the *Externestiene*.

It was high time now that we finished breaking out our prize, for the sun was well down in the west and would soon be hidden by the mountain wall rimming the coast of the mainland.

Brash ice choking the track through which we had already broken offered no great impediment. We drew close to the prize and made a lunge at her stern, pivoting ship and ice as a unit and heading the vessel into our old channel. This put us bow to bow. A hawser was quickly roused out, made fast on the captured ship and secured on our own deck, and the ticklish business of backtracking was begun.

Captor and captive were lying side by side in the lake by nightfall. And it was none too soon, for new ice already was building up on its surface. Montrello announced he was ready to commence raising steam. Knocking off work for a few minutes during the afternoon, our men aboard the *Externestiene* had piped the United States ensign to her main gaff and cracked a bottle of enemy champagne against her hull to christen her *Eastbreeze*.

Montrello had a full head of steam at the throttle by dawn. A carefully selected crew of thirty-two men had been put aboard and shaken down on emergency drills. The ship was ready for sea.

When seven bells on the morning watch heralded full daylight the *Eastwind* smashed into the pack with the *Eastbreeze* steaming astern, bound for Hochstetter Bay and rendezvous with the *Southwind*.

Chapter 28

# WINTER TAKES OVER

THE principal mission of the Northeast Greenland Patrol Force was to deny the enemy a foothold in the most remote corner of the Western Hemisphere. In carrying it out we were about to have an ally—old man winter. The events of October 15 and 16 had convinced me that this ally was preparing to shoulder the onus of the task.

Henceforth until summer we could expect continued sub-zero temperatures and icy Arctic gales. These gales, of course, would break up the ice fields and brush an occasional lead into the coast. Given time, an icebreaker like ours could make it through the pack even in the dead of winter. But an iceworthy vessel without breaking qualities would never make it after the first of November. Perhaps even now it might be too late to get our hard-won prize out onto the open seas. Both her ice escorts were cripples.

At any rate it was high time to shift operations from inside the pack to outside the pack. First, however, I needed ice information from which to plot a course through it.

Shortly before noon, October 17, the *Eastwind* brought the *Eastbreeze* to rendezvous with the *Southwind* in Hochstetter Bay. We found our sister ship lying to in a little patch of open water, one large enough for a plane to take off from. I ordered both ships' planes away on an ice-reconnaissance mission.

We began to prepare our prize for service under her new flag, in-

stalling armament and setting radio frequencies. A permanent crew
of thirty-two men was put on board. I placed Lieutenant Curtis Howard in command.

Just before dark the planes returned with their ice charts. There
were no leads. The entire ocean was frozen for a distance of 100
miles offshore. But there were some soft spots—ice pools separated
by new ice. I plotted a course which tended roughly east.

During the night final adjustments were made to the *Eastbreeze's*
machinery and boilers. Boats were filled with water and covered
tightly, and an electric heater was installed in each to prevent freezing.
A full head of steam was raised, and at the break of dawn everything
was ready for getting under way.

In the meantime I had a little chat with Lieutenant Rother.

"I did not think it was humanly possible to get my ship out of the
ice," the German skipper declared. "It was a marvelous piece of
ice seamanship, Captain, but I am not happy about it. If I am ever
recaptured and returned to Germany, I will face a firing squad for
letting my ship fall into your hands."

"No danger," I commented. Then I asked, "How did you get
stuck?"

"I tried to escape to Norway," Rother explained, "but we ran into
the main pack northeast of Cape Bismark. New ice formed almost
at once, but the *Externestiene* is a good ship. She rose to the pressure."

Later Mueller supplied me the details of the *Externestiene's* abortive
attempt to escape. He translated the diary of one of our prisoners,
Heinrich Henke, radio mate. The literal account read:

October 2, 1944. After we unloaded the whole night through we
were finished with everything and can consider our trip back. At 1550
the weather troops have left, all boats are picked up and the anchor
is hoisted. We have covered exactly 50 m. Immediately a sharp lookout is posted and we see an American seaplane that is observing us.
Speedily our ship is camouflaged with all colors and the American flag
is raised. After that the airship flew around several times and then
disappeared. Up to now everything went along all right. As it was
we were finished with unloading and the stuff was ashore but was not
camouflaged. If the expedition was seen and later was attacked we,
unfortunately, do not know.

We now take course 60 degrees and navigate straight along the

Sometimes we had to blast our way.

Docking facilities in Antarctica. Craft on quarter of *Northwind* is a "Greenland Cruiser."

coast and try at 1800 to get through the ice. At first the going is all right even though several floes have to be hit to get through. But the ice is getting thicker and thicker and at 2100 we have to give up any thought of going farther. We are now lying trapped in the ice. Wherever one looks all that is to be seen is ice and snow. However, the coast of Greenland can be seen.

October 3, 1944. At 0500 it is getting worse and that means the ship will have to be abandoned. In a hurry the sailors are busy with paint and brushes and the ship is hurriedly painted all colors. Then the whole crew is assembled and put out of the way so that the whole ship will resemble the landscape. In case we do have to abandon ship several provisions are made. The ice skiff is packed with tents and living materials; the skis are being made ready and other provisions made.

October 4, 1944. That we will still be fast in the ice and that no thoughts are being made of getting free, emergency matters are being prepared. There is nothing for us left to do. In the evening we are nice and comfortable with a nice liquor and gin together. [Last entry.]

At 6:45 A.M., October 18, our little fleet steamed out of Hochstetter Bay. We intended that the *Southwind* tow the *Eastbreeze*, with the *Eastwind* smashing a trail in the van. But the rake of the transport's bow prevented her being snubbed into the *Southwind's* towing crotch. Our plan was modified so the prize followed under her own power close astern the *Southwind*.

At the end of the second day we felt the rise and fall of the ship under wave action. It was nice to hear the whisper of each sea as it caressed the floes. To the eastward of us the sky was black and forbidding. We were nearing the edge of the pack, and this was the time and place to issue patrol instructions.

I believed it was high time the *Eastbreeze* earned her own salt. She was seaworthy and, in fact, far more comfortable than either of her escorts in a heavy sea. Moreover she had radar which fitted her for patrol work. I assigned her a station between Latitude 73° 30' North and 74° North. The *Southwind* was given the sector between 74° North and 75° North to patrol, while the *Eastwind* took the northernmost sixty miles—75° to 76°—as her station.

In the early morning, October 20, we burst out of the pack and scattered to our stations. Huge seas swept in from the northeast, lashed by a wind that was heavy with snow. Visibility was practically zero. There was much scattered ice flanking the margin of the outer pack which the ships could not avoid striking from time to time. This ice could not be seen against the sea return on the radar, but any ship—any enemy transport—would show up as a solid pip. Ours would be a difficult gantlet for him to run.

On October 25 difficulty developed. The *Eastbreeze* was having steaming trouble. Howard radioed that he was out of fresh water. The evaporators could not be made to function and the water we had pumped into his boats was already salted. Seas which swept over the decks of the prize had penetrated even the tightly lashed boat covers. The *Eastbreeze* must leave the area.

I ordered the *Southwind* to replenish the *Eastbreeze's* water supply and prepare her for the long trip to Iceland. I asked the Commander Greenland Patrol to send an escort to take our prize to Iceland.

ComGrePat replied that no escort vessels were available and suggested we scuttle the *Eastbreeze*. This I refused to do. We had gone to enough trouble to get her out of the pack. The *Eastbreeze* was a new ship—a valuable prize and well worth the risk of running the U-boat gantlet off the Icelandic Claw.

I decided the risk was justified and ordered Howard to proceed to Iceland without escort. The *Southwind* would take her south as far as Latitude 70° North, then return to her patrol station. From that point Howard would be on his own.

Howard carried out his orders well. On October 30 he reached Reykjavik.

As October 1944 slipped into history it was obvious that winter had taken over the task of keeping the Germans out of northeast Greenland. Our work here was done. But there still remained a little matter of unfinished business in Spitzbergen. If the German Polar Sea command had carried out its plans, *Haudegen* was doing business in King Carl Land. Someone should knock it over.

Of course, practical operations were opposed by technicalities—too often a source of frustration. Spitzbergen was in the area of the British home fleet. It was their pigeon, not ours. But I knew the British Navy had no icebreakers worthy of the task of getting into Spitzbergen in dead winter. We had two icebreakers, even though crippled, less than 400 miles away. Moreover we had the enemy's plans, his land-mine layout and the disposition of his weapons. A night attack would be a pushover for us!

I decided to sail for Spitzbergen.

As a sort of afterthought I informed ComGrePat—and others who needed to know—what the *Eastwind* and *Southwind* were up to.

The answer I received was disappointing. We were ordered to keep in our own area. At first I was a trifle huffy about the inflexibility of command areas. Then it occurred to me that, since we had compromised the Germans' code, perhaps the U. S. high command wanted the Germans to do the work of weather reporting. I hoped this was so.

I ordered the *Southwind* to rendezvous with us at Latitude 70° North. Thence the two ships limped southward.

I watched the *Southwind's* blunt bows rise and dip into the seas behind us, fascinated by each puff of spray they cast over her foredeck. I felt a gentle tug at my sleeve. It was O'Hara, grinning about something.

"Beggin' the captain's pardon," O'Hara began, "we've still some work to do. King Boreas will be mighty unhappy if we bring a cargo of ice worms back across the Circle. Everything's set up, sir, for making Polar Bears out of 'em."

"Put the show on the road then," I said. "By the way, Mr. O'Hara, please be so kind as to have the Royal Baliff remove Mr. Kelsey's pants and halfmast them at the yard as a signal to the *Southwind* that we will shortly cross the Arctic Circle."

Kelsey, Land, Montrello, McCormick and more than 300 of their shipmates were still ice worms in name and would be until the initiation ceremonies were over. But in experience in Arctic know-how they were now qualified ice seamen. I was proud of every one of them.

The *Externestiene* reached Boston on December 14. The vessel is now on the active list of U. S. Navy ships—the U.S.S. *Callo*. But to 360 officers and men who were in on her capture she is still the U.S.S. *Eastbreeze*.

*Part Four*

SOUTHWEST GREENLAND OPERATION

*1944*

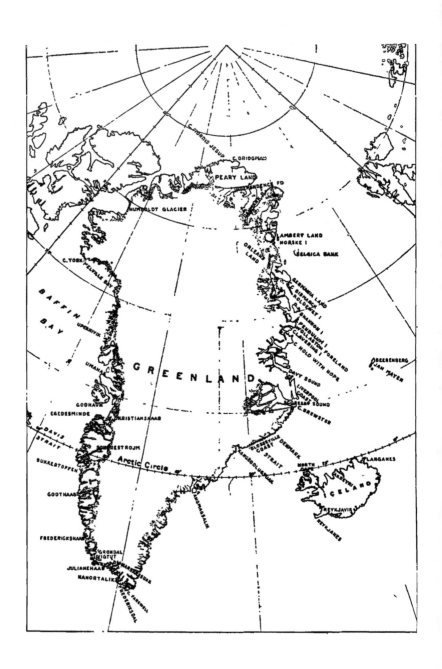

Chapter 29

# SEAGOING DIPLOMATS

IT HAS been said that a United States Coast Guard officer must combine the characteristics of a navigator, marine engineer, lifesaver, sea-fighter, international lawyer and diplomat.

It was largely in this latter capacity—as a diplomat—that I found myself ordered ashore in Greenland on February 7, 1945. I packed my sea chest and moved from the *Eastwind's* cabin to quarters at Narsarssuak. There I found Von Rosenvinge, now holding the rank of lieutenant commander and serving as flag secretary to Commodore E. G. Rose, USCG, Commander Greenland Patrol. My orders stated that I was to serve as the commodore's chief of staff.

Three months after I went ashore Germany surrendered. This immediately relegated the Greenland Patrol to a position of relatively minor importance in the United States' war effort. But a tremendous task still faced the Navy in the North Atlantic.

Thousands of ships and planes had to be returned from Europe for refitting and manning with newly trained crews so that they could be thrown into the offensive against Japan. Aiding the movement of these ships and planes became the primary function of the Greenland Patrol.

Despite the importance of all this, the Greenland Patrol was undeniably caught in the backwash of the war. Admiral Smith was transferred to the continental United States. His former post, as Commander Task Force 24, with headquarters at Argentia, Newfoundland, was assigned to Commodore Rose, who received a promotion to rear admiral. I was ordered to take over as Commander Greenland Patrol with Commander C. F. Edge, USCG, as my chief staff officer.

Our first job, of course, was attending to the hundreds of details created by the unprecedented number of ships and planes moving across the Atlantic from Europe. Beyond this, we were faced with helping plan and establish the United States' peacetime role in Greenland.

The basis for retaining a foothold on the island, to guard against future aggression from Europe, hinged on the Greenland Agreement. We suspected that, now that Germany had surrendered, the covenant would be in constant jeopardy from adverse influences on both sides of the Atlantic.

It seemed to me that the logical place to begin bolstering the agreement was in Greenland itself. Our relations with Danes and Greenlanders were already extremely friendly. We must keep them that way and, if possible, make them even more friendly.

To this end I made a point of touring the western settlements: calling on the Honorable C. F. Simony, governor of Greenland, and paying official, but somewhat social visits to the various colony managers, Danish functionaries and numerous Greenlanders. We also provided these dignitaries with man-of-war transportation to Narsarssuak.

But in the matter of social intercourse with Danes and Greenlanders I needed help. Consequently the real missionary work devolved to a large extent on numerous Greenland Patrol personnel. Two who were ideally suited to the task were a rough old salt, Carl Jensen, chief machinist's mate, USCG, and Von Rosenvinge.

Jensen, a Dane by birth, had been an enlisted man in the Danish Navy prior to World War I. Emigrating to the United States in 1921, he enlisted in the Coast Guard as a fireman. I am not certain of Jensen's age. By the time I met him in Greenland he had taken on years and weight, achieving the appearance and good humor of a Santa Claus without benefit of beard. He had a sparkle in his eyes which matched the gleam of his gold rating badge, his service stripes and the brass buttons of his chief petty officer's uniform.

Jensen was a habitual user of snuff. For this reason he was known throughout the Coast Guard as "Snus," the Danish word for snuff. He was of the school of iron men and a mechanical genius. We could rely on him in any emergency.

In accordance with service custom Snus had the left sleeve of his uniform jacket adorned with gold hash marks—six of them, representing twenty-four years of perfect conduct. To Snus those hash marks implied a status far above that of an ensign with his single gold stripe. Consequently Snus spurned a commission. Eventually he was transferred ashore from the *Northland* and designated as "commanding officer" of the United States naval oil barge at Narsarssuak.

Because Snus was fond of people, particularly Danes and Greenlanders, I decided to include him in my diplomatic corps. His love of his native land and its king had not been dampened by his transfer of allegiance to the United States. This attitude toward Denmark would be valuable to us. The imposing array of gold on his left sleeve and his unabashed manner even in the presence of those of the highest position tended to suggest that Snus was an officer of considerable rank and importance. Moreover Snus had served in Alaska for many years before coming to Greenland and was well informed about Eskimo psychology.

My reasons for appointing Von Rosenvinge to the diplomatic corps were equally sound, I believe. American-born of Danish parents, Von Rosenvinge—a lawyer in civilian life—had been Danish vice-consul in Boston before the war.

It was my intention in conducting our good-will tours that Von Rosenvinge and I would call on the higher echelons, leaving it to Snus to mingle with the Danish workers and Greenlanders. As it turned out Snus was integrated into all our activities. His fluency in the Danish tongue, his working knowledge of the Eskimo language, his quick wit and jovial laugh—and, as I have said, his unabashed manner—leveled all barriers of caste.

More than once I heard Snus relate a story which never failed to charm his democratic Danish listeners. He would tell of his days in the Danish Navy and how he had served in a ship with His Royal Highness, the Crown Prince (now King Frederick IX).

"His Highness was a midshipman," Snus would continue. "One

day he said to me, 'Jensen, I might have to be king someday. I want to know all classes of my fellow citizens. Let me make a liberty with you and meet the kind of people you meet on shore.' "

Snus's eyes would sparkle and his mouth broaden in a grin. "His Highness must have guessed that I didn't associate with the nobility or the clergymen when I went ashore. I lent him one of my blue-jacket's uniforms and stuck close to him to see that he didn't get into trouble. Well, it turned out that His Highness was the one who took care of *me. What a man!*"

Yes, Snus was welcome in the executive mansion of Governor C. F. Simony and in the "castle" of Oscar Corp, the cosmopolitan manager of the cryolite mine at Ivigtut. He was just as welcome in the neat little cottages of the Greenlandic hunters and in the lowly hovels of the Greenlandic fishermen. Most of all, I think, he was loved by the children.

I still like to recall Snus trudging through a village like a Pied Piper of Hamelin, followed by scores of Danish and Greenlandic youngsters shouting: "Ønkel Snus! Ønkel Snus! Chew gum! Chew gum!"

There was only once when I wondered if I had made a wise choice in sending Snus afield. A personal letter I received from Ivigtut told of a Greenlandic woman in the near-by village of Arsuk having just presented her husband with a fine daughter. The letter continued: "She has decided to call the baby Ønkel Snus."

I read no farther. Jumping out of my chair, I rushed to the operations log and fanned back through the pages of a calendar. It was not until I had checked on the dates of Snus's trips to Arsuk that I breathed a sigh of relief.

I later informed Snus of his little namesake and how she had momentarily had me worried.

"I wouldn't worry, even so, Captain," Snus answered, laughing. "All Skeemo gals want kiddies by a foreign poppa. And they prefer Americans to Danes because they figure America is a bigger country than Denmark. Their menfolks don't care, either. They just want to know who to put the finger on for the hundred and forty bucks the Greenland Administration 'fines' every poppa."

"Even so," I growled, "none of our personnel had better be involved—ever!"

"No, sir, Captain!" Snus agreed. "No sailor would ever be mixed up in anything like that!" He picked up his cap, walked to the door and hesitated. Turning a grin-widened face to me, he said: "No, *sir!* Sailors are too smart ever to get *involved* like that!" He wheeled and strode down the hall, chuckling.

I think that Snus and Von Rosenvinge contributed more to preserving America's position in Greenland than ever will be apparent on the surface. But to say that these two alone produced a lasting, favorable sentiment toward the United States would be unfair to others.

I cannot forget the hospitable manner in which Commander Henry U. Scholl, USCG, treated Danes and Greenlanders. Scholl succeeded me in command of the *Eastwind.*

Scholl developed the warmest of all American acquaintances with Governor Simony. In fact the *Eastwind* virtually became the governor's flagship so long as Scholl was her skipper. And Ønkel Henry, as Simony called him, did not overlook the "little people." He became the idol of many Greenlanders.

Commander C. F. Edge, USCG, my chief staff officer, was eccentric in many ways. Yet there was something inherently warming about his eccentricities. This, combined with an inborn suavity, won him a universal popularity among the Danes and considerably advanced our cause.

Lieutenant Kensil Bell, USCGR, who served as staff historian, often traveled with me. We soon learned that the surname Bell is unknown in Denmark. The Danes, puzzled by Bell's name, invariably asked for an explanation. Perhaps we were inept. Or perhaps the Danes were highly amused that anyone should have the name of a metallic instrument usually found in a church steeple. At any rate, to the Danes Bell became Lieutenant Ding-Dong, and they always addressed him with a smile. But we did not mind this, for to win smiles is essential to diplomacy.

Lieutenant Commander James M. Leroy, USN, Greenland Patrol survey officer, was also one of our diplomats. Leroy had been a member of Louise Boyd's expedition to Jan Mayen Island and northeast Greenland in 1937. His knowledge of the latter coast served the United States admirably when he joined the *Bear* as navigator in 1941. This, of course, was in the earliest days of the Greenland Patrol, when the *Bear* was flagship of the task unit consisting of herself, the *North-land* and the *North Star*. But it was later—after the commencement of hostilities—that Leroy made his greatest contributions to our hydro-graphic and diplomatic efforts in Greenland. And this stemmed di-rectly from Admiral Iceberg Smith's farsightedness.

Over the years the Danes had conducted numerous hydrographic surveys of Greenlandic waters. But, in keeping with Danish policy to isolate Greenland from the rest of the world, their charts had been withheld from international distribution. And with Germany occupy-ing Denmark, all known hydrographic knowledge pertaining to Greenland was denied us. As a result the principal sailing directions available for the coasts was the sketchy *Arctic Pilot* published by the British Admiralty. Some small coasting charts and a few harbor charts also were available. But these were highly inaccurate, for they were based on rough surveys made sixty to ninety years before.

Admiral Smith was alert to the necessity of expanding the hydro-graphic information about Greenland. But with the initiation of hostilities Coast Guard cutters were occupied with too many other duties to continue the work. Consequently Admiral Smith prevailed on the Navy Hydrographic Office to assign the schooner *Bowdoin*, with an Arctic expert, Commander D. B. MacMillan, USNR, in command, to continue the survey.

Later the admiral also procured the survey boat *Splash II* and, aware of Leroy's knowledge, experience, abilities and proficiency in the Danish language, had him placed in command.

The *Splash II* and her skipper soon became a familiar and welcome sight in Greenlandic settlements up and down the coast: from Ang-magssalik around Cape Farewell to Thule. Leroy willingly rendered any service the Danes and Greenlanders required, from repairing antique boat engines to towing kayaks and umiaks. Steadily his charts expanded, and sounding figures formed neat patterns across their faces.

Noteworthy among Leroy's diplomatic achievements was his co-operation with Danish survey officers after the liberation of Denmark in 1945. Making available all his findings, he saved the Danish gov-ernment a vast amount of effort. And it was not only the material he supplied, but the spirit with which he supplied it that went far to cement the Danish-American relationship.

There were officers in the Army, besides Colonel Eugene Rice, Greenland Base Commander, who also contributed immeasurably to our diplomatic efforts. Among them was "Ice Cap" Pete Hostmark. To appreciate Hostmark and his exploits it is necessary to backtrack in history and review the attempts of man to survive on the Greenland Ice Cap.

# Chapter 30

# ICE IN THE CLOUDS

MUCH of what I know about the white man's adventures on the Ice Cap prior to World War II—and during the war, as well—I learned from "Ice Cap" Pete. Summed up briefly, it amounts to this

For 161 years a procession of adventurers and mountaineers attempted to overcome the challenge of one of Nature's most formidable barriers—to cross the Greenland Ice Cap.

Among those who made the attempt and failed was Edward Whymper, the greatest mountaineer of his time, whose conquests of Mont Blanc and the Matterhorn made mountaineering history. Whymper undertook the crossing in 1867 and again in 1872. Despite his defeats, he clung to the belief that the ice could be conquered and that a government-financed expedition would insure the availability of sufficient funds to make the crossing successful.

It was Fridtjof Nansen who made the first complete crossing from Angmagssalik to Godthaab in 1886. Nansen had five other men in his party. They ascended the Cap on August 16. It was not until the end of September that the hardy little group finally fought its way in to Godthaab.

The Nansen expedition traveled on skis. The equipment was crude and the clothing inadequate. The men suffered intensely during the arduous trip. But Nansen was a scientist. Even when the hardships were at their worst he took advantage of every opportunity to collect meteorological data. Then, obliged to winter in Godthaab, he utilized his time to study the Eskimo and gather the material which resulted in his book, *Eskimo Life*.

In 1892 Robert E. Peary, later rear admiral, USN, crossed the northern end of Greenland. He charted the coast and explored Independence Fiord. There have been several successful crossings of the Cap since Peary's time. Probably the most notable were those by Ejnar Mikkelsen in 1910 and by Knud Rasmussen in 1912.

With the advent of the aviation age excursions onto the Ice Cap achieved a new kind of importance. No longer were they motivated by scientific reasons and man's inherent desire to surmount obstacles.

Exploitation of the northern air route to Europe—the shortest route through the skies—brought with it a humanitarian obligation for government to aid fliers whose aircraft were forced down on the icy desert. The first forced landing was made by Bert (Fish) Hassell in 1926 when his plane ran out of gasoline over the difficult marginal zone of the Cap. After easing down without mishap Hassell and his partner, Parker Cramer, made their way on foot to Holsteinborg.

Until the advent of World War II only single planes in sporadic flights had flown across the Ice Cap. But the war put myriads of craft into the air, thousands of them bound for Europe via Greenland. It follows that the number of forced landings on the Cap increased proportionately. Rescues of surviving airmen, victims of forced landings, gave rise to a crop of heroes—men who willingly risked their lives to snatch plane crews from death by cold and hunger.

Teamwork in which all services co-ordinated their efforts attended the rescue of the crews of two B-17s and six P-38s from death on the Ice Cap early in 1942.

This squadron set out from Narsarssuak, Greenland, to England via Iceland. About halfway across Denmark Strait it received orders to return to Sondrestrojm Base in west Greenland. Actually these orders originated from the German radio station at Sabine Island, but the unsuspecting pilots believed them to come from the Commander, Greenland Base Command, at Narsarssuak. The Germans brought the squadron close to Sondrestrojm, then ordered it to proceed to Iceland. Again the flight wheeled about and headed east. By this stratagem the Germans kept the American fliers chasing around on orders and countermanded orders until all planes ran out of gasoline.

A Navy squadron led by Lieutenant George Attebury and navigated by Lieutenant James M. Leroy located the beleaguered airmen. Major Frederick Crockett, U. S. Army, with his dogs and sledges was transported to the nearest fiord in the Coast Guard cutter *Northland*.

Crockett was guided over a treacherous crevasse-scored area, which lay between the fiord and the surviving fliers, by Colonel "Fish" Hassell of the Air Force. From his plane Hassell could spot the snowbridged crevasses. He conducted Crockett safely among them by "buzzing" him in the proper direction.

Crockett reached the survivors and fetched them to the *Northland*. Then it was learned the bombardiers had failed to properly destroy their bombsights. Someone had to go back onto the Ice Cap and salvage them. This task fell to Major Norman Vaughn, rescue officer of the Greenland Base Command.

Travel on ice was nothing new to Vaughn. He had left Harvard to go to the Antarctic with Admiral Byrd and had since spent most of his time in the Polar Regions. Vaughn set out with a sledge and dog team—but there was no Fish Hassell overhead to buzz him when he was about to make a false step. Vaughn was obliged to ski ahead of his team in an effort to detect crevasses. Time and again he plunged through snow bridges and dangled in his harness over bottomless crevasses until dragged to safety by Captain Strong, his companion.

Colonel Bernt Balchen and Lieutenant Aram Y. Parunak, USN (pilot), in the summer of 1942 made a spectacular rescue of a plane crew by landing a PBY-5A on a "dimple" or lake in the Ice Cap. Balchen traveled over the ice and led the survivors back to Parunak's plane. They took off—and not an hour too soon. Shortly after they soared into the air the dimple emptied itself into a crevasse.

The most daring Ice Cap rescue was made by Lieutenant John A. Pritchard, USCG, flight officer of the *Northland*, in December 1942. Lieutenant Commander Francis J. Pollard, the cutter's commanding officer, received information that a B-17 was stranded on the Ice Cap. He fought his way into Comanche Bay and was on the point of sending a rescue party ashore when Pritchard insisted that he could land his J2F (Grumman "Duck") on the Cap by sliding in on pontoons.

He took off, located the bomber and, ignoring the airmen's plea not to attempt it, came down for a successful landing. Two men were returned to the *Northland,* and Pritchard returned for the next load. He landed, picked up Corporal L. A. Hayworth and took off. Pritchard, his radioman, B. A. Bottoms, and Corporal Hayworth were never seen or heard of again.

In the meantime Lieutenant Max Demarest and Technical Sergeant Tetley left the Army auxiliary weather station at Comanche Bay in a motor sledge to proceed overland to the stranded plane. Neither Demarest nor Tetley was experienced in Ice Cap travel. Demarest, who was driving the sledge, decided to follow a "gully," where the ice appeared to be smoother. It was a snow bridge! The sledge plunged through the hard snow, carrying Lieutenant Demarest with it into a bottomless crevasse. Luckily Tetley, who was sitting on the rear of the sledge, was thrown clear onto firm ice.

Ultimate rescue of the remaining crew members came when Lieutenant Bernard Dunlop, USNR, and Colonel Balchen adopted Pritchard's technique of belly-whopping their amphibian planes onto the ice.

There were other heroes of Ice Cap rescues and attempted rescues. Among these were Captain Willie Knudsen and Captain Peter Hostmark, both of the Air Force. I heard of both and of Norman Vaughn long before I ever met them. The source of their nortoriety originated in England and was spread across the North Atlantic by westbound pilots. The event occurred in late January 1945. Later the yarn was confirmed. It ran like this:

A raw wind howled across Prestwich Airfield, driving a mixture of rain and sleet which bit into the faces of three even rows of khaki-clad soldiers. Standing apart from the troops, a little group of ranking officers huddled close to a dignified gentleman in a tall silk hat, whose umbrella offered some scant protection to himself and his companions. A pendant suspended from the civilian's neck glistened in the light reflected on the wet pavement of the airstrip.

Something momentous must have been afoot to bring out the lord mayor of Prestwich, the commanding general and his staff on such a wretched night—and at such an unusual hour! The general's aides had done well, and on extremely short notice, to handle all arrangements for receiving the dignitaries who were now expected to arrive any minute! For it was only a few hours since any inkling of their arrival had been received.

Word had been flashed to Prestwich in a top-secret dispatch which (paraphrased) read: "Four planes with Colonel Vaughn: 209 VIP dogs arriving your station."

"What do they mean, *dogs?*" the deciphering officer asked.

"Shoot it down to GHQ. It must be garbled," ordered his commander.

In London cryptographers pondered the message and concluded it must be a code within a code. Top priority was reserved for the White House. Yes, that was it! The key was contained in the words "Colonel Vaughn . . . 209 . . . dogs." The President of the United States and who else? Colonel Harry Vaughn was White House aide. Naturally Mr. Roosevelt would be on board the colonel's plane. Obviously there were 209 VIPs (very important persons) in the four planes. Prestwich must be alerted!

The first plane set down and taxied over to the waiting throng. The pilot cut his motors, the door opened. Somewhere a voice commanded, "Present . . . arms!" A column of motor vehicles moved up, the limousine in the van stopped close to the plane. The mayor and general stationed themselves appropriately to greet the arrivals.

A chorus of howls rose from inside the plane as the crew began pushing Eskimo sledge dogs, one by one, out the door. The mayor, the general and his staff melted into the darkness. Measured footfalls of troops being marched hurriedly away were swallowed by splattering raindrops. Only an aide remained.

Norman Vaughn, now a lieutenant colonel, was in charge of the flight. Hence the impression that the Vaughn mentioned in the dispatch was Harry Vaughn.

Norwegian-born Captain Peter Hostmark was in charge of the canine cargo carried in two of the planes, while another experienced dog driver, Captain Willie Knudsen, was custodian of dogs in the remaining two planes. Each officer knew his business thoroughly. Willie was rescue officer in Labrador, while Pete was his Greenland counterpart. In civilian life Ice Cap Pete headed the Hostmark Engineering Company of Seattle, Washington, with civil engineering as his profession and skiing as a hobby.

Engineers were plentiful in the Army, but ski experts like Peter rare. So after a course in dog handling Captain Hostmark was posted where the Army felt his services could be used to best advantage.

The top priority assigned this flight to England was no mistake. The allied front had advanced into the Belgian woods. Vehicles could not penetrate the forests to evacuate the wounded. Stretcher bearers, struggling to wade through knee-deep snow, were unable to keep pace with the heavy toll in casualties. Dog teams were the only answer, and these must be put to use without delay. The stop at Prestwich had been made only because it was necessary to service the planes and await better terminal weather in Belgium.

In mid-December 1943 an Air Force training plane took off from Sondrestrojm Base, over the Arctic Circle on the west coast of Greenland, and headed south for Narsarssuak Base. A routine report from the aircraft fifteen minutes after its departure informed the control tower that she was on the beam and gaining altitude. The plane was never heard from again. After an hour or so of silence officials became alarmed. A rescue plane left Narsarssuak and sped north with emergency supplies, but was forced back by a violent snowstorm which raged over the Ice Cap.

Captain Peter Hostmark was ordered to proceed with his surface team. Taking three dog teams with sledges, the captain and his men boarded a Coast Guard icebreaking tug and sailed north. After fighting through heavy seas and newly formed ice the little vessel finally reached a narrow fiord, from which Captain Hostmark and his crew made their way onto the Ice Cap. Because the weather was so bitter throughout the month all planes were grounded, so the rescue party had no air reconnaissance to guide it. This was a serious handicap because only a very rough estimate could be drawn of the plane's probable position.

There followed a search which lasted two dreadful weeks. Hostmark and his men were hampered by perpetual darkness, furious icy gales and treacherous crevasses. Once the captain felt the snow sink beneath his skis. Only his momentum carried him with his sledge to firmer snow beyond the crevasse. He glanced around to see a yawning pit immediately behind him.

With his crew and dogs suffering intensely from the cold and hunger, Ice Cap Pete was on the point of abandoning the search when the party stumbled on the wreckage of the missing plane in the Arctic darkness. Its entire crew was dead. Reverently the rescue team hollowed graves in the ice, buried the victims and marked their last resting place with parts of the broken plane.

Ice Cap Pete's value to his government was not confined to search and rescue. His personal charm and fluency in Danish contributed materially to the continuity of friendly relationship with Danes.

The village of Sukkertoppen is situated on Sukkertoppen Island, a barren place covered with ragged sandstone, bushes and tundra, lying a few miles off the west coast near the Arctic Circle. It has a well-protected harbor and is one of the principal Greenlandic settlements.

By July 1945 I had visited most of the villages on the west coast of Greenland, but had never been to Sukkertoppen. Because of its location near the coastal approaches to the U. S. air base at Sondres-trojm, I considered Sukkertoppen to be a strategic place from a standpoint of ocean search and rescue. In order to tie its facilities into my planning I felt I should go there and gain firsthand knowledge.

When Peter Hostmark learned of my plans for visiting the settlement he asked to go with me. I consented with pleasure, for Pete was always a jolly companion. By the time we climbed on board one of my Catalina bombers to make the flight, another officer had joined us. This was Commander Delwyn Hyatt, USN, commanding officer of a Navy tanker. The three of us were clad in our best service uniforms in an effort to be congruous with Danish formality. Because we anticipated no hiking, we carried suitcases.

The plane reached Sukkertoppen Island about two o'clock in the afternoon. We found all of it, except the extreme end opposite the village, enveloped in a heavy fog bank. Looking down, I saw a native in a skiff not far from shore and instructed the pilot to land. We motioned the skiff to come alongside the plane, and as it drew near Pete leaned out and asked in Danish: "Is there a good trail to the settlement?"

The native grinned and said, "Yes."

"Can we get there quickly?" Pete asked.

"Yes," the Greenlander replied, nodding his head eagerly.

The native brought his skiff alongside the plane, and the three of us piled in. The plane took off and was out of sight by the time we reached shore. Captain Hostmark gave the native a pack of cigarettes for his trouble and we sprang ashore. We looked around for the trail we expected to find, but there was none. In the meantime the Greenlander had left and was already out of earshot.

At length we gave up hope of finding a trail and began struggling through brush in the direction of the village. Then something Captain Von Paulsen had once told me flashed across my mind.

"Whenever you seek Eskimo pilotage," V.P. had said, "never ask him if your ship can navigate the uncharted body of water you wish to enter. He will always smile and say yes, because he figures that is the answer you wish to hear and a Skeemo never wants to say anything he thinks will be displeasing to you. So your proper approach is to ask him if he fishes in the fiord or whatever it is you wish to know about. If he says yes, you keep on asking indirect questions until you get your answer. Never take an Eskimo on your bridge because he will be lost with the change of perspective. Have him paddle his kayak ahead of you in water he knows is deep."

It occurred to me that our Greenlander had wanted to please us by the answer he thought we wanted. I told my companions, and the three of us enjoyed a hearty laugh.

Had we known what was ahead, we would not have thought it so funny. The settlement was five miles, as the crow flies, from the place where we landed. But we must have traveled thrice as far. We climbed through jagged rocks, we scaled cliffs, we waded through swamps and boggy tundra, we forced our way through thick brush and we splashed through soft mud which was halfway to our knees. Thanks to our K-rations, however, we were spared the necessity of subsisting on louse wort, Greenland celery, roots and fungi—Arctic survival food.

It was after midnight when at length we staggered into the village and knocked on the door of the first European house we came to, the doctor's house.

Dr. Norgaad must have been taken aback at the sight of three crazy

Americans in uniform covered with mud from head to foot, carrying splattered suitcases. But he was too good-natured to evince any surprise. Instead he greeted us as though he had been expecting our arrival and invited us to come in. While the doctor filled a tub with hot water (there is no running water in Sukkertoppen) Mrs. Norgaad prepared a hot supper, and we soon felt warm, clean and comfortable.

Commander Hyatt sank into a chair and exclaimed, "If I have to return the way we came, I'm going to marry a Skeemo woman and never leave Sukkertoppen!"

He could have included both Pete and me and not have been wrong!

A few weeks later Captain Hostmark and I climbed a glacier and began shuffling on skis on the Ice Cap. The wind moderated, and we were attacked by swarms of mosquitoes. Crevasses are something to reckon on, but mosquitoes cinched the argument. I began to retreat toward the glacier.

When Pete overtook me I told him the Ice Cap was the last place I had expected to find mosquitoes. "A tribe of wild Skeemos up here wouldn't surprise me now!" I added.

"Tommy," Pete remarked seriously, "if a Skeemo is ever dangerous, it's the white man's fault. Only one thing will make him wild, and that's liquor."

# Chapter 31

## *CHILDREN OF THE NORTH*

PERHAPS Pete's remark that an Eskimo is naturally docile offers one more clue to the disappearance of the Norse colonists during the 300-year void in Greenland's history.

Whether it does I cannot say. But in pondering the great Greenlandic mystery it seems worth while to consider the numerous attempts—largely guesses—to answer the riddle.

Some have felt that the Black Death must have spread to the island from Europe and wiped out the descendants of Erik the Red's original settlers. Others have believed that they perished from malnutrition. Still others—and this is a widely held theory even today—declare that the Norsemen were decimated by hordes of warring Eskimos who descended on them from the north.

It is interesting to note at this point that no one knows whether Erik the Red or any other Norse colonist ever saw an Eskimo. We cannot be certain that southwest Greenland was inhabited in those days, for there is no written history of the times either by Norsemen or Eskimos.

Is it tenable that the Norse colonists were attacked and exterminated by warriors native to the area or coming from a distance? To anyone who has made a study of Eskimo psychology and folklore the theory is ridiculous. As Pete said, the Eskimo is a natural pacifist. And it is likely he always has been. We know of no experience in history that would have "tamed" him and turned him from savagery.

Fridtjof Nansen's theory of the extinction of the Norse colonists by amalgamation with the Eskimos is the most logical. Perhaps there were Eskimos in southwest Greenland when Erik the Red arrived. Or perhaps they came into the region sometime afterward. Ultimately when the Norsemen were cut off from Europe and unable to maintain their normal way of life they probably were forced to join with the Eskimos in order to survive.

That interbreeding and absorption by the Eskimos occurred is borne out by the observations of Gustav Frederick Holm, who found that the southern Greenlanders have certain un-Eskimolike physical characteristics. These features included attractive teeth, prominent noses and beards.

Though an Eskimo may commit an act of manslaughter when he is under the influence of white men, he normally is not given to violence toward another human being. Certainly he never would commit murder or massacre on a scale so large as to exterminate a colony of several thousand people. Settling a dispute by *fighting* is, to the Eskimo, ridiculous. Still, *we* call him uncivilized!

Differences among Greenlanders are generally settled by peaceful discussion or by arbitration. If an agreement cannot be reached, the case is held in abeyance until the governor or colony manager arrives to judge it. But even today some villages, particularly on the east coast, are not accessible to colonial jurisprudence. In such places it is reported, the traditional drum dance decides the more serious disputes.

Challenge to a drum dance is delivered by one of the parties involved. Both disputants then are permitted one sleep (one day) to compose a song ridiculing his opponent. At the end of twenty-four hours the two men meet in the presence of the entire village, each armed with his song and a tambourinelike drum.

The challenged man sings his song first. His opponent stands facing him with his feet firmly planted apart. To move both feet is to forfeit the dispute. Beating his drum rapidly, the challenged man dances about while he sings. From time to time his lyrics are varied with the words, *"Ay! Ay! Ay!"* Occasionally he delivers his foe a body blow with his head.

After a stipulated period the man who issued the challenge is given an opportunity to sing his song.

Challenged and challenger thus alternately sing and dance until the villagers decide the dispute in favor of the one who elicits the heartiest laughs. If, during the dance, one of the contestants laughs, he is declared the loser and is forever exiled from the village.

The conversion of Greenlanders to Christianity has largely dispelled their pagan metaphysical dogma. But there still remains a half-belief in a world of spirits, wizards and taboos. This is particularly noticeable in those isolated places which are visited only occasionally by an itinerant clergyman.

I encountered an instance of native superstition one night when we were asked to quarter three transient Greenlanders at Narsarssuak.

It was summer and the weather was warm. But, because Greenlandic weather is likely to change abruptly, we lighted the oil heater in the Quonset hut and showed our guests how to turn it higher if the night got cold.

The officer of the day came to my quarters about midnight and told me, "I think you had better take a look at our Greenland friends, sir."

We went to the Quonset together and found the door and windows locked and the lights burning brightly. A blast of hot air stifled us when we opened the door with a pass key. Inside, the Eskimos were sleeping peacefully with the heater turned to full capacity.

In the morning I asked Snus Jensen about this.

"They are afraid for the ghost, Captain," Snus explained. "Skeemos always sleep with their windows and doors locked at night, and they have it hot with the lights on to keep him away." "Ghost" is Snus's word for "evil spirits."

Among Captain Von Paulsen's many gems of Arctic advice was an injunction that the ice navigator learn as much as possible about the Eskimo. A working knowledge of his language is especially important because the native names of geographical points inscribed on our charts are descriptive and convey a definite visual impression. The word *uminak*, for example, means *heart-shaped*. An excellent hydrographic guide to Arctic pilotage is a glossary of Eskimo words and phrases compiled by Commander Donald B. MacMillan, USNR. It is published by the Navy Hydrographic Office.

I must confess that during nearly four years of service in the Greenland Patrol I learned too little about Eskimos. The fragments I do know were gleaned largely from Frederick, who speaks a jargon of Danish and Eskimo. And I always talked to Frederick with either Snus or Miss Magnella (the Danish nurse at Ivigtut who is now my wife) serving as interpreter.

Frederick, a kayakman and renowned hunter, is chief of the village of Arsuk. As such he occupies the uppermost niche in the social caste of Greenlanders and is a power behind the throne of local colonial administration.

In 1941 the Danish motorship *Julius Thomsen* was about to sail for New York with a cargo of cryolite. Frederick asked Mr. Oscar Corp, manager of the mine, for permission to go along.

"Why, Frederick?" Mr. Corp inquired.

"Time me get married. Maybe I find better wife in America."

A number of Danish functionaries were sailing in the ship and could keep an eye on Frederick. Consequently Mr. Corp consented.

After the *Julius Thomsen* reached New York Miss Magnella piled Frederick into a taxi cab which whisked them to Battery Park. On the way the Greenlander voiced his disappointment. Americans rushed about like madmen—and no one was catching seals.

The Battery Park Aquarium held a fascination for Frederick. Fish were something he understood. They fascinated the nurse as well, and she failed to notice that Frederick had left her side until she was startled by an outburst of screams in the ladies' room. Rushing to the rescue, the nurse found Frederick being shooed away by a crowd of angry women. Miss Magnella apologized for Frederick and led him outside.

The Greenlander did not know how to explain his requirements in Danish, so he used a few of the English words he knew. "I want *piss!* This place they do it!"

The nurse informed him that men and women used separate places for such purposes in America and showed him the proper room.

"Americans fools!" Frederick grumbled. "Should use extra room for put more fish."

Frederick and his custodian later had lunch at an automat. The Eskimo was highly amused and kept using the nurse's nickels to refill his cup with coffee. Miss Magnella finally pried him away, and they proceeded to Central Park Zoo. When they neared the seal pool

Frederick excitedly yanked at Miss Magnella's sleeve. "Quick! Me go to *Julius Thomsen!* Get harpoon. Catch seal!"

The nurse endeavored to explain the impossibility of that.

"Americans crazy people!" the Greenlander grunted. "No eat seal. No use skin. Buy much food, feed seal. Cost many kroner [Greenlandic money]."

Mr. Albert Fischer, a cryolite-mine official, had Frederick as his guest in his hotel suite one evening. Mrs. Fischer was present. Frederick puffed nervously on a cigar Mr. Fischer had given him. Sensing that the Greenlander was ill at ease, Mr. Fischer asked, "What is the matter, Frederick?"

The Greenlander made known his wants.

"There it is, Frederick," Mr. Fischer said, indicating the bathroom.

Frederick shook his head. "I see Mrs. Fischer go *kumarfik.* I see Mrs. Fischer come out. In America men no use same *kumarfik.* I no see other little room."

Among those who greeted the *Julius Thomsen* when she returned to Ivigtut was Mr. Christian Jensen, the Danish manager of Arsuk village. "Where is your wife, Frederick?" Jensen shouted from the dock.

"I marry Arsuk girl!" Frederick replied. "American girl bad wife like Danish girl. No understand how clean and cook seal!"

Frederick went to Arsuk, but came back to Ivigtut the following day looking somewhat crestfallen. When Mr. Corp asked what was wrong Frederick answered: "In Arsuk they laugh and call me big liar. They believe all I say about America until come to place I put kroner and out of pipe come coffee. They say big wizard can no do that. I come get Miss Magnella tell them I no big liar!"

Frederick frequently did odd jobs for some of the Danish families at Ivigtut. One day he was washing clothes in a bucket for Mrs. Oscar Corp. The mine manager's wife found him doubled over with his knees unbent, scrubbing away in typical Eskimo style. Thinking to make the work easier, Mrs. Corp directed Frederick to fetch a bench and place the bucket on it. Then she went about her chores.

Mrs. Corp returned later to see how Frederick was getting along. The bucket was on the bench, just as she had indicated—but so was

Frederick! He was standing on the bench, doubled over with his knees unbent and scrubbing as before.

Mrs. Corp ultimately learned that Greenlanders for untold generations have had to keep their knees and posteriors out of the snow and ice. Consequently positions of kneeling and squatting are unknown to them.

Like so many primitive people the Eskimo frequently tends to exhibitionism in the presence of the white man. Kayak turning, while always entertaining to the white man, is not merely an Eskimo stunt. Rather, as Jette Bang in her magnificent volume of photographs entitled *Greenland** states, it is a very difficult but useful accomplishment, especially in the south of Greenland where seal hunting is the year-round occupation. It is important, Jette Bang continues, for the hunter paddling alone to be able to right his kayak without assistance if it should capsize. Otherwise he would most certainly drown.

Probably the majority of male Eskimos aspire to be great kayakmen and hunters, proficient in the chief skills of the only way of life they knew. Yet Greenland has produced—and undoubtedly will continue to produce—gifted artists, musicians, theologists, nurses, schoolteachers and artisans.

In the larger settlements of Greenland, such as Julianehaab and Godthaab, every child is required to attend school until the age of fourteen. The education provided is on the grammar-school level, with the Danish language a required subject. Among these children there are always some capable of absorbing higher learning. Such children attend the seminary of high-school level at Godthaab and are instructed by Danish and Greenlander teachers. The most intelligent of those attending the seminary usually continue their education on a university level in Denmark at the expense of the Greenland Administration. All educated at government expense outside the island are required to return to the homeland. I am told no Greenlander has ever permanently left the island.

The Honorable Eske Brun, ex-governor of Greenland, is now di-

---

* *Greenland* by Jette Bang. Steen Hasselbalchs Forlag, Copenhagen, 1940  The comments on kayak turning are a free translation from the text. Translated and used here by permission.

—

rector of the Greenland Administration. Mr. Brun has summed up Greenland's most acute social problem:

We must clearly understand that Greenland is at present a poor country, and poverty leaves its mark there in exactly the same way as elsewhere. Above all, it results in bad houses, bad clothes and bad food which bring about poor health conditions. We have established a medical service in Greenland with doctors and hospitals. Some of the hospitals are good, others are bad, but we are striving to change them all into good ones.

Our attack on disease and, above all, on tuberculosis, which has wrought havoc in the country (and which unlike many other diseases up there does not seem to be decreasing), must be concentrated first and foremost on raising the Greenlander's standard of living.*

---

\* *Arctic* (Journal of the Arctic Institute of North America), Volume II, Number 1, May 1949.

Chapter 32

# ONE MAN'S BURDEN

HAD Mr. Brun's high office not demanded his exercising the utmost of tact, he might have added: "We have good doctors, too, and one of these doctors is outstanding among the men of
his profession."

This "outstanding" doctor has quietly led a crusade against both
tuberculosis and its root—the Greenlanders' standard of living. To
appreciate fully the handicaps under which this "colony doctor" has
worked we must roll back the years.

It is 1919. The place is Copenhagen, Denmark.

An old wooden ship slid slowly away from her dock. Her big brass
whistle boomed out a prolonged blast to warn the Copenhagen water
front that she, the king's steamer *Hans Egede*, was backing out of
her slip. For five seconds which seemed like minutes the brazen note
baffled the exchange of farewells between the passengers who thronged
the rail and their multitude of friends on the dock. The blast faded,
and the shouting and waving resumed.

Here and there a handkerchief fluttered in a dab at its owner's eyes.
This was not a pleasure cruise. Everyone on board was in the service
of the Danish crown, otherwise he would never have been permitted
to land on the shores of the vessel's destination—Greenland. A Dane
not under government orders cannot set foot on this island, whose
rulers seek to preserve its natives against exploitation. All contracts

were for one year, but it would be many more before some of the passengers returned to Denmark.

A tall young doctor stood apart from the people at the rail. The expression on his handsome face reflected neither joy nor sadness over his departure from his homeland. No friends mingled with the crowd on the quay to bid him good-by. To Dr. Axel Laurent-Christensen this voyage to Greenland was an economic necessity. It was not easy in 1919 for a newly licensed physician to break into practice. Perhaps after a year in Greenland he would be able to return to Copenhagen and at least be able to eat while waiting for patients. While he was in Julianehaab the pay would not be too lucrative, but he would have a roof over his head, and living expenses would be light. There was a hospital in the settlement, and he, as colony doctor, would be in charge.

In charge! The thought conjured up a little smile of satisfaction, for Dr. Christensen had just finished his internship. His mind pictured spotless tile floors, smart nurses, a well-equipped operating room, laboratory, X-ray, dispensary, pharmacy and all the other components of a modern clinic.

Three weeks later the *Hans Egede* anchored in Julianehaab Fiord. The doctor whom Laurent was to relieve was on hand to meet him, eager to get about the business of relief. Together they jumped into an umiak, which a couple of Greenlanders paddled across the ice-packed water to the bleak little village. They rushed along a narrow street lined with native huts and turned off to climb a steep hill on which was situated a ramshackle building the old doctor referred to as a hospital. Dr. Christensen's heart sank when he entered and stared at its hodgepodge of rooms and the pitiful crowd of humanity that filled them. Cots of all descriptions were everywhere, packed into the rooms and overflowing into the halls, and every cot was occupied by a patient. Outpatients were obliged to wait outside, for there was no space inside where they could sit. There was no electricity, no running water, not even an inside toilet or bath. A single room served as laboratory, dispensary, pharmacy and surgery.

The hospital, the new doctor learned, was but one corner of his field of ministration. His purview extended to the whole of Julianehaab colony, which spread over the entire southern tip of Greenland.

A good deal of his time must be spent in traveling from settlement to settlement. Only about a fourth of his patients were concentrated in Julianehaab village, the colony capital. This meant his professional ratio would be one doctor to 4,000 inhabitants.

An examination of hospital records showed the preponderance of cases were tuberculosis—first, pulmonary; second, of the bone and joint. There was a high incidence of other respiratory diseases, malnutrition, accident cases and, finally, venereal diseases. The building reeked with the mingled odors of cooking food and medicine. One tired Danish nurse was in attendance, assisted by a few *keefak* native orderlies.

It is little wonder the new doctor was seized by an impulse to return to Denmark and face the consequences of a breach-of-contract suit. But Dr. Christensen was made of sterner stuff. He knew someone must be on hand to care for the health of the natives to the best of his ability, and such a responsibility was plainly his—at least for the ensuing year. But he would lose no time getting away when his contract expired.

Dr Laurent-Christensen stayed for more than a quarter-century.

The young doctor settled down to his new duties, used the outmoded instruments of his profession, traveled over his district, began an intensive study of the Eskimo tongue. He was impressed by the universally high incidence of t.b and, in isolated settlements, by the terrific death toll of childbirth. He determined to inaugurate a medical crusade, but first he must have facts. His year had sped by before he was ready to begin. He must stay on another year to see it through. Dr. Christensen is still crusading.

A new hospital must be built and provided with running water, steam heat, electricity, X-ray, modern therapeutical and other appliances  A complete set of new surgical instruments must be obtained and the library stocked with the latest volumes on all branches of medicine. Greenlandic girls must be brought in from outlying settlements and given a two-year nurse's-training course. On graduation they would be qualified to return to their villages, render emergency treatments, improve sanitation and bring to their female patients proper obstetrical care. War must be declared on the colony's worst enemy—tuberculosis.

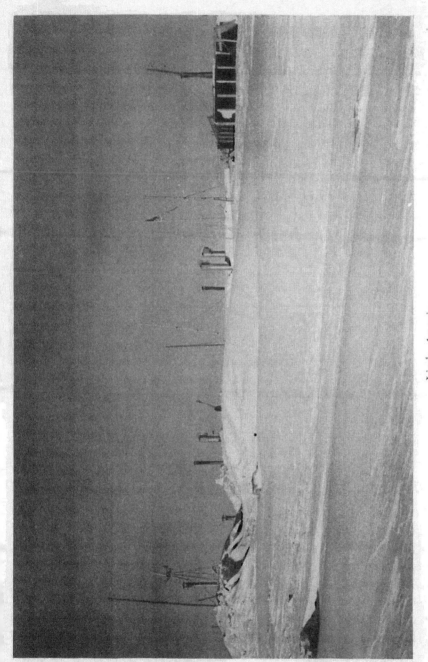

Little America.

Penguin conference.

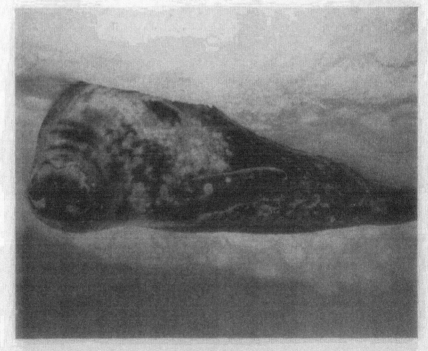

Antarctic wild life.

This was a big order, far more than the Greenland Administration's medical budget could stand. But over a period of years improvements trickled into Julianehaab, and a new, spacious annex to the little hospital was completed. For a short time the original structure was used exclusively for clinical, surgical and laboratory requirements, but eventually it was invaded by an overflow of patients from the new sixty-bed addition.

Within a few years the first class of native nurses was graduated and sent out into the colony to carry on the war against infection and premature death.

In the meantime Dr. Christensen learned the native language, studied new methods tirelessly and made an extensive research into tuberculosis. Later he published a paper on the disease and won the commendation of eminent authorities the world over. The colony doctor was confronted with pathogenic conditions embracing every branch of medicine except tropical diseases.

A Greenlander will submit uncomplainingly to any medical treatment a doctor prescribes, provided he knows the practitioner to be a doctor. This was not always true, for as late as 1925 one isolated settlement clung to its faith in the village Angatok, or medicine man. Dr. Christensen tried hard to make inroads into the inhabitants' traditional superstition.

One day the Angatok approached the young doctor furtively and in strict privacy. The medicine man was ill—the time-honored charms had failed to produce favorable results. Could the white doctor help him? The diagnosis was simple. A few tablets brought prompt relief to the patient. But word leaked out that the Angatok had been successfully treated by the doctor. The medicine man lost face with his people and his job as well.

Anyone less energetic than Dr. Christensen would have been invalided home after a few years of the kind of grueling work demanded of the Julianehaab colony doctor. Even on circuit, life was punishing.

Often it was necessary to camp on the trail, sometimes during a roaring blizzard. Dr. Chirstensen soon learned that Eskimos are the most hospitable people in the world. Living with them, sharing their simple fare and common sleeping shelf, he found them to be a happy, carefree lot. The natives came to adore the new colony doctor.

It was not only Dr. Laurent-Christensen's kindly understanding of Eskimos that earned him their love and devotion. His surgical skill played an equally important part in gaining their confidence. Whenever possible, he brought his patients to the hospital for surgery, but frequently an emergency operation had to be performed under the dim light of a kerosene lantern. In such cases he was lucky when there was a native nurse in the village to assist him.

One night, following a busy day at the Julianehaab hospital, the doctor was aroused from his sleep by an excited native. An ax murder had just been committed in one of the Greenlandic huts. He dispatched the native to inform the colony manager. After all, except for the death certificate, the case was one for the civil authorities rather than himself. However Laurent-Christensen dressed leisurely, picked up his bag and walked down the hill to the scene of the crime.

A young Greenlandic hunter was slumped on the floor, his head lying in a gory pool. Blotches of crimson were splattered over the wall, and from some of them little rivulets of blood oozed slowly downward. The lethal weapon was quite in evidence, its blade tinged with bits of brain. The doctor perfunctorily knelt down and adjusted his stethoscope. Suddenly he tensed. The man was still alive! For no earthly reason, of course. But it was no longer a corpse on the floor. The man was a patient.

"Get him to the hospital at once!" the doctor ordered.

Dr. Christensen sprinted to the hospital, summoned the Danish nurse, flung on his gown, scrubbed and was ready for the patient when he was carried in. Still alive? Yes! Surgery would be a hopeless gesture, without a Chinaman's chance for success. But the doctor knew he had nothing to lose and must proceed on the assumption that there was some hope for the victim.

A large piece of the hunter's skull had been pressed into the brain. This had to be lifted out, the jagged edges dressed and a silver inlay inserted to replace the missing parts of bone. Much to everyone's surprise, the young native made a complete recovery. His mind seemed to function better than before the accident. While convalescing, he organized a Greenlandic hunters' guild and established cooperative prices for the sale of skins. Later he studied music and within ten years became the colony's foremost musician.

While brain surgery was not infrequent, one case amused Laurent. The patient had a brain tumor which must be removed without general anesthesia. Notwithstanding an Eskimo's inherent impassiveness, the doctor realized it would be extremely difficult for the man to keep quiet while undergoing such a nerve-racking operation. But there was no alternative, so the surgeon talked incessantly in an effort to keep the man's mind occupied. At length he was through the bone and about to begin the most delicate phase of his task. The slightest motion might prove fatal.

"What do you want me to give you after you leave the hospital?" Dr. Christensen asked.

"I would like a new pair of pants," replied the patient, taking a profound interest in the turn of conversation.

"You may have a pair," the doctor offered. "What else do you wish?"

"A new *amorak*," the native answered.

By the time the tumor was out the Greenlander had been promised a complete new outfit of clothing from shoes to cap. Two days later he was ambulatory. Dr. Christensen, amazed at his speedy recovery, asked him how he felt.

"Fine," said the patient sadly. "But I wish the operation had taken longer."

"Why?" the doctor asked. "Was it not long enough?"

"No," asserted the native emphatically. "You finished the operation before I had time to ask for a nice, fat young wife."

The assignment of an assistant doctor to the Julianehaab colony in recent years has eased Laurent's burden to some extent and made possible added time for study and research. While t.b. occupies first place on his agenda for such pursuits, Dr. Christensen seeks the answer to two major enigmas. These involve an occasional case of poliomyelitis on the west coast and the complete absence of cancer among the east-coast natives. The doctor does not expect to hit on a solution during his lifetime. He hopes his notes will help future research to stamp out both of these dread evils.

To augment funds made available to his hospital and to provide industrial therapy to patients the doctor purchases their hospital-made products. These include Eskimo dolls, kayak models, beaded goods, *kamicks,* bags, slippers and clothing. A ready market at the U. S. post exchange in Narsarssuak some sixty miles away is always eager for such products. The profits earned by the doctor go to the hospital.

Shortly after World War II the profits paid for a complete outfit of the crimson blankets so adored by the natives.

"Red blankets improve the patients' morale," Dr. Christensen explained. "After all, morale is an important factor in the treatment of any ailment."

"Do your patients ever grow impatient or despondent?" I asked Dr. Christensen.

"No," the doctor answered. "They are fatalists. Most of our t.b. patients will recover. Some whom we failed to catch in time will die here. Would to God I could be as complacent as they! Sometimes I feel so insignificant, so helpless when I realize I am only scratching the surface. They need and deserve better care—much better."

We moved on to the next ward—the woman's pulmonary t.b. ward. All were propped up in bed making little trinkets for the exchange. I walked over to one woman and admired her handiwork. She grinned her pleasure.

"You will have to admire all of them now." Dr. Christensen laughed. "Otherwise the rest will lose caste."

My chief staff officer, Commander C. F. Edge, USCG, was probably closer to Dr. Christensen than any of the other Americans in Greenland. In mid-1946 Laurent confided to him that he was a tired man, sick of fighting for adequate medical facilities, despondent over his inability to hospitalize any except the advanced cases of tuberculosis.

"I am going home this fall," the doctor told Edge, "never to return to Greenland again. My mind is made up. I'm through."

"Laurent," the commander replied, "time has so fettered you to Greenland that you cannot escape for long. The people you love are here. Your work is here. Denmark will be like a foreign country to you, and you will be irresistibly drawn back to Greenland. I'll give you two years. Then you will be back—right here in Julianehaab!"

"No," the doctor said with emphasis. "I'll never come back."

In April 1948 Dr. Laurent-Christensen returned to Julianehaab.

*Part Five*

THE ANTARCTIC EXPEDITION

*1946-1947*

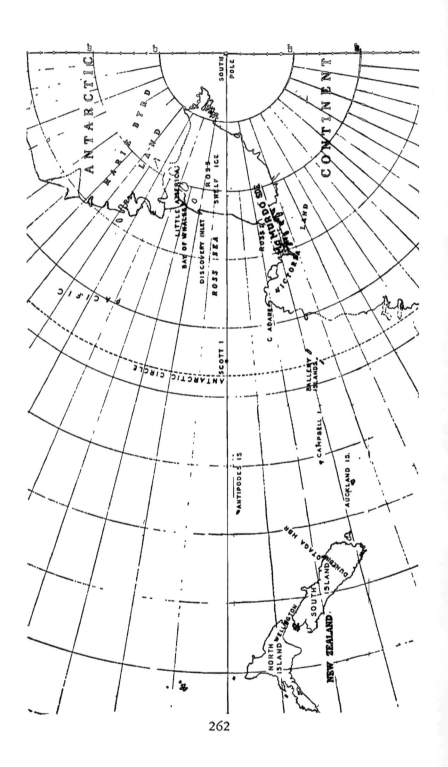

# Chapter 33

## *ANTARCTICA, 1947*

*Clang, clang!* 1:00 P.M., November 25, 1946. Commander Peter F. Smenton, USCG, executive officer of the United States Coast Guard icebreaker *Northwind,* stood on the wing of the bridge and slowly gazed along the full length of the ship's starboard side. Satisfied that all was in readiness, Smenton spoke softly to the talker beside him.

The talker inclined his head and repeated the executive officer's order into the mouthpiece of the telephone set he wore. "Let go all lines," he said.

On the dock sailors lifted the mooring lines from their bollards. The heavy lengths of manila came streaming on board the *Northwind.* Then the ship moved slowly astern as her whistle boomed a prolonged blast.

Back on the fantail a wild chorus of howls took up when the note of the whistle died away. A sprinkling of laughter broke out amid the throng of people who crowded the dock, and many shifted their attention to the several dog teams tethered on the afterdeck.

The explosion of an occasional flash bulb among those who had come to bid the *Northwind* good-by denoted ample representation by the press. And for Boston, Massachusetts, here was news in the making. The *Northwind,* recently returned from the north Polar Regions, was now bound for the opposite end of the world—the Antarctic.

While the ship maneuvered into the channel I stood near Smenton and regarded my new command and her crew who were mustered in even rows at quarters.

Only three weeks ago I had flown out of Greenland and sadly watched her icy mountains fade into the blue haze. My order detaching me from the now nonexistent Greenland Patrol had been vague. They merely directed me to arrive in New York and report to Rear Admiral E. H. Smith for further assignment.

Iceberg Smith had a smile on his lips and a sparkle in his eyes when I was ushered into his office. I knew he was pleased about something. Then in his usual right-to-the-point manner he instructed me to proceed to the Boston Naval Shipyard and assume command of the *Northwind.* He added that the ship was soon to sail on an Antarctic expedition being organized by his friend, Rear Admiral R. E. Byrd, USN.

The following day, November 9, I boarded the *Northwind,* had the ship's company mustered, read my orders and assumed command. Then I plunged into the task of outfitting her with the implements which my experience had convinced me were needed on such a cruise. In addition to these implements there were two men who I felt were particularly necessary—Snus Jensen and Harry Wisnieuski.

Now, eighteen days later, as my ship stood down the channel I felt a little tug at my heart when I saw an icebreaker identical in every respect to the *Northwind* moored at one of the docks. She was the *Eastwind,* my old command. We had been through a lot together, the *Eastwind* and I. In running off with her sister ship I felt that I was doing her wrong.

But I was happy to be in the *Northwind,* and not only because of her destination and the thrills which I knew must lie ahead. Another reason for me to rejoice was that Rear Admiral Richard H. Cruzen, USN, was to command this expedition.

Cruzen was an officer with wide experience in the Arctic and the Antarctic. During the 1940-1941 expedition to Antarctica as lieutenant commander, he commanded the *Bear,* Admiral Byrd's expeditionary flagship. In the summer of 1946, as captain, he was task-force commander of Operation Nanook, the Arctic expedition from which the *Northwind* had recently returned.

It was from this latter expedition that my acquaintance with Richard H. Cruzen stemmed. Support of Operation Nanook by my Greenland Patrol had brought us into close contact, and we had grown to call each other by our nicknames—Dick and Tommy. But now that Dick was to be my chief, I must henceforth speak to him—and of him—as Admiral Cruzen, the rank to which he had just been promoted.

Rear Admiral Byrd chose Cruzen to command Task Force 68 on this voyage to the south Polar Regions. The selection was indeed a wise one, for, in addition to being an experienced ice man, Admiral Cruzen had earned a reputation during World War II as an efficient organizer and a fearless leader.

The *Northwind* put in at Norfolk, Virginia, on November 27 for final preparation, briefing and rendezvous with other Atlantic units of Task Force 68. Those of us at Norfolk were the *Mount Olympus*, flagship; the *Pine Island*, a seaplane tender; the *Northwind*, icebreaker; and the *Brownson*, destroyer. We would rendezvous with others in the Pacific.

In order to encircle the Antarctic continent as completely as possible Admiral Cruzen had set up four major subdivisions or task groups within his task force. These were:

*Central Group:* Rear Admiral R. H. Cruzen
*Mount Olympus* (Command Ship)
*Merrick* (Supply Ship)
*Yancey* (Supply Ship)
*Northwind* (CG) (Icebreaker)
*Burton Island* (Icebreaker)
*Sennet* (Submarine)

*Western Group:* Captain C. A. Bond
*Currituck* (Seaplane Tender)
*Henderson* (Destroyer)
*Cacapon* (Oiler)

*Eastern Group:* Captain G. J. Dufek
*Pine Island* (Seaplane Tender)
*Brownson* (Destroyer)
*Canisteo* (Oiler)

*Carrier Group:* Captain D. S. Cornwell
*Philippine Sea* (Aircraft Carrier)

On December 2 Admiral Cruzen's two-star flag fluttered from the main truck of the *Mount Olympus*. The *Northwind, Pine Island* and *Brownson* formed column behind the flagship and moved out of Lynnhaven Roads on the first leg of a long voyage to the Antarctic.

On our departure from the Canal Zone we were joined by the submarine *Sennet* and oiler *Canisteo*, while the *Pine Island* and *Brownson* detached to proceed in company to their operating area near the eastern end of the Antarctic continent. Our immediate destination was now Scott Island, far across the Pacific.

Scott Island was recorded on our charts as a small dot in the middle of nowhere. The nearest land, the mysterious Antarctic continent, lay over 700 miles to the southward. Yet because of its very loneliness this island could hardly be called insignificant.

On the contrary, Scott Island is an important landmark, sought by all mariners who would enter the icy waters of the Ross Sea. It is the very gateway to the great Ross Ice Shelf, which fans out for hundreds of miles from the heart of Antarctica. This shelf is a vast, endless sheet of ice which Nature had offered as a springboard from which men may have access to the desolate terrestrial fastness of a mighty continent—a continent so scored by glaciers and so heaped with snow that if it were suddenly to melt, the waters of all oceans would rise 105 feet! The Greenland Ice Cap, it will be recalled, would add another 23.8 feet if melted.

The Ross Ice Shelf is constantly on the march. It builds up at its roots, advances and calves to form mammoth icebergs. Some of them attain a length in excess of twenty miles! These bergs drift out through the ice pack to loll in the long Antarctic swells and dwarf to inconspicuousness the quarter-mile stretch of Scott Island.

Scott Island is a wind-swept mass of rocks whose perpendicular sides are capped with perpetual ice. It is therefore difficult to pick it out among the many bergs which habitually surround it. For this reason the island remained undiscovered until recent years.

In 1902 Captain Colback, sailing in the *Morning*, one of Scott's expeditionary ships, discovered Scott Island, which he named in honor of his chief. This was the same Captain R. F. Scott who was to reach the South Pole some ten years later with his little party of five men and their man-drawn sledge.

Imagine the disappointment Scott and his frostbitten men must have felt when they staggered to the Pole. A Norwegian flag had been planted there only a short time before their arrival. This, Scott must have known, was accomplished by Ronald Amundsen, whose dash to the Pole only one month before, had been made in sledges drawn by dog teams. Amundsen established his base at the Bay of Whales, carved in the Ross Ice Shelf, which materially reduced his distance of travel over that of Scott's long trek from McMurdo Sound.

Amundsen returned alive. Scott and his party never returned. Because the Englishman refused to abandon his weakened companions he perished with them.

Sometimes it requires more courage to lose than to win. Two years earlier—in 1909—Sir Ernest Shackleton, with three companions, fought his way to a point less than 100 miles from the South Pole. And there he made his heartbreaking decision to turn back. Had he pushed on to the Pole, his party would have succumbed to starvation. As it was they escaped such a fate only by the narrowest margin.

Shackleton's mission was to experiment with means for polar travel. To this end, he brought with him to his base at McMurdo Sound an *automobile*. This motorcar was custom-built according to Shackleton's specifications and equipped with oversize tires for snow travel. But automobiles were then in their infancy, and Shackleton's proved a failure.

Shackleton conceived the use of motorized equipment to conquer frozen wastes. He lighted a torch—a torch which Lieutenant Commander (now Rear Admiral) Richard E. Byrd, USN (Ret.), picked up after Sir Ernest's death in 1916. Byrd shared Shackleton's vision of turning ice foe into a friend through modern machines and devices. To him the Ross Ice Shelf was not the great barrier geographers commonly called it. Byrd saw it as a usable springboard.

In 1928 Byrd's Little America Number One rose on the shores of the Bay of Whales out on the great ice sheet far away from any known point of land. The leader and his men set about preparations for his epoch-making flight over the South Pole. Byrd accomplished the flight in November 1929, together with Bernt Balchen, A. C. McKinley and Harold June, the third expedition to gaze on the ice-covered 9,500-foot heights at the south end of the world.

Further experiment and progress were made during Byrd's two succeeding expeditions to the Antarctic. Finally he convinced President Harry S. Truman and his naval leaders of the importance of a large-scale exploration of the Antarctic continent to our military and economic potential.

Because Antarctica is an enormous continental land mass, for the most part a lofty plateau, its temperatures run about twenty degrees colder, latitude for latitude, than those encountered in the North Polar basin. Only during the brief Antarctic summer is it possible to carry out any extensive work in this region. To explore it on a large scale over a short season would require an unprecedented organization of ships, men and machines. Such a task was clearly a naval one. Fleet Admiral Chester W. Nimitz, Chief of Naval Operations, tabbed the expedition with a name—Operation High Jump.

The work of Operation High Jump must naturally fall into two categories: (1) collection of scientific and geographical information, and (2) supporting operations with ships, aircraft and vehicles. It was necessary that the former task be carried out by a group of scientists and technicians. Responsibility for its accomplishment was vested in Rear Admiral Byrd. He assumed the title "Officer in Charge of Scientific Projects." Supporting operations fell to Task Force 68 under Rear Admiral Richard H. Cruzen.

In his operation order Cruzen defined the mission of the central group, the one to which the *Northwind* was attached. This was to push through the Ross Sea ice pack and establish a base on the Ross Ice Shelf. Using land planes on skis, Admiral Byrd could carry out an air reconnaissance of the continent from this base. Operations of the central group were to be flanked by those of the eastern and western groups. Flights from both these latter groups were to be launched from the open sea. Each flanking group had three PBM flying boats.

It was planned to send the aircraft carrier *Philippine Sea* from Panama to Scott Island with six R4D (C-47) planes, two Piper Cubs and a helicopter with their spares and crews. The large R4D planes were to be flown from the deck of the carrier to the base at Little America or wherever it might be established. Arrival of the *Philippine Sea* at her Scott Island rendezvous was to be synchronized, as nearly as possible, with completion of the base.

To test the feasibility of submarine operations in ice it was determined to send the submarine *Sennet* into the Ross Sea pack with the central group. This group was the only subdivision of Cruzen's command scheduled to operate in ice.

Operations of this central group in ice presented a serious problem, one with which I was directly concerned. At the time the United States had only two heavy seagoing icebreakers. These were the *Eastwind* and her new sister ship, the *Northwind,* both Coast Guard ships. The rest of our icebreaker fleet had been awarded to the Russians under Lend-Lease. The *Eastwind* had seasonal commitments in Greenland and could not be spared. This left only the *Northwind.* The Navy was rushing construction of the *Burton Island,* another icebreaker of the *Wind* class, but it was evident that she would not be ready in time to be of any aid in providing escort for the central group during its inbound movement through the Ross Sea ice pack.

This meant the *Northwind* must do without help.

# Chapter 34

# TASTING ANTARCTIC ICE

FROM his station on the signal bridge Chief Signalman Mavor translated a rapid succession of dots and dashes. They
were being flashed to us from the lead ship in our column, the flagship *Mount Olympus.* Behind us the tanker *Canisteo* plowed heavily
through the long westerly Antarctic swells. Astern of her an occasional burst of spray scattered over the cigar-shaped hull of the submarine *Sennet.*

The message read something like this: *"Desig* [nate] *Northwind
scout ice pack south of Scott Island. Canisteo fuel Mount Olympus
then Merrick and Yancey when latter two rendezvous."*

"Execute" followed, and the *Northwind* wheeled out of column
with increased speed. Ahead of us was Scott Island, barely distin-
guishable among the big bergs which drifted lazily in the vicinity.

On the clear horizon to the northward two hazy objects were rapidly
resolving into the familiar gray outlines of ships. These would be
the *Merrick* and the *Yancey,* keeping rendezvous with clocklike precision and in true Navy fashion. They had steamed under forced
draft all the way from Fort Hueneme, California, to join at the exact
time stipulated in their orders—noon, December 30, 1946.

As it developed, Admiral Cruzen had estimated very closely on
time losses during the trans-Pacific voyage. Delays had been oc-
casioned by fueling at sea and collection of oceanographic and magnetic data. His ships reached the approaches to Scott Island with only
an hour to spare.

In obedience to her orders the *Northwind* sped southward. Shortly after the curvature of the earth swallowed the ships grouped in our rear the easily recognized blink of the Ross Sea pack loomed ahead.

I realized now that the admiral had implied far more responsibility than appeared on the surface of his orders. Not only must I return with a true picture of ice conditions, but I must also be prepared to say whether or not the ships of the central group might navigate the pack. Save for the *Northwind*, these ships had not been built for work in ice. The *Mount Olympus, Merrick* and *Yancey* were thin-skinned, difficult to maneuver, and were neither reinforced nor protected against collision with ice masses. And the same characteristics held for the *Sennet*. With most of her body abulge below the water-line, the submarine would be even more vulnerable than the other ships. My job required imagination in addition to mapping the ice as I saw it.

Throughout the day a gentle breeze from the southeast kept the pack fairly open, so the *Northwind* was obliged to break ice only when passing from lead to lead. Moreover I noticed that the ice was of a far softer texture than any I had encountered in the Arctic. Each floe we struck seemed to crumble in two as the ship sliced through it. My officers, nearly all of whom had had considerable experience in the Arctic, agreed with me that this was "sissy" ice.

At midnight the visibility was still good enough for a reconnaissance flight. The *Northwind* carried an outmoded HOC-4 helicopter in addition to her J2F-6 airplane. I took off in the helicopter with Lieutenant James Cornish, pilot.

With pontoon landing gear our cruising radius was reduced to sixty miles, so after about twenty-five minutes of flight the pilot banked into a turn for the return trip. I drank in the icescape while we swung about. As far south as the eye could reach the endless field of white was streaked with wide avenues of deep blue which were invaded here and there by a berg or a windrow of brash. Yes, conditions looked good.

On our return to the *Northwind* Cornish and I were congratulated lightly by several of my officers on being the first men ever to fly a helicopter south of the Antarctic Circle.

I made the ship fast to an iceberg while Dr. Jack Hough and Lieutenant William G. Metcalf took an oceanographic station. Another party "keel-hauled" the ship with a magnetic device. By its use the terrestrial gravity at a particular latitude could be measured. This project—under Captain George F. Kosko, USN—was being carried out by Dr. J. R. Balsley. It had begun on board the *Northwind* at Latitude 81° 26' North.

Another group of scientists on board the *Northwind* was concerned with submarine transmission of sound waves. Its leader was Dr. A. H. Taylor, whose famed sire had invented radar. Taylor was every inch a scientist, lived in a scientific world of his own, talked science, thought science and probably dreamed science. He was typically representative of the school the laymen tabs "long-beard." Dr. Taylor did wear a beard, a very impressive one.

To me this beard was a matter of considerable concern. I was mildly superstitious about beards. Moreover they are not hygienic in the Polar Regions. Ever since the *Northland* was trapped in Hochstetter Bay back in '43 beards had been second only to obscenity on my list of taboos. Regardless of service regulations, I denied all military personnel in my ship the privilege of wearing beards.

Our official passengers bowed to my antibeard edict in spite of their civilian status—all, that is, except Dr. Taylor. With Dr. Taylor no argument could prevail. His beard was a trade-mark as vital as that of the Smith Brothers; he simply could not live without it, and that was that. So I crossed my fingers and allowed the situation to appeal to my sense of humor.

When we returned to Scott Island I reported to Admiral Cruzen in the *Mount Olympus*. The commanding officers of the *Merrick*, *Yancey* and *Sennet* were already assembled in Admiral Cruzen's flag quarters.

The admiral and his commanders listened to my report on ice conditions for a distance of 150 miles south of the group's present position. I told Admiral Cruzen confidently that he could proceed safely with his entire force. I added, however, that *ice is where you find it* and conditions might change without notice.

"I favor proceeding at once with all ships," Cruzen said, "but before I give the order I would like to know how you gentlemen feel about it."

The admiral asked each one of his commanding officers in turn: Captain John Hourihan of the *Merrick,* Captain James Cohn of the *Yancey,* Captain Robert Moore of the *Mount Olympus* and Commander Joseph Isinghour, the submarine's skipper. Each voiced his concurrence.

Admiral Cruzen then gave final instructions. He would shift his flag to the *Northwind,* the better to avail himself of ice information, while Captain Robert S. Quackenbush, his chief of staff, remained in the *Mount Olympus* to handle the many administrative matters which constantly beset the task force. The icebreaker would lead the column in which the *Mount Olympus, Yancey, Merrick* and *Sennet* were to follow in the order named. Speed of advance would be tentatively five knots, and the route would follow, as nearly as possible, the 180th meridian.

An hour later the admiral's gig bounded across an agitated swell which was being whipped up by an increasing southwesterly wind. I did not like this turn of weather, recalling the effect of Corioli's force. A southwest wind would tend to pack the ice in tightly.

Neither Admiral Cruzen nor two officers who accompanied him, Commander James Minny and Lieutenant Commander George Kittredge, needed an introduction. The *Northwind* had been Cruzen's flagship during his Arctic expedition only the summer before. Beyond these, the admiral's staff consisted largely of well-known news correspondents and columnists.

Admiral Cruzen shared my concern over the shift of wind. But the die had been cast, and, after all, ice *is* where you find it. His flag sprang to our masthead. The signal was made for getting under way.

# Chapter 35

# *THE TOUGHEST ROSS*
# *SEA PACK IN HISTORY*

LIEUTENANT (j. g.) JAMES P. VAN ETTEN, USCG, blotted his signature, breathed a sigh of relief and closed the ship's logbook. Naval tradition decrees that the first watch of the New Year must be written in rhyme, and on January 1, 1947, the officer who had the middle watch was a radar expert, not a poet. But in spite of this handicap Van Etten had composed his verse well. His record of events read:

> 0000-0400
> Under way as before,
> Making slightly more than four (knots),
> Steering 190 p.g c.
> This Antarctic is no place to be.
> Turning three six r.p.m.
> Ice is trying to hem us in.
> Using pilothouse control
> With Little America the ultimate goal.
> The good ship *Northwind* in the lead,
> The others following at top speed.
> At forty minutes past New Year
> Other ships have stopped through fear.
> *Northwind* circling to clear a path,
> But the mighty *Sennet* is in due wrath.
> Claims that she could pave the way,

But breaking ice takes more than say.
    Channel cleared and vessels freed,
Proceeding now at lessened speed.
    At four bells—course is set
One, three, five seems the best yet.
    Zero three hundred finds new lead:
On 185 the ships proceed.
    Twenty minutes has gone by
When helicopter takes to the sky.
    Admiral Cruzen is aboard
And it ain't New York he's headed toward.
    And now with 'copter drawing near
Here's to all A HAPPY NEW YEAR.

It was nearly eighteen hours before I had an opportunity to read the log because not all my officers were experienced in ice escort work. This required that either myself or Commander Smenton be in constant attendance on the bridge. We had to be alert for any order the officer of the deck might give which would put a sharp turn or "hair bender" in the channel we plowed for the less maneuverable ships following astern of the *Northwind*. Moreover the speed over ground must be so maintained as to keep the icebreaker at a distance not greater than 400 yards ahead of the *Mount Olympus*. If we got too far ahead, the ice would close in behind us.

My mind skipped over the events recorded by Van Etten as well as other log entries up to 8:00 P.M., January 1.

Shortly after we entered the pack it was apparent that the wind had closed most of the leads which had existed the previous day. It was necessary, therefore, to break a channel through close-packed floes of young ice. As Van Etten poetically expressed it, the *Mount Olympus* became stuck, which halted the ships following her and allowed the ice to fill the space between them.

This was where the *Northwind* began to earn her salt. First the icebreaker broke out the *Sennet*, then the others from rear to van. When the lead ship of a column is stuck, ice quickly fouls those behind her. So all vessels must be broken out. To break out a column of vessels under normal conditions the icebreaker approaches the rear ship at an angle of thirty degrees to her bow, straightens out im-

mediately ahead of her, then backs down to smash remaining ice
against her stem. The ship so broken out is then ordered to move
ahead. The icebreaker swings on to the next ship and quickly repeats
the process before the one immediately astern of her has to stop
moving.

As we broke out the submarine Joe Isinghour shouted, "Those guys
up ahead are all that's holding *us* back."

In a few minutes the *Merrick*, *Yancey* and *Mount Olympus* were
freed, and the column moved on.

After tussling with the ice for two days we fought our way through
a blinding snowstorm into a large ice lake. Meanwhile the column
had been broken time after time, so the navigating personnel in the
fleet were pretty well exhausted. Admiral Cruzen and I knew we
could expect a heavy ice beyond such a large body of water. This is
because ice lakes are caused by strata of heavy ice which lie to the
windward of lighter ice. The wind separates the ice fields because it
sweeps light floes along at a more rapid pace. Here we had a temporary haven. The little fleet was ordered to heave to and await improved
visibility.

On the morning of January 3 the southwesterly gale subsided.
While snowfall still reduced visibility, both the admiral and I were
anxious to explore the ice beyond us. The helicopter could not be
flown in this kind of weather, so I decided to make a reconnaissance
with the ship.

What we found astounded everyone.

A stratum of heavy floes which towered as high as the bridge formed
a seemingly impenetrable barrier along the south shore of the lake.
We skirted it for miles in both directions. It seemed endless. Finding
no hole in the wall, I selected a crack and began the tedious task of
prying the *Northwind* through it.

Several hours were required to worm through a half-mile or so of
this mammoth ice. Beyond it the ice was tightly packed, but the floes
were lighter and yielded readily to the smashing impact of the *Northwind's* heavy blows. In the evening we returned to the ice lake. Approaching it, we stumbled onto a "gate" through the barrier. Only one
heavy floe had to be opened to break into the lake.

The visibility had improved during the day, so Admiral Cruzen decided to take advantage of the weather and push on toward our destination. He gave the order to form up.

We opened the gate for each ship, then parked her in a position in column beyond the barrier. But the wind seemed determined to fight it out with our admiral. As the last ship, the *Yancey*, was passing through the "gate" the wind made up with a vengeance. The big, unwieldy supply ship was slammed against an adjacent mass of ice with a terrific impact. The ragged underwater edge ripped through the ¾-inch plating of the ship's hull.

On board the *Yancey* a well-drilled damage-control team sprang into action. It battled bravely against the tons of water which poured into the hold. Soon the men had a soft patch shored firmly against the gaping shell plating. Captain Cohn reported that he was ready to continue duty assigned.

Again the *Northwind* cleared the ice from the ships, and the column moved on. But progress was extremely slow. By 6.00 A.M., January 4, nearly twelve hours after our departure from the lake, we had made only five miles. The *Sennet* was having a particularly difficult time of it and had to be broken out constantly. Ice persisted in climbing up her turtleback and threatened to sweep away her conning tower.

It was now obvious to Admiral Cruzen that the submarine could never be got through the Ross Sea pack. He decided to have her towed to Scott Island. The stem of the submarine was snubbed into our towing crotch, and the two vessels started in tandem on their long journey to Scott Island.

Admiral Cruzen was deeply concerned over having to leave the *Mount Olympus, Merrick* and *Yancey* at the mercy of the pack in the presence of icebergs, but he had no alternative. Yet this was not his greatest worry. Somewhere on the ice, far to the east, a PBM was down. Whether or not its crew of eight men was alive no one knew. The Navy must proceed on the assumption that at least one man was alive. The plane had last been seen taking off from the *Pine Island* with the tender's skipper, Captain H. H. Caldwell, along as observer. Captain Dufek, the commander of the eastern group, was scouring the area with his two remaining PBMs. But it was a vast region, and the weather was treacherous. To locate the missing plane would be like finding a needle in a haystack.

Throughout the night the *Northwind* and *Sennet,* joined together like railroad cars, smashed and wormed their way northward at a speed of ten knots. With the submarine's bow filling our towing crotch it was possible for officers and men of the two vessels to exchange visits. Lieutenant Henry Wiensettle, my assistant engineer, had served in the "pig boats" of the distant past. He returned after his first visit feeling much like Rip Van Winkle. "Why, they've even got staterooms and showers," he declared. "And they can smoke below hatches!"

About noon, January 5, an urgent message was received from the *Mount Olympus* with an appeal for help. The *Merrick* and *Yancey,* it said, were drifting helplessly down on bergs and in immediate danger. The admiral summoned me, together with his flag watch officers, Jim Minny and George Kittredge, to discuss the situation.

"Two courses of action are open to us," he announced. "Course one: take the submarine out of the ice before proceeding to the assistance of the other ships. Course two: drop the submarine in the ice lake through which we have just passed, aid the other ships and then return to the *Sennet* to take her the remaining forty miles or so through the pack. Tommy," he said to me, "what would you do?"

I replied that I would first see the submarine to safety before assisting the *Mount Olympus, Merrick* and *Yancey* and voiced my belief that the beset vessels would drift around the bergs, though they might experience some pressure before they cleared them.

Minny agreed with me.

Kittredge declared that he, as a submariner himself, would not hesitate to puddle-jump a submarine through the remainder of the pack if conditions warranted.

The admiral thanked us for our advice and announced his decision. This was to leave the *Sennet* in an ice lake about two miles back and speed to the assistance of his main body. I hastened to the bridge. We ran back to the little ice lake and let go our tow. Then I had two more engines warmed up in order to give the ship full power with all six generators.

I realized now the wisdom of Cruzen's decision. Anything might happen to ships beset in ice. If the pack closed in on the *Sennet* while we were absent, she could reach for open water by diving beneath the ice. I remembered the Nazi submarine whose torpedoes had been fired at the *Northland* during the northeast Greenland campaign of 1944.

The commander of Task Force 68 was now faced with the following situation: (1) the vanished plane still missing with its crew of eight persons; (2) his main body of the central group helpless in the ice and drifting down on bergs; (3) the *Sennet* behind him in a small ice lake which might close and necessitate her undertaking a hazardous underseas voyage to open water. On the heels of this, another blow fell on our admiral which was so staggering that Commander Minny consulted me about the advisability of delivering the news to Cruzen.

A dispatch addressed personally to Rear Admiral Richard H. Cruzen informed him that his son had been accidentally killed.

I shared Minny's view that this was no time to burden our commander with such a heartbreaking message. I instructed Jim: "Keep the news of this tragedy from Dick [we all referred to Admiral Cruzen, affectionately, as Dick] until he is satisfied that his ships are safe."

I sent for Lieutenant (j.g.) Henry Langenbeck, my communications officer, and ordered him to deliver the messages of condolence, which were certain to pour in, directly to Commander Minny. Moreover he must suppress any leakage of information from his men. The admiral might despise me for it later, but I didn't think he would. Until we could break the news it would be hard on Jim and me because we were messmates with our commander and therefore very close to him at all times.

Throughout the night the *Northwind* roared through the ice, smashing through floe after floe with such force that her foredeck was continually splattered with particles of ice. Once I turned from my window to find Admiral Cruzen standing beside me.

"Are you giving her all she's got, Tommy?" the task-force commander asked.

I replied that I was "goosing 'er to death!"

By midday, January 6, we were hammering at the barrier of shelf ice near where we had taken the *Sennet* in tow. Already we had the gray hulls of the ships in sight, lifted above the horizon by a mirage effect. The two supply ships had drifted off to eastward about three miles away from the *Mount Olympus.* Several bergs were spread over the intervening distance.

An hour later we were close aboard the *Merrick,* which, it was reported, had sustained some slight damage while drifting around the berg.

The admiral directed that the three ships be escorted far enough to the southward to assure their being clear of all icebergs. This was tedious work, because each ship had to be broken out and led to an ice channel about five miles to the south.

In an effort to expedite the operation the icebreaker's two-inch wire-rope towing cable was made fast to the *Yancey.* But the supply ship's freeboard was higher than the designers of our towing equipment had reckoned on. She could not be snubbed close enough to our stern.

It was past midnight before we had the *Mount Olympus, Merrick* and *Yancey* parked in a narrow, slushy channel in a field of young, soft ice. This was about five miles south of the group of bergs in whose vicinity the ships had previously drifted.

In the meantime the admiral's spirits had been bolstered by a heartening bit of information. The broken wreckage of the PBM, missing for one week from the eastern group, had been found. Six of its crew members, including Captain Caldwell, were still alive. Already Captain Dufek was proceeding with rescue operations.

Now, with the main body of Cruzen's central group in a position of relative safety, we could make a quick dash back to the submarine and have her out of the pack in short order. I put the *Northwind* on a northerly course and called for full speed.

"Well, Tommy, things are looking rosy now," the Admiral remarked. "Let's go below for a spell."

I motioned to Minny. "Come along, Jim, and fetch the message."

Down in the cabin we removed our parkas. Mustering courage, I drew a breath and began. "Admiral, sir, things are not altogether rosy. We have been keeping some bad news from you." I always kept a bottle of whisky in a drawer for use by exposed men coming off watch. I reached for it and poured out a half-tumblerful, then handed it to the admiral.

"You're kidding," Admiral Cruzen said, laughing.

"No, sir," I insisted.

"Well," Cruzen said, "I'll take it standing—without the spirits."
Jim handed the admiral the message.

Admiral Cruzen read it. "Excuse me, gentlemen," he said, "I want
to be alone awhile—and thanks to you both for holding it. I really
mean that." He retired to his stateroom.

In no more than ten minutes the admiral returned to 'the cabin and
plunged immediately into a discussion of future operations of his
task force.

*Gad, what a man!* I thought. *No wonder he's an admiral.*

# Chapter 36

# MORE OBSTACLES

WHEN the *Northwind* returned to the *Mount Olympus, Yancey* and *Merrick* on the morning of January 8 we were amazed to find that the central group was actually farther from its goal than it had been five days before! Scott Island, from which we had just returned, gave us a fixed reference point plus well-clocked reckonings. This was the first clear weather we had thus far experienced in the Antarctic. Lieutenant (j.g.) Robert B. Moore, my navigator, confirmed the thirty-mile northerly drift established in his reckoning by an observation of the sun. We were not disappointed. From a standpoint of ice miles the group had made good a fair distance of thirteen miles during the five-day period.

Throughout the day the column crept slowly southward through a winding riverlike ice channel.

The admiral's interest lay first in getting his central group through the Ross Sea pack. He must then seek a favorable location for a base from which flight operations might proceed. It was by no means certain that the Bay of Whales would be available for the establishment of a Little America Number Four. Climatologists predicted it would be completely swallowed by 1947. This prognosis was based on observations of previous expeditions. It had been determined that the jawlike walls of the bay were closing at a rate of four feet per day.

In spite of the admiral's reluctance to accept this theory he could not help being concerned. There might be no indentation in the ice shelf suitable for a seaport so essential to his base. Of course McMurdo Sound remained. But both Shackleton and Scott had been greatly hampered by the ice in setting up their camps during favorable ice years. We knew already that 1947 was the worst Antarctic ice year on record.

Admiral Cruzen's anxiety over the operations of the central group was not his only one. A stream of dispatches which flew between him and his eastern and western-group commanders and his traffic with Washington preyed on his time. It was clear to me that he needed at least one good night of well-earned rest. On the evening of January 8, Lieutenant James A. Hunter, USPHS, my medical officer, prevailed on him to take some sleeping tablets. The channel was fairly navigable, and I promised to call him if we experienced any difficulty.

About midnight, when I was satisfied that the task-force commander was sound asleep, I went to the bridge. The four-knot speed we were making seemed tantalizingly slow. Using the admiral's radio code name, I ordered the ships behind us to increase to eight knots. The task group leaped ahead. By 4:30 A.M. we had clipped off twenty-eight miles!

As the quartermaster who had the morning watch moved out to strike one bell I saw the channel's end in a small ice lake ahead. The ice beyond the lake looked soft and mushy, so I determined to push on and called for full power. The *Northwind* rushed through the lake and crashed into the ice, which split, then crumpled easily. Our speed slackened some, but still it was ample.

We had penetrated the ice a few hundred yards when a row of hummocks loomed up ahead. This, I knew, would slow us materially. The *Merrick* was following immediately astern in the canal we were slicing. Minny had the flag watch. I yelled at him to stop the convoy. He barked the order into the TBS—short-range radio. No acknowledgement came. There was no outgoing signal!

By this time the *Northwind* was leaping onto the hummocks, being slowed gradually to a standstill. I looked aft in alarm. The *Merrick* was still charging ahead. She rushed at full eight knots toward our stern. The groove we had hewed in the ice would permit no other heading.

U

"Signalman!" Minny shouted. "Speed zero! Quick!"

The officer of the deck jumped to the whistle, pulled the lever. No sound issued from the stack. The whistle was frozen. The danger signal could not be sounded.

Again I looked at the *Merrick*. She still plunged ahead. My gaze flew to the signal yard. The emergency pennant had been broken out. The signal to halt was being hoisted. This signal implied stopping the engines, not necessarily checking headway by reversing them. I hoped the *Merrick* and the ships steaming behind her would size things up and ring full-speed-astern. So far they had not done so.

I snapped at the officer of the deck to rock his helm. Maybe it would help get the ship in motion. The *Merrick* was now only 100 yards astern and still charging. Yet I could see the frothy wash at her stern and knew her engines were backing. But she had a lot of momentum to overcome! Too much, I thought. A collision appeared inevitable. I sounded the general alarm.

"Now hear this," the junior officer of the deck bellowed into the public address microphone. "Collision aft! Collision aft!"

This alarm was intended to get the passengers who were accommodated aft up on deck before the *Merrick's* stem invaded their living quarters.

Lieutenant (j.g.) Stanley Russell, who had the deck, drawled, "It's only a bunch of news hawks." The humor of his statement failed to register.

As he spoke four pressmen tumbled out of the afterhatch—Hearst's Robert Nichols, the *Post's* Thomas Henry, Scripps-Howard's Jim Lucas and *Collier's* Fred Sparks.

I looked again at the *Merrick,* only fifty feet behind us. I glanced over at the ice which hissed along our outer skin. The ship was moving! Rocking the rudder had turned the trick. But would we gain ample headway before the *Merrick* struck? It seemed as though she must already have made contact with our stern. Still I had felt no impact. We were moving faster now. The *Merrick's* lofty stem seemed a trifle farther away. Collision had been averted—by a margin of inches! I sought the *Yancey* and *Mount Olympus.* Both ships had sheered off before entering our canal and were hove to in the ice lake.

No more eight knots! Four knots was good enough for the admiral. From now on it would be good enough for me!

At 8:00 A.M. the admiral came on the bridge looking much refreshed. The clamor of our general alarm had not roused him. His eye fell on two shiny speed cones, or speed indicators, which are sometimes used by vessels in formation. "Why are you using speed cones, Tommy?" Admiral Cruzen asked.

It took courage to tell him.

The commanding officers were getting the "feel" of the ice. By now they had learned that the stems of their ships could stand a good deal of punishment. No longer were they timid about calling for power when the situation demanded it. Moreover my own officers were becoming used to anticipating ice masses. They learned to gauge power and rudder to offset any tendency of the ice to toss the ship violently to port or starboard. It was pleasing to see the entire task group working together as a team. Each ship had learned to *anticipate* the movements of the others. After all, this was one of the major objectives of Operation High Jump.

At 7:30 P.M. the force plunged into a large body of open water. A clear horizon spread before us, its sharp line accented by a watercloud. This meant no ice ahead—not for ten miles at least.

"Maybe we have reached the Ross Sea,*" I told the admiral.

"Not yet," Cruzen replied. "When we see emperor penguins we may be sure we are near the south end of the pack. None have been sighted so far. They are much larger than Adelies."

Since leaving Scott Island we had passed many flocks of Adelie penguins, happy comedians of the feathered world. From the *Northwind* we had enjoyed a close view of their humanlike antics.

Once I saw a bevy of nine Adelie penguins playing King of the Hill on a pile of ice. This is a game children have enjoyed since the Middle Ages. A boy stands on a mound while the others try to dislodge him. Whoever succeeds becomes King of the Hill until he is forced down by another player.

---

* Cartographers have not clearly defined the boundaries of the Ross Sea. Admiral Cruzen described it as "that body of open water between the Ross Ice Shelf and the southern edge of the Antarctic pack."

Several times we passed a flock of a hundred or more penguins asleep on the ice. They always posted sentries against attack by their archenemy, the sea leopard, a large, carnivorous seal. Whenever we drew near a sleeping flock it was alerted by the sentries. The penguins always stood up and regarded the approaching ship with curiosity. Then caution would impel them to waddle out of our track. When the vessel was only twenty-five yards or so away caution gave way to panic. They would get down on their bellies and scoot away over the ice, propelled by their feet and steered by their flippers.

Once when the ship intruded on a sleeping flock one bird was slow in making his getaway. He became separated from his companions by a crack the *Northwind* had made in the ice. He scooted around frantically, seeking a bridge over which to join his comrades, but found none. They saw his plight and halted, then stood up and faced the danger. Finally the marooned one dove into the water and popped out across the crack, landing on both feet. Then he got down on his belly and flipped toward his fellows. As soon as they were assured of his safety, all slithered away together.

We often came upon a big "crab-eater" seal asleep on the ice. These monsters are completely white and quite harmless. They always managed to sleep near an escape hole through the ice. Like the penguins, the crab-eaters regarded the ship with curiosity at first sighting. Then they would slowly flip toward the escape hole, accelerating their speed as the ship drew nearer.

I thought for a while Cruzen might be mistaken about emperor penguins, that we might at last have reached the inside of the Ross Sea pack. But soon a white aura spread from shore to shore before us. There was more ice ahead.

We found ice in abundance. There were no southward leads. However helicopter observations showed some wide blue-water leads which tended in a *southeasterly* direction. These were separated from the big ice lake by a chain of pools. By smashing a track from pool to pool we could get into one of the leads. The admiral figured it was worth a gamble.

We had no difficulty reaching the nearest lead. But I noticed that the ice grew heavier as we followed it to the southeast.

Finally the admiral asked, "What do you think of it?"

"I don't like it," I replied. "Consolidated polar ice scares me."

It was enough for Admiral Cruzen! He snapped a few orders to his flag lieutenant. The ships virtually turned in their tracks and began a hurried retreat back to the lake.

As far as I was concerned the retreat might have been a rout. The wind made up and began to close the leads. We came very near to losing that race. When consolidated ice closes on a ship something is going to give—and it isn't going to be the ice.

We hammered our way into the ice lake none too soon. With the ice closing steadily the *Northwind* had been obliged to lead one ship at a time across the shrinking pools. The last two ships, the *Merrick* and *Mount Olympus* were stove in by ice while we fetched them to safety. Here again good damage control saved them from sinking.

In the afternoon of January 10 I made an air reconnaissance in our plane 200 miles south of the lake. There were no leads. Where we had attempted to work southward the previous night only pressure ridges remained to mark the edges of heavy fields. I thought of what might have happened, had we not retired, and shuddered.

On January 11 our ice lake vanished. We were obliged to push on. After twenty-four hours of fighting we were no more than five miles from the starting point. I realized with a shock that the central group had made good less than 200 miles since leaving Scott Island. We had been in the ice for twelve days.

Admiral Cruzen still had to make 500 miles before reaching the Ross Ice Shelf. After this he must find a suitable harbor, unload his ships and get them started back—all within a month's time. The brief Antarctic summer was already drawing to a close. Fall would bring falling temperatures and violent gales. I marveled at our commander's ability to detach his mind from a situation which would unnerve the average officer. He found a retreat from realities in "whodunits." These he read avidly.

Somehow the admiral's manner of relaxing imparted confidence to the ship's officers. It spread throughout his fleet. We knew he would succeed.

On January 12 a helicopter flight showed close-packed ice ahead of us along the 180th meridian. Over to the southeast the leads were broad and ice-free. But the ice grew increasingly heavy in that direction. By continuing south, it would take us at least three days to reach the barrier. On the other hand, we might make it in one day by steaming southeastward.

The admiral prudently chose the long way.

January 16 found the central group still steaming south. We were presumably only thirty miles from the barrier. Still no open water. I wanted to see how close we really were and had the helicopter called away with myself as observer. On this flight Lieutenant David Gershowitz, USCGR, was pilot. Dave was Brooklyn born and bred, a Jewish lad who had fought his way up from the ranks. He had pioneered helicopters and was considered to be an ace rotary-wing pilot.

Soon we sighted the Ross Ice Shelf! This was the El Dorado! We were through the pack! Both Gershowitz and myself were spellbound for a minute.

Then Gersh found his voice. "Cheez," the pilot exclaimed. "What a sight! Quick, Captain, take the stick! Take the stick!"

I protested. "I can't fly this contraption, Dave!"

Gersh only repeated, "Take the stick, Captain!"

I refused. Gershowitz forceably took my hands and, placing them on the stick, let go and called the admiral by radio. "Open water ten miles ahead of you! Ice barrier——"

"Dave," I interrupted, "take this stick before I put your windmill into a spin."

"But, Captain, sir," Dave yelled. "Cheez, I gotta make a report, and I can't talk without my hands!"

At these words an outburst of laughter poured over the receiver. This was followed by wild hurrays! Our conversation had been broadcast over the command circuit.

The barrier was like a dazzling desert of white sand dunes which rolled inland from chalky cliffs. Crowding our cruising radius, we flew westward over its face to an indentation which had once been Discovery Bay. Now it had nearly disappeared. Perhaps the Bay of Whales would also have vanished! Maybe the climatologists were right. Tomorrow we would know.

Throughout the rest of the night the central group skirted the barrier to the eastward. We were approaching the place where the

Rear Admiral Richard H. Cruzen, the commander of Navy's Task Force 68 (otherwise known as the Byrd Antarctic Expedition), studying the World of Ice aboard the Coast Guard's icebreaker *Northwind*.

Rear Admiral Richard E. Byrd leaving plane on return from South Pole.

Bay of Whales should be. There must have been some anxious moments for Admiral Cruzen. If there were no Bay of Whales, McMurdo Sound was the only alternative. It lay nearly 500 miles west of us. Cruzen knew McMurdo Sound could offer him only an open roadstead. His ships would be in constant peril. It was unlikely he would find McMurdo Sound open this year.

Admiral Cruzen had fought his fleet through 700 miles of pack ice—an achievement never before equalled in the annals of ice navigation. Was victory over the Ross Sea pack to result in failure to find a base? Cruzen himself, engrossed in the pages of a whodunit, seemed the least worried of any of us.

# Chapter 37

# THE SEAPORT TO
# LITTLE AMERICA NUMBER FOUR

THE Bay of Whales existed. But it had shrunk to a mere three miles in length by a width of one mile, with its entrance narrowed to 200 yards. It was completely carpeted by a layer of thick bay ice. At the distal end several rows of huge pressure ridges marked the juncture of bay ice with shelf ice. There the shelf rose gently to an elevation of about 300 feet and leveled off to conform with the surrounding elevations.

In theory, at least, the climatologists had not erred. The bay should have been completely obliterated. They had reckoned, however, without the heavy layer of bay ice which formed the floor of this basin. It held the jaws and sides of the bay apart and thus preserved a seaport for Operation High Jump. But before it could be used, the bay ice must be removed. This was a job for the *Northwind*.

"How long will it take you to break the ice out of this bay, Tommy?" Admiral Cruzen asked.

"Just a minute, sir, and I'll tell you," I replied. I called for full speed and put the ship into a charge at the bay ice. She struck with her full momentum. The impact was like hitting a stone wall which yielded grudgingly to her force. It shattered the ice along the outer end of the bay and carved a groove two shiplengths deep into which the *Northwind* spent her strength.

Lieutenant R. I. Price, the first lieutenant, measured the ice. It was six feet thick, with one foot of frozen snow on the surface. This snow would cushion the breaking force of the vessel and slow down the operation ahead of her.

"I'll have the ice out in twenty-four hours if the wind holds fair," I told the admiral. As long as the wind was from the south it would carry the chunks of ice we broke out of the bay.

My optimism seemed to please Cruzen. He shifted his flag to the *Mount Olympus* and sent over a reconnaissance party to select a site for Little America Number Four.

The reconnaissance patrol consisted of some distinguished members. It included Dr. Paul Siple, who had represented the Boy Scouts of America on Byrd's first Antarctic expedition. Dr. Siple was now an eminent climatologist. There were Commanders Charles O. Reinhart, USN, and J. C. McCoy, USN, both civil engineers with wide experience in the Arctic. Commander C. M. Campbell, USN, was a Navy flier who was slated to command the base to be established at Little America Number Four. The fifth member was Captain V. D. Boyd, USMC, who had been Byrd's dog driver during his third expedition. Boyd was now in charge of all canines.

The reconnaissance party climbed down our rigid ladder to the ice and donned skis. Then it struck out across the frozen surface of the Bay of Whales to ferret out a roadway from the inner end of the bay to the heights on the ice shelf above. An emperor penguin which stood by watching curiously fell in behind the single file of men and waddled along to see what was up.

The *Northwind* began her task of icebreaking.

After an absence of six hours the reconnaissance party returned. It was followed by a half-dozen emperor penguins, which seemingly herded the men toward the ship. The explorers marked a trail up the barrier, then skied a couple of miles farther south to Little America Number Three. Beneath the tops of radio towers the party found the 1940-1941 expeditionary hut covered with snow. They cleared away an entrance and found everything, including fresh meats, just as Byrd left it six years before.

Siple estimated that Little America Number Three had drifted one and a half miles northwest of its original position. This was due to the movement of the Ross Barrier.

For sixty-three hours the *Northwind* hammered away at the stubborn bay ice. As she worked inward from the entrance to the Bay of Whales the ice became thicker. Each time she lunged the impact was more terrific than before. After two days the ice became *ten feet thick,* with the usual foot of frozen snow on the surface. The ship could never have handled it if she had been burdened with a bow propeller.

Whenever the vessel was about to strike ice the warning went out from the bridge over the PA: "Now hear this. Hold tight!" This was necessary to keep the ship's company from being bowled off its feet.

I lived through the period in constant fear of damaging a propeller. The loss of a blade or two might put an end to the expedition. Yet the risk had to be accepted. After the first day I kept the bridge only at infrequent intervals. My officers now knew the business thoroughly.

I think the continuous pounding played on everyone's nerves. I was thankful that all hands had been subjected to psychiatric screening before the expedition began. My ship's surgeon, Lieutenant James A. Hunter, USPHS, was a psychiatrist as well as a skillful surgeon. With his blessing I extended the privilege of an occasional slug of whisky to all hands. All a man had to do was sign for it. The practice was never abused.

After sixty-three hours of nerve-racking work the ice was getting even thicker than before. We had cleared an area one mile wide and two miles long.* We had plainly reached the point of diminishing returns. After beveling off an embarcadero for the large ships I moored the *Northwind* with ice anchors and set about to plant "deadmen" for the rest of the force. "Deadmen" consist of heavy timbers having a long, stout wire strap secured to them. They are buried horizontally in the ice with a bite of the strap sticking out. Ships which have no ice anchors can then make fast to them.

This nineteenth day of January was a "scorcher" for Antarctica, with the mercury soaring to 20° F. My ship's company of 200 officers, men, scientists and correspondents had been cooped up for more than a month. While the deadmen were being planted I granted shore leave for recreation. Several baseball games were started. Lieutenant

---

* Rear Admiral Richard E. Byrd estimated that the *Northwind* removed 15,000,000 tons of hard ice in breaking out the Bay of Whales *(National Geographic,* October 1947).

(j.g.) Stanley B. Russell and I had brought our golf clubs along. We laid out a three-hole golf course on the frozen snow and allowed others to share our clubs. Save for the low temperature which burdened us with alpaca jackets and gloves, conditions were excellent. The lighting phenomenon made white balls stand out in clear relief.

While I have never got out of the dub class, I can boast having played golf through more degrees of latitude than any other person in the history of the world. On an afternoon in 1944 I played a game with Niels Jensen at Sandotten in Latitude 74° North. My score, while wretched in both Polar Regions, was better in the Arctic. There the ice surface was hard. *This* gave me good distance no matter how badly I dubbed my strokes.

The *Yancey* and *Merrick* came in and moored, then began unloading dog teams, tractors and materials for bridging the crevasses which lay between the bay ice and the top of the barrier. For the time being, at least, the *Northwind's* work in the Bay of Whales was finished.

By this time the aircraft carrier *Philippine Sea* was rushing across the Pacific with Admiral Byrd on board. She had six R4D (C-47) planes on her flight deck which Byrd proposed to fly from Scott Island to Little America. My orders were to rendezvous with her on January 27, take on mail, freight and passengers and support the flight.

I decided to allow us five days for the outbound voyage to Scott Island. This would leave two days in which to make repairs to our machinery. These repairs were urgently needed. Lieutenant Commander Clyde D. Goodwin, my chief engineer, knew we had several cracked bearings which would have to be replaced. Moreover repeated impacts on hard ice will jar loose electrical terminal connections no matter how well they are tightened. Goodwin wanted to make a thorough check.

I launched the Greenland cruiser in order to make more cargo space available and left the craft in charge of Snus Jensen. Harry Wisnieuski, who had been my Greenland Patrol yeoman, was selected to be his crewman. Harry had boated with Snus in Greenland and was a qualified mechanic as well as a good ice sailor.

At 4:00 P.M., January 22, we were ready for getting under way. A raw wind swept in from the south, unleasing snow flurries which swirled about the deckhouse. Dr. Taylor stood at the gangway, oblivious of this miserable weather. His mind was wrestling with some scientific problem, no doubt. I don't believe he was aware that he wore a Panama hat and carried an umbrella under his arm.

Smenton asked Dr. Taylor if he had all his luggage. The scientist replied abstractly in the affirmative. He boarded the Greenland cruiser and was taken to the flagship outside the bay.

Later as we passed the *Mount Olympus* she made a signal that Dr. Taylor had forgotten his suitcase. Would we please deliver it? I was tempted to heave it over the side and ask Dr. Taylor to go fetch it. Somehow the situation tickled my sense of humor. I burst out laughing and complied with his request.

Without a convoy to care for, the voyage to Scott Island was easy. But visibility was wretched and necessitated our navigating a good deal of the time by a special short-range radar.

At 2:00 P.M., January 27, we groped onto Scott Island Bank. The coal-black cliffs of the island popped through the mists. Even at a range of 200 yards its icy heights were lost in the fog. As far as I knew, no ship had ever before come within a mile of this mass of rock and ice. We made a rough hydrographic survey of the waters around Scott Island. I concluded that, small as the island was, it might offer a lee in which to transfer cargo and passengers from the *Philippine Sea* to the *Northwind*.

We anchored close under the lee side of Scott Island. Gersh then asked for permission to fish. It was granted. Without waiting to bait his tri-hooked leader, he cast his heavy line over the side. As it fell to the bottom he felt a series of forceable tugs. Pulling it up, he found he had caught three large blue cod.

"Cheez!" Gershowitz exclaimed and darted about the ship to exhibit his good fortune. He had never before caught a fish. In nearly as little time as it takes to tell, all fishing gear on the ship was in use. My crew members pulled up fish as fast as they could lower their lines.

A signal from Admiral Byrd in the *Philippine Sea* interrupted the sport. Byrd informed me that the arrival of the carrier was delayed by numerous icebergs and established rendezvous 100 miles east of Scott Island in about twelve hours. The *Northwind* was ordered to make contact with the *Sennet* and escort her to the rendezvous.

The submarine was operating about twenty-five miles north of Scott Island on a weather-reporting mission. Notwithstanding the fog, contact was successful, and we proceeded together to our rendezvous with the aircraft carrier.

When I reported on board the carrier Captain Cornwell pointed out the tremendous stack of cargo—150 tons of it—which must be transferred to the *Northwind*. In addition there were two cub planes to be taken on board. I nearly went limp.

Although the wind held gentle, as it had for the past few days, the seas along the Antarctic Circle are continually rough. My idea was, therefore, to seek a lee. Behind shelter, transfer of the cargo could be made by merely lowering it from the carrier to the deck of the icebreaker.

My number-one suggestion for effecting transshipment was the anchorage close under the east bank of Scott Island. Captain Cornwell explained that the cruising radius of an R4D, even when light, would not stretch from Scott Island to Little America. Admiral Byrd was determined to take off at the earliest favorable weather. Cornwell was obliged to hover within the plane's flying limits.

I played my next card. The *Northwind* could take the *Philippine Sea* into the sheltered fastness of pack ice where the sea was completely dampened. The captain of the carrier vetoed this idea, and I can't say I blamed him. He had never been in ice.

The third course of action remained. To me this was an arduous one. Both vessels must steam side by side into the sea and transfer everything and everybody while under way. Because of an icebreaker's stubby length and broad beam she can be relied on to handle miserably in any kind of a seaway.

Captain Cornwell and I agreed on base course, speed and distance between ships. Details were passed to our first lieutenants for working out. I was then escorted to Admiral Byrd's quarters. Admiral Byrd explained that the icebreaker on station midway between the *Philippine Sea* and Little America was essential to his proposed flight. She would be an aircraft beacon and a mobile rescue unit as well. At best he could expect close sailing on fuel supply. If the planes were to wander off their course, they might not reach their destination.

The direct route to Little America would take the flight over ice which I believed was unnavigable, even for the *Northwind*. I made known this opinion to Admiral Byrd, but hastened to say we would do our best to comply with his wishes. The latter qualification was added because to Admiral Byrd there is no such word as "can't."

For the next three hours Admiral Byrd held me spellbound. He discussed informally the subject nearest his heart—polar operations. He asserted his belief that God has hidden untold wealth beneath ice masses against such time as we may be intellectually prepared to unlock His secrets. The admiral emphasized that ice is present for man to use rather than fear.

The impression I gathered of Admiral Byrd that day has persisted ever since. He is a great visionary, and his imagination is supported by energy, tenacity and organizing ability.

Byrd thinks in terms of science as well as operation. He delegates responsibility freely, particularly in the treatment of specialized tasks. He knows how to size men up and how to make them work for him. His enthusiasm is infectious, and his smile inspires his subordinates to double their efforts. Byrd's interest in polar development is humanitarian and his motive basically altruistic. He believes the Polar Regions offer both economic and military potential to the peace-loving nations of the world.

I returned to the *Northwind* as the *Philippine Sea* swung lazily into the sea, steadying on a north-northwesterly course, and settled down to a speed of exactly five knots. We then saddled up to her waist, regulated our speed to match hers and steered a parallel course with a distance of fifty feet separating the two ships. The ticklish operation of transferring cargo on an overhead cable began.

About 8:00 P.M. a north-northwesterly breeze made up, dissolved the fog and splashed the seas with whitecaps and streaks of foam. Throughout the night it continued to blow, forcing the *Northwind* to roll so heavily that at times I thought we must surely crash our mast into the carrier's flight deck. With the exception of Smenton, Moore, Russell and myself, who doubled on ship control, my officers pitched in with the crew to expedite rustling oncoming materials below hatches.

Because our men were continually soaked by the sheets of spray which whipped across the deck, Dr. Hunter was on hand every two hours to administer a ration of ardent spirits to the ship's company.

The doctor's purpose in prescribing this treatment stemmed from psychological considerations. Gratifying results fully supported his theory.

On January 28 the thirty-hour task of getting everything on board and secured for sea was finished. We had avoided personnel casualties, and that was little short of miraculous. The only damage sustained was the loss of a half-netful of supplies. But it is an ill wind that blows no good. I believe we cleared our books of every missing item of property since the ship was commissioned. Our survey accounted for missing equipment which would have filled a dozen cargo nets.

Next thirty-six military passengers were brought aboard. This was done by using a breeches buoy. Many of these passengers had been carefully grooming beards of all descriptions. I made them shave. It must have made them very happy. The last person to come on board was Captain Harry R. Horney, Admiral Byrd's chief of staff. Harry Horney was an old Greenland Patrol sailor. This put him in solid with me.

After receiving fuel from the oiler *Cacapon,* which had joined us during the night, the *Northwind* hastened south to define the outer limits of the pack between Longitude 168° West and 155° West. Admiral Byrd's purpose in making a survey of the outer edges of the ice was to get the *Philippine Sea* into a lead, or indentation, for launching his planes. This would reduce the distance of flight to Little America.

The destroyer *Brownson* had been reconnoitering the edge of the pack for the past day. Admiral Byrd felt that she could not produce optimum results because of her thin skin and the dense fog which still hovered over the pack. But on January 30 I was pleased to confirm the *Brownson's* earlier report on ice conditions. This frail vessel had done a splendid job.

The icebreaker then plunged into the pack at approximately 165° West and commenced working in on a base course of 158° or south-southeast. As we ran deeper into the pack the ice became more and more ponderous. By noon, January 31, I was forced to change our axis of advance to a trifle west of south. Consolidated fields of tough polar ice were estimated to average 400 square miles in area. Fortunately the weather was clear and calm, with narrow channels of brash-flaked water separating these enormous masses of ice. We were able to make fair progress.

Our situation, however, was precarious. Should a wind spring up and the ice become lively, the *Northwind* might easily be crushed! Had the stakes not been so high, I would have fought my way post-haste to the navigable ice along the 180th meridian. As it was I dismissed eventualities from my mind and kept plugging.

Calculations at 7:00 P.M. showed that we were nearly halfway through the pack. I sent the helicopter aloft to see if we could work east a few miles. This would approach the optimum for homing the admiral's flight. It was now awaiting our "tallyho." The helicopter got into trouble. Gershowitz sent a distress signal. He was five miles east of us and losing altitude rapidly. The rotor blades were icing. If he landed on ice, his pontoons would stick. He must land in the thread of water over which he was flying.

We made good two miles in the direction of the distressed helicopter. Then we came on an ice floe which was jammed between two fields of consolidated ice directly in the channel. I rushed at this floe in an effort to break through. The *Northwind* struck violently. Her bows rose high and stayed there. She stopped so suddenly and with such force that many men were thrown off their feet. I called for a second lunge. Engines were reversed to full-speed-astern. Nothing happened. Not even by rocking the helm could we budge the vessel. I glanced anxiously at the anemometer rotor. The cupped blades were revolving! It was clear that a wind was making us. The ice would move—and we were stuck!

The situation called for immediate action. Ice was already hissing at our sides. Tiny pressure slabs began to fold upward. The heeling tanks were full of water for ballast. It would take an hour to half-empty them for heeling! This was too much time. I sent for Lieutenant (j.g.) Ricardo Ratti, my gunnery officer, and ordered him to prepare to blast.

I was thankful for the northeast Greenland precaution of keeping five mines and detonating outfit on the foredeck. I was thankful, too, for the rigid ladder lashed to the forward bulwarks. We had never practiced blasting. I must be a teacher, as Captain Von Paulsen had been. I made my way out on the ice with Ratti and his gunner's mates.

In a few minutes the mine was planted and we were pouring back on board. The officer of the deck led me to the bridge-wing and pointed to the helicopter. It was again air-borne and headed our way. The pilot had somehow got rid of his ice in good time. I waited until the helicopter landed, then exploded the mine. The anemometer rotor was spinning more rapidly! The crackling of large pressure slabs creeping up the ship's sides could be heard above the din of our engines.

A muffled roar rocked the ship. A shower of ice fragments rained on the deck. The *Northwind* began to move! Her bows sank back to their normal draft, and the vessel shot rapidly astern.

I gave Admiral Byrd a "tallyho." But we had to get out to the westward—as fast as possible.

At midnight, February 1, the first R4D, piloted by Lieutenant Commander McCoy, a veteran Antarctic flier, zoomed overhead on her way to Little America. Byrd was on board this plane. He sent me a personal dispatch of greeting and included a report of heavy ice to the north and east of us. But we had already learned this—the hard way. Before the last plane flew over us, threatening clouds were moving overhead and the wind was steadily on the increase. Moreover the serpentine stretches of open water between consolidated fields were narrowing rapidly.

By 4:00 A.M. the skies were completely overcast, and a southeasterly wind was whistling savagely. We fought desperately to get clear of heavy ice. By 8:00 A.M. we had worked into a region of broken floes. At noon we were in large fields of young ice—endless fields, but soft, safe and easily navigable for an icebreaker.

On February 2 the *Northwind* slipped into the Bay of Whales. Our reception was one which might have attended the return of a hero. I was puzzled. Why all the to-do? Then I remembered with deflated ego that there were several tons of mail on board for the central group.

*Well, anyway,* I thought, *Snus will be pleased to see us again.*

Indeed the jovial Dane was happy—but it appeared that his reason was far from being sentimental. "We were just about to run out of beer, Captain," Jensen explained. "You returned just in time."

The wind was completely out of my sails.

# Chapter 38

# UNEXPECTED DIFFICULTIES
# ON THE WAY OUT

ONE of the objectives of Operation High Jump was the blazing of a trail in a new branch of medicine—Arctic medicine. Quite naturally the onus of research, as far as the *Northwind* was concerned, devolved on Dr. Hunter. And his background ideally suited him to such a study. He divided Arctic medicine into two principal categories: hygiene and psychiatry.

Hygiene had to do with proper diet, exercise, clothing, care of eyes, ventilation, temperature of living quarters and sanitation. To institute suitable measures toward observance of these requirements he made recommendations to the division officers and lectured all hands.

Psychiatry, on the other hand, required specialized treatment which the doctor himself must take care of. To this end Dr. Hunter watched his binnacle lists carefully. He noted that most physical complaints proceeded from the men's mental attitude. For example, when all hands were constantly busy the line-up at sick call was either nil or very short. During slack periods of work the line of ailing men lengthened in spite of the means we provided for keeping them occupied. We had done our best to provide attractive furnishings, games, music, instruments, hobby craft, courses of study and a ship's newspaper—the *Midnight Sun*.

The doctor psychoanalyzed each patient whose presence at sick call was not absolutely necessary and treated him individually. Eventually the ship's morale reached a high plane.

The doctor and I shared a belief that if the officers at the top of any organization are jovial and happy, their spirit will be reflected down through the ranks. It was for this reason that we founded the Antarctic Owls' Club. Every night after the movies the Owls met in the Chief Owl's Roost, which, in our case, was the chief engineer's stateroom. A meeting was called a "flight." These "flights" of the Owls were "gam sessions" at which soft drinks were consumed.

In the meantime Admiral Cruzen was anxious to get the central group unloaded and out of the ice. It must get clear before the early fall could make the pack unnavigable. Moreover the *Mount Olympus*, *Merrick* and *Yancey* were needed on stations stretching along the outside of the pack from which weather data might be flashed to Little America. Weather charts could be constructed from this information and Byrd's program of aerial exploration greatly facilitated. Still another supporting implement was needed—an emergency landing field—a job for an icebreaker.

Byrd and Cruzen settled on Ross Island in McMurdo Sound as the place best suited for this emergency field. It was proposed, therefore, to have the *Northwind* escort the central group to Scott Island. The ships would then deploy to weather stations. The new icebreaker *Burton Island* could be expected to make contact with the central group during its outbound passage through the ice. She would provide additional escort. The *Northwind* and *Burton Island* were to return along the most navigable route to the inside of the pack. One icebreaker would continue on to Little America while the other set up the small emergency base. After the season's work was completed both icebreakers would rendezvous at Little America to evacuate its personnel.

In anticipation of the *Northwind's* assignment to the McMurdo Sound task I set about organizing and training a search-and-rescue team. Sixteen men, headed by Lieutenant (j.g.) Russell, were selected, and we devoted our remaining days at the Bay of Whales to infantry drill on skis and practical instruction in first aid.

After consultation with his commanding officers Admiral Cruzen established February 8 as our tentative date of departure. Already a miniature tent city, completely self-supporting, had sprung up on the fleecy barrier heights above the southeast end of the Bay of Whales.

This city, with its airstrip, had been duly commissioned Little America Number Four by Admiral Byrd. By February 5 all ships of the central group were unloaded. They were allowed three days to prepare for the arduous journey ahead.

On the eve of our departure we held a smoker on board the *Northwind* as a sort of farewell celebration. The well-rehearsed acts would have done credit to an old-time vaudeville. One of the star performers was Dr. Hunter as a hypnotist. He expedited his demonstration by mesmerizing his subjects during the afternoon and impressing a post-hypnotic suggestion. When the show began he had only to make a few dramatic passes to regain his subjects. Lieutenant Commander William J. Menster, fleet chaplain,* was another star. He entertained with guitar and song. This smoker, like all others we had, was followed by a snack of beer and hot dogs.

At 6:00 P.M., February 8, Admiral Cruzen was piped on board the *Northwind,* and at 8:00 P.M. "Execute!" for getting under way was flashed to the central group. Ships let go moorings from the deadmen, maneuvered into a column and steamed slowly out of the Bay of Whales. Admiral Byrd, his plane crews, scientists and supporting personnel, about 200 men in all, were left at Little America.

Forty-eight hours later the fleet twisted northward among scattered ice which stretched along the 180th meridian. Ahead of us loomed the uninterrupted white blink which warned us that we were about to enter the pack. The radar showed something metallic in the pack. It was distant nine miles and moving our way. A few quick stabs of purplish light from our searchlight challenged the intruder. It was the *Burton Island.* She was our brand-new sister ship, commanded by Commander Gerald L. Ketchum, USN.

Our meeting at this point was most opportune, for the central group was about to plunge into the pack. Now, with a second icebreaker to follow the *Northwind* and smooth off the rough edges, the fleet was able to make good progress. Moreover it soon became plain that the pack was not nearly so obstinate as it had been during our inbound passage.

---

* Commander Menster wrote an excellent book about Operation High Jump entitled *Strong Men South.*

On the night of February 13 a furious gale burst upon the fleet. The ice became lively. Agitated floes scurried into the lead we were following and fouled the ships repeatedly. The *Northwind* and *Burton Island* darted about, trying to marshal the vessels into column. The *Merrick,* in the van, was thrust violently against a heavy floe by a terrific gust of wind. Her rudder was torn off. Two holes were smashed in her side.

I knew at once we were in for a tow job—an arduous one. Not only must the big supply ship be taken clear of the ice, she must be towed all the way to New Zealand. Getting her out of the ice would present a multitude of problems because she could not be snubbed into our towing crotch. After that, a trip of nearly a thousand miles across the screaming sixties and furious fifties (degrees, south latitude) during the hurricane season promised to be unpleasant. But one thing at a time. First we must care for the immediate situation.

The admiral ordered the *Burton Island* to take the *Mount Olympus* and *Yancey* out of the pack. The *Northwind* began her task with the *Merrick.* Getting our wire-rope hawser made fast to the *Merrick* was only a matter of ten minutes' work. Then our troubles began. On February 15 the *Burton Island* reported she had cleared the ice pack with the *Mount Olympus* and *Yancey.* She would return and give us a hand.

The next day our sister ship joined. At this point we were trying to grope our way through a stratum of icebergs which so studded the pack as to form a nearly impenetrable wall. The *Burton Island* attempted to clear a track for us by pushing them out of the way.

Once I was obliged to make a sharp turn with the towing cable hove short. The *Burton Island* began to push on a berg that threatened the turn. The berg slipped off her stem the wrong direction and came charging down toward the *Merrick.* Under the spreading white cloak of this berg I saw beneath the water the ragged green submarine shelving. If it struck the *Merrick* it would rip out her bottom.

Lieutenant Moore had the con on board the *Northwind.* He saw the threat at the same time as I. Moore grabbed the control handles and threw them back halfway.

"Goose 'er," I yelled at Moore. He threw the controls back full.

The *Northwind* shot wildly astern. Our stern struck the *Merrick* with a sickening crash, buckling frames and dishing in shell plating. We thrust her clear of the charging berg only by a bare margin.

In the afternoon we fought our way clear of the ice and joined the rest of the task group. Now that we were out of the pack, we could think about the next leg of our journey.

I asked Admiral Cruzen to let me take the *Yancey* to New Zealand. We were certain to encounter storms, and I could use her to cruise in the lead, spreading an oil slick. He granted my request and set up a special task unit of *Northwind, Merrick* and *Yancey*, all under my command.

Four members of his staff were left on board the *Northwind*. These were: Lieutenant Commander Charles R. Dale, meteorologist; James Lucas, Scripps-Howard's news representative; Jack Hough and Lieutenant Bill Metcalf, our oceanographers. My orders were to return to the Antarctic after leaving the *Merrick* and *Yancey* at Dunedin. The *Mount Olympus* was ordered to take station in the vicinity of Scott Island and report weather. This was necessary to Admiral Byrd's operations at his Little America base. Cruzen shifted his flag to the *Burton Island* and ordered her to go to Ross Island as a supporting unit for Admiral Byrd's exploratory flights.

At 5:00 P.M. "Execute" was flashed from the *Burton Island*, now flagship. All units proceeded on their assigned tasks. The weather was excellent, and I wanted to take advantage of it. We worked up to ten knots (over the bottom) and our towing cable stretched out to 300 fathoms.

During the night a wind swept out of the west and whipped up white crests on the deep waves. I signaled the *Yancey* to begin pumping oil. Her slick enabled us to maintain a ten-knot speed in spite of the heavy lurching which comes with steaming in a trough.

Daylight broke to show our world shrunk to a radius of less than one mile. Around us the wind drove boiling wave tops into troughs and showered our weather side with sheets of spray.

My eyes followed the smooth slick stretching like a path ahead of us until it was lost in the blurred stern of the *Yancey*. Abaft of us the *Merrick* tended off to leeward, her bows dipping rhythmically and throwing white fountains of sea water across her foredeck with every plunge. Over our laboring stern I watched the towing cable as it worked up and down with the movements of the ships.

At noon the anemometer accelerated to register a whole gale. The *Merrick* was being swept more and more to leeward, and her increasing resistance to our pull caused the cable to break water occasionally. I decreased speed to five knots. By the time the 8:00 P.M. reports were mustered we were barely creeping into pounding seas. With the wind howling with such force, heavy oil was instantly atomized. This made the *Yancey's* slick ineffectual. I ordered her to cease pumping and authorized discretionary courses.

When night fell the storm reached hurricane force. The sea raged about us with such fury that its waters became a sheet of boiling foam, broken only by a sharp blending with the pitch-black sky. Behind us an intermittent burst of white shot skyward as the *Merrick's* bows buried themselves in each onrushing comber. But for this we could not see her, and the *Yancey*, only a mile away, was completely swallowed by the darkness.

I clung desperately to the splinter shield. The deck beneath me rose high, trembled as though in fear of the next convulsion, then sank with a sickening plunge. The bows intermittently buried themselves beneath tons of sea. On each plunge water broke against turret and deckhouse with an impact I thought would surely sweep them away. When the bows were unburdened of the seas they had scooped up, the ship would roll over dizzily.

On one of those convulsive lurches the wheelhouse door flew open. A figure emerged, groped for a dog handle, missed and fell sprawling to the deck. The door crashed shut. I hand-over-handed my way along the splinter shield, grabbed the man as he rolled against my feet. I thought he would rise, but instead he vomited. I snatched at him as the ship flung herself the other way. My feet shot out from under me, and my unidentified companion and I careened about the slimy deck like so much loose baggage. After a complete cycle of ship's motion we regained our feet.

I now knew this man was the messenger.

"Sir," he said, "Mr. Goodwin says we've lost all the turns on our towing windlass. They are doing everything they can to hold on to the bitter end."

No use sending the messenger back with instructions. I had no order to give. Nothing we could do would lessen the strain on the cable. It would be stupid to tell Captain Hourihan in the *Merrick* to cut the bridle. No man could possibly stand against the seas which poured over the *Merrick's* bow.

There is something spellbinding about a storm at sea. I was fascinated by the blob of white which spread intermittently into the dark sky. But soon these bursts of spray became gradually weaker. I knew the towing cable had parted. I waited for the downroll, then dashed to the door and flung myself inside the wheelhouse.

"Sir," the telephone watch greeted me, "Mr. Goodwin just called to say the cable has *parted.*"

Day broke on February 17 as the hurricane reached the height of its fury. The *Merrick* rolled wildly as each sea battered her side. Still, a seaman's sixth sense told me she appeared to be riding the waves satisfactorily.

At times the wind reached ninety miles an hour. If it took a turn for the worse the *Merrick* would indeed be in difficult straits. But I had a plan for fendering down and removing all hands by placing the *Northwind* along her lee side. I knew this could be done, because I had once tried it while extinguishing a fire on a burning tanker at sea.* This experience had shown me we could expect severe damage to our side and top hamper.

However the storm moderated a trifle throughout the day while the *Northwind* and *Yancey* plowed back and forth on the most comfortable courses we could find. Running before the sea, the icebreaker was fairly steady. "Snake" Meyer, the chief boatswain's mate, and his petty officers spliced a thimble in the end of the towing cable. Fortunately the break had occurred so near the end that practically its entire original length was intact.

By 7:00 P.M., February 18, the wind was down to moderate gale force. While towing conditions were far from satisfactory, I felt they were about as favorable as we could expect along the sixtieth (south) parallel. I decided to resume towing at 8:00 P.M. and signaled my

---

* U S. Coast Guard Cutter *Hermes,* rescue of *American Fisher* off the California coast, June 17, 1937.

intention to Captain Hourihan, instructing him that we would make fast to his anchor chain instead of a bridle.

In the evening of February 18 I put the *Northwind* before the sea and crept slowly across the *Merrick's* bow while the cable was passed and made fast. In ten minutes' time we were again under way, paying out our cable and working up to a speed of seven knots.

The following day the seas smoothed out. Commander Dale could now copy weather from Campbell Island and New Zealand. Today his weather chart showed another storm speeding toward us at twenty knots. I made a radical change of course ninety degrees to the right to dodge it and increased speed to ten knots. When the storm passed we felt only the tail.

At 8:00 A.M., February 21, I received a TBS call from Captain Hourihan. "Tommy," the *Merrick's* skipper said, "my calculations show we will reach Dunedin about eight o'clock tonight. Today is Friday, and everything stops for the week end at 6:00 P.M. Do you think we can get to port before saloon-closing time?"

"Hold tight!" I replied. "You're going to be goosed!"

Thenceforth we made good thirteen and a half knots over the bottom.

In explanation of my excessive fuel consumption I was happy to report that we beat the saloon-closing deadline.

# Chapter 39

# THE ANTIPODES ·

ON March 3, 1800, Captain Waterhouse of H.M.S. *Reliance* climbed into his rigging, braced himself in the ratlines and shrouds and focused his spyglass on some small islands his ship had just stumbled upon. Only one of this group was large enough to merit the definition of "island," and on it he bestowed the name "Principal Island."

Principal Island was roughly four miles long by nearly as wide, with palisading sides reaching to an elevation of 600 feet in places. Beyond them the island was undulating and green to its 1,300-foot crest.

Captain Waterhouse named the group "Penantipodes," because it was the nearest land antipodal to the position of Greenwich, England. Later, cartographers tabbed the islands "Antipodes."

Shortly after the middle of the century the New Zealand government established a refuge hut for shipwrecked sailors at Depot Anchorage on the northeast end of the Principal Island.

The *Northwind* had made a quick turnabout at Dunedin and returned to the Antarctic. Now on March 1 we were steaming northward again in company with the *Mount Olympus* and *Burton Island*, bound for Wellington, New Zealand.

A westerly wind howled with strong gale force, causing us to roll and lurch violently in the trough. Indeed the seas were flinging us from side to side with rolls which at times exceeded fifty degrees. In the *Mount Olympus* Admiral Cruzen saw the difficulty with which the icebreakers were holding their station and authorized them to proceed independently. The *Burton Island* chose to ease into the seas, while I decided to steer a zigzag course with seas alternately on bow and quarter.

From their position reports I found on March 3 that zigzagging had gained us about a ten-hour lead on the *Mount Olympus* and *Burton Island*. A zag should take us close to the Antipodes. I wanted to see these islands. I radioed the admiral that we were putting into the Antipodes to repair some storm damage. I forget just what this damage was, but we required rationalization of some kind to avoid international embarrassment.

The morning of March 4 was foggy when the *Northwind* felt her way into the quiet waters of Ringdove Bay on the southwest side of Principal Island. As though Nature condescended to reveal a portion of the mysteries concealed in the mists, she raised the curtain about 500 feet. Before us stretched the cathedrallike grandeur of pastelled cliffs, with arches, spires, templets and flying buttresses. Thousands of birds perched on every accessible rock formation. Several groups of winged creatures plunged porpoiselike past us through the water, leaped ashore and landed squarely on both feet. We knew then they must be penguins.

I scrawled out a message to Admiral Cruzen informing him of my whereabouts and of the thousands of penguins we found there. I asked how many he wished us to take.

In a matter of a few minutes his reply came: "Desire fifty-four penguins."

I was pleased that the admiral imposed no qualifications as to sex. There is only one way to determine a penguin's sex, and that is to watch the egg roll out.

We proceeded to Depot Anchorage. A surge swept around the rocky promontory on the northeast end of Principal Island, lashing the wall of Depot Anchorage with a margin of white spray. This was broken only by a short gap which formed a cleft. A suggestion of beach could be seen through it. Here, then, was the landing place— the only one on the island.

We organized our forces into parties. The first, led by Lieutenant (j.g.) Russell, would make a reconnaissance of the northeast end of the island. Lieutenant (j.g.) Moore would take two boats on a hydrographic survey of the islands—east of Principal Island. Our helicopter would accomplish such air scouting as the fog might permit. The task of collecting data for a historical chronicle fell to James Lucas, while Dr. Hough and Lieutenant Metcalf studied the geology of the island.

The fog showed every indication of remaining with us throughout the day. I was determined to carry out our survey program in spite of this obstacle. Chief Photographer E. E. Mashburn, USCG, took off in the helicopter to photograph the coast line below the fog line. The aircraft made a circuit of the perimeter of Principal Island.

In the meantime Lieutenant (j.g.) Robert B. Moore, with Signalman First Class Andrew Petriokowski, called away the motor surfboat and gig for exploration of the waters surrounding Horseshoe Island, one mile northeast of Principal Island. Actually this fortresslike island resembles a broken horseshoe in that there are now two islands whose combined length is something near a mile. Both spring abruptly from the sea and rise to an elevation of 880 feet. At one time they were united by a natural bridge with midchannel piers. But one span has fallen into the sea, leaving its twin still intact, appropriately called "Remarkable Arch."

The Depot party, under Russell, found the refuge shack in a sorry state. High winds had demolished a part of the roof and blown off its door. Elements swirling into its interior had reduced the tinned rations with which it had been stocked to piles of rust. A chronological sequence of names inscribed on the walls fixed the date of the latest visit as 1921. The list of eight names was led by Edward Marin, 1886, followed by James Kelley, S.S. *Stella,* 1901. Posterity will note that "Kilroy was here—March 4, 1947."

A boat box was hoisted up the cliff nearest the shack, and, after repairs were made, five cases of U. S. K-rations were installed.

Russell radioed to report his detail unable to proceed with a reconnaissance of the northeast end of the island because of grass conditions. This sounded ridiculous to me. I recalled a surfboat and went ashore to see for myself. Running a gantlet of sea elephants on the beach, I started up a defile which led to the cliff tops and found its sides virtually covered with penguins.

The first bird I brushed against taught me something about the disposition of his species—the rock-hopper penguin. This bird is a highly spirited penguin who will use his hawklike beak freely and vigorously on any intruder rather than retreat. I learned this the painful way. The rock hopper is easily distinguished from any other bird of his genus by tufts of yellow feathers which protrude from the temples. Before I reached the grasslands above the cliffs I longed for the safer company of the sea elephants on the beach.

Vegetation consisted entirely of tall tussock grass and razor-sharp reeds which towered above a man's head. It made travel exceedingly difficult. All one could do was flop around in it. When I succeeded in reaching Russell and his party, who were resting near the Depot, I could fully appreciate what he meant by "grass conditions."

After sailing out of Depot Anchorage the *Northwind* coasted along the northwest side of the island, twisting among the Windward Islands while Van Etten made radar photographs on which to base our chart construction of the group.

The first outlying island we passed was a basalt cone of striking contrast in its several parallel colors. Its elevation of 425 feet exceeds the diameter of its sea-battered base. This island had never been located on the sketch chart of the group. Later we named it in honor of Colonel T. O. Lees of Wellington, New Zealand. The colonel is a survivor of Shackleton's *Endurance* expedition (1914-1916).

By the time we ended our circuit of the islands at Ringdove Bay night was beginning to creep over the Antipodes. Only one task remained—to collect fifty-four penguins. While I pondered how to go about it, Snus offered a suggestion.

"Captain," Jensen said, "I've seen the Alaskan natives catch birds. They use a big net. We could do the same—with a fish net."

Within an hour fifty-seven furious penguins were brought on board. These were incarcerated in the makeshift aviary we had made of the forward forty-millimeter "quad" splinter shield.

The *Northwind* then got under way and shaped course to intercept the *Mount Olympus* and *Burton Island*. Her broad bows dipped rhythmically into the heavy swell to shower her bridge and foredeck with recurring clouds of spray. From the rail forward of the wheelhouse I watched our penguin prisoners stomping about in their pen. Commander Smenton stood beside me. With each burst of spray we ducked in unison.

"Someone will have to look after our zoo," I remarked. "Have we any ornithologists on board?"

"No, Captain," Smenton replied. Then he grinned. "I think I have it," he continued. "The helicopter pilot! We know Gersh studied agriculture in college. Now, agriculture must include poultry husbandry in its curriculum. Gersh is our man!"

So Lieutenant Gershowitz was appointed curator. He went about his new duties like an expert. Taking an interest in the rock hoppers, he nursed them with motherly care, cut their fish into strips that could be jammed down their throats and inserted vitamin tablets to compensate for lack of fish liver in the normal diet. He rigged swinging perches to prevent the birds' becoming seasick. Not knowing whether penguins drink fresh or salt water, Gershowitz provided basins of each and observed carefully to determine which they required. He never did find the answer, but concluded that either will suffice.

Lieutenant Gershowitz's interest in his penguins, while of little apparent significance, typified the work of the unsung heros of Operation High Jump. Zoologists, biologists, geologists, correspondents and scores of other specialists made possible the over-all success of the expedition. It is impossible to gauge intrinsic benefits by immediate returns. Like the voyages of Captain Cook, the trail blazed by Byrd and Cruzen will, if exploited determinedly, lead to infinite treasures in resources.

The expedition, in but a fraction of 1947, mapped an area more than half as large as the United States; charted 5,400 miles of coast line; located vast deposits of coal, iron and other valuable minerals; tested and developed mechanized equipment essential to surface support of exploratory aircraft; determined the effectiveness of explosives in dealing with ice; and gained valuable information concerning Arctic hygiene.

Then there were the intangibles which result from training and experience. Officers and men in ships learned how to handle their vessels, when to apply power and rudder, how to keep station and how to respect ice rather than fear it. Many of these lessons were learned the hard way. But, as Captain Von Paulsen once said, "Lessons learned the hard way last the longest."

Unquestionably the high degree of success achieved by the expedition was largely due to the genius for planning, organization and leadership of two truly great men: Rear Admirals Byrd and Cruzen. Sharing laurels for the success of the central group were the skippers of the *Merrick, Yancey, Mount Olympus* and *Sennet*.

It is an easy job to slam an icebreaker around in the ice without too much fear of her being holed, particularly when her officers have had long experience in this type of work—but it is difficult with a thin-skinned vessel.

But I was proud of my own ship, her officers, men and aircraft pilots. I was still more proud when we left New Zealand to begin our long homeward voyage across the Pacific. A dispatch addressed to the *Northwind* was received from the commander of Task Force 68. It read:

"Well done."

*Part Six*

BERING SEA PATROL

*1948*

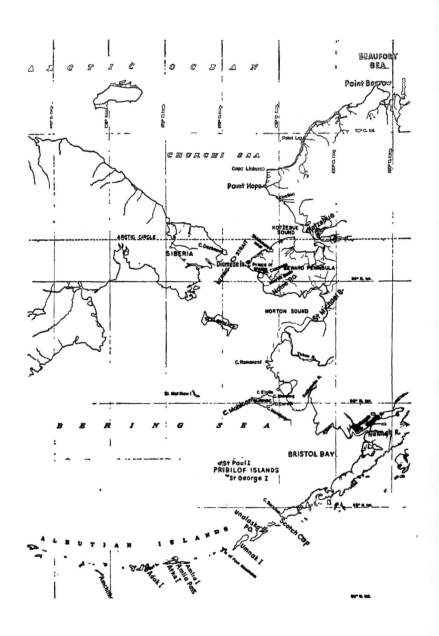

# Chapter 40

# *SAILING NORTH WITH*
# *LAW AND ORDER*

THE work of the United States Coast Guard has traditionally been closely linked with the development of the Arctic Regions. Among outstanding contributions to the work of our government in the north was the role this service played in the growth of Alaska.

In 1867 when the territory of Alaska was purchased from Russia it was scornfully referred to as "Seward's Ice Box." Popular belief held that it was a land of snow and ice, too far from the United States to be of any value. Few people at the time knew of the tempering effect of the Kurishio current. Its warm waters wash the shores of southern Alaska and shoot fingers between the Aleutian Islands to hold the Arctic ice pack at bay.

Four months after the Alaska purchase treaty was signed the Revenue cutter *Lincoln* left San Francisco with a government inspection party. Its members were instructed to determine what sort of country Seward had acquired for $7,200,000.

In the years immediately afterward the cutters *Corwin*, *Wolcott* and *Rush* followed the *Lincoln*, bringing to Alaska a procession of surveyors who represented many physical sciences. Most of the work of these officials was conducted on shore. Meanwhile the cutters busied themselves with exploring the shore line and rivers which drained the coastal area.

317

By 1880 canneries began to spring up along the south coast of the new territory. These and the pelagic fisheries attracted an influx of workers. On their heels followed a procession of lawless men who lived by exploiting native and worker alike. Quarrels, mutinies, fights, shipwreck, piracy and murder were the order of the day. The Revenue cutters were assigned the job of bringing law and order to places that had been beyond the reach of the arm of law.

To carry out this new duty more cutters were needed—faster ones. The *Corwin* and *Lincoln* were too slow to cope with lawless ships. Accordingly the Greely Relief Expeditionary bark, the eleven-year-old *Bear*, was transferred from the Navy to the U. S. Revenue Cutter Service. After reconditioning in New York she sailed around the Horn to San Francisco and was there placed under command of Captain Michael A. Healy. Her new skipper was already a veteran of Alaskan waters, having commanded the smaller *Corwin*. He was a seaman of the first order and had established the reputation reflected by his nickname—"Hell-Roaring Mike."

Captain Healy was proud of the *Bear*. She had been built for ice, and she had fine lines, auxiliary steam power and was a good sailer as well. Moreover she had two modern three-inch breech-loading rifles. Healy would be able to deal with ships which had defied the *Corwin*.

The *Bear* arrived in Alaska in 1886, and Healy set about bringing order out of chaos. His first act was to suppress the sale of liquor to natives. While the courts were sometimes corrupt and often too lenient with offenders, Healy insured a full measure of justice. His method of throwing known violators into the *Bear's* brig for transportation to Sitka discouraged lawbreakers because Healy saw to it that the ride was long and unpleasant.

Captain Healy made Unalaska his base of operations. All trade with the Aleutians and the Bering Sea flowed through Unalaska. At such a natural crossroads the *Bear's* skipper could avail himself of the information essential to his mission—news of mutinies, disaster and illicit sealing.

Healy rode herd on the seals wherever he could and punished poachers severely, but he could not be omnipresent. One reason for his frequent absences from the Bering Sea lay in the far north—in the Beaufort Sea.

Whalers were beginning to flock to the Arctic Ocean, north of Alaska. Large-scale fisheries in areas of sea ice could not be carried on without considerable risk. Healy learned of trouble in the Arctic— bad ice and mutinies. This was a job for the *Bear*. Healy coaled his ship and set her on a northerly course. Shortly after she reached the Beaufort Sea the *Bear* rescued survivors of the wrecked whaler *Napoleon,* towed the *J. H. Howland* free of dangerous ice and suppressed a mutiny on the bark *Lagoda.*

Each year the *Bear* repeated her Arctic cruise, administering justice and attending to the medical needs of the Eskimos. Her hold was always stocked with food, not only for her own crew, but to tide native settlements over lean years as well. Captain Healy earned a reputation as a fair administrator and stern disciplinarian. Of the *Bear's* officers and men he required rigorous adherence to his doctrine: "Never make a promise to a native you don't intend to keep."

Nearly every village in northern Alaska has a record of famine within the memory of its existing population. Healy hit on a solution. On the Siberian side of the seas the Eskimos had a reliable source of food available to them—reindeer. He sailed to Siberia, transplanted ten head of reindeer to Alaska and landed them at Teller. They thrived as well as on their native soil. Healy urged the government to undertake the project on a large scale. It did. Today reindeer husbandry is an important Federal industry. No famines have since occurred among the native population.

In 1911 the International Pelagic Sealing Treaty was signed by the United States, Canada, Russia and Japan. The covenant outlawed pelagic sealing and provided an equitable sharing of skins among the four countries.

With a firm basis for seizing poachers thus established, the Bering Sea Patrol of the U. S. Revenue Cutter Service came into being. The duties of the patrol were numerous, but could be divided into two general categories: (1) enforcement of all U. S. laws in Alaska and jurisdictional waters, and (2) the traditional saving of life and property at sea and medical assistance to natives on shore.

In 1915 the Revenue Cutter Service became the U. S. Coast Guard.

The Bering Sea Patrol continued until 1941, when the force went to war. In the meantime several new generations of cutters had grown old and outmoded in service, but the old *Bear* was still going strong. In 1927 the historic cutter was decommissioned and replaced by the *Northland*. The *Bear's* retirement was short-lived. In 1940 she joined the squadron under Rear Admiral Byrd in the Antarctic Service. In 1941 when war clouds broke she was assigned to Iceberg Smith's Greenland Patrol.

The *Bear* rendered her traditionally high quality of service in the harsh sea area off Greenland until 1944. Upon commissioning of the *Eastwind* she was retired and sold. Today the *Bear* is back where she began her career—in the seal fisheries. Perhaps she will complete another cycle of useful service to the United States. At least that is the prayer of hundreds of officers and men who knew and loved her.

In 1948 the *Northwind* was assigned the work which had in the late nineteenth century been the *Bear's*. Would the vessel be up to this task? I was to find out and make suitable report with recommendations as to whether or not future patrols were justified.

In keeping with established practice the commanding officer of a Coast Guard cutter assigned the Bering Sea Patrol sails with a commission as United States Commissioner, justice of the peace, probate judge and coroner. In 1948 I was duly vested with these multifarious powers in order to carry on the work of my predecessors.

A Commissioner's Court is one of limited jurisdiction. Felonies and civil suits of similar gravity must be bound over to a District Court. The majority of cases arising in legal jurisprudence occur in the southern part of Alaska. In the southwestern part, along the peninsula and in the Aleutians, a special District Court visits annually the isolated settlements. This court is transported in a Coast Guard cutter and hence has come to be known as the "floating court."

The *Northwind* was assigned the court cruise as a preliminary to the Bering Sea Patrol. After this initial phase of our work was completed I had to carry out all the duties previously assigned the Patrol. Moreover there were more added since the war as a result of increased Armed Forces activity which required our logistic support. While nominally bearing the title Commander Bering Sea Patrol Force, I

Two little Alaskans say "Aaah" for Dr. Wm. J. Braye of the U. S. Public
Health Service.

Supplies and mail for the Coast Guard station at Attu.

Street scene, Little Diomede, less than a mile from the "Iron Curtain."

Alaska's governor, Ernest Gruening, talks it over with citizens of Skagway.

found it actually an empty one, since I had only the *Northwind* under my command, rather than the several ships of the prewar patrol.

A chain of Coast Guard loran (electronic beacon) stations, together with a number of Navy and Air Force outposts, had sprung up along the Aleutians since the wartime disestablishment of the patrol. These, plus two isolated lighthouses on Umnak Island, must be supported logistically.

Without natural obstacles the task of fulfilling all Coast Guard obligations with one icebreaker would not have been difficult. But there would be storms, fog, surf, ice and shallow water to contend with. Moreover the *Northwind* was actually poorly prepared for an Arctic venture. Lack of funds reduced our complement far below that which the ship had previously enjoyed.

In 1948 only one of our three engine rooms could be continuously manned. On-board aviation was nonexistent. For the want of personnel and operating expenses the indispensable helicopter and useful Grumman "Duck" were both gone. Without full power, without our "eyes," and with only a handful of seamen we would be greatly handicapped when it came to bucking the Arctic pack this year.

I decided to consider the relative importance of each of our tasks, together with the equipment at our disposal and the services we were best prepared to render. This estimate would govern our proposed itinerary.

Unquestionably the alleviation of human suffering was of prime importance. There was a vast area of Alaska which had seen neither doctor nor dentist since before the war.

Until July sea ice would spread over the entire northern part of the Bering Sea and Arctic Ocean. While the ship might readily cope with it, the shores would be inaccessible to boating. Moreover after a long winter of activity outposts on the Aleutian chain would likely require logistic support as soon as we could render it.

I decided, therefore, to work the southern part of the Bering Sea after the conclusion of the court cruise in early June. In July I would sail for the Arctic.

Chapter 41

# *THE LAND OF THE ALEUT*

BEGINNING at Umnak Island the Aleutian Islands stretch westward some 1,300 miles from the Alaskan peninsula to Kamchatka on the Siberian coast. While the Alaskan Aleutians cover a lineal distance of about 900 miles, the Russian-owned Komandorski group is properly included in the chain. The Komandorskis lie roughly midway between Attu, the westernmost American island, and Kamchatka.

The Aleutian Islands are remnants of a submerged mountain system and form a chain of active cones. While devoid of trees, the lower slopes are covered with a luxuriant growth of grasses and soft moss. In general the topography of the islands is rugged and precipitous. The coasts are bluff and exposed; the shores are bold with many off-lying islets, rocks and reefs; the beaches are rocky and narrow, and the water is usually deep close to shore. The weather of the Aleutians is characterized by persistently overcast skies, high winds and violent storms. Fog persists much of the time.

In 1741 Vitus Bering, sailing westward from Kodiak on his return voyage to Kamchatka, discovered the Aleutian Islands. Soon afterward Russian fur traders began visiting the islands, drawn by reports of fox and sea-otter furs. They found a nation of some 25,000 inhabitants whose diet consisted mainly of fish. The natives were well formed and mild mannered. They were first called *elaets*, but the name was later corrupted to *aleut*.

322

The Aleuts found by the Russians were peace-loving but spirited in their resistance to attempts of the traders to enslave them. As a result in a short span of fifty years all but 1,100 had perished.

Today there are about 4,000 Aleuts in Alaska. Most of them have been attracted to the mainland by the salmon-canning industry.

It was on the Alaskan peninsula, where I worked in 1920 as a cannery hand, that I made the acquaintance of the Aleut—and, incidentally, the Coast Guard, too.

Twenty-eight years passed.

Now I was winding up the cruise of the "floating court" in the *Northwind,* a cruise which had taken me from Seward to Bristol Bay—to familiar old canneries, but few familiar faces.

This floating court was presided over by Judge Joseph Kehoe of Nome, Alaska. Years of experience on the bench in Alaska had stamped Judge Kehoe with a natural dignity which left no doubt in the mind of any person in the courtroom as to who was the judge. The brand of justice he dispensed was tempered with common sense and an understanding of native psychology. Its quality merited the respect of plaintiff, defendant, defense counsel and district attorney.

Now, as daylight of June 4, 1948, was dawning I wished Joseph Kehoe had been a Bristol Bay pilot instead of a Federal judge.

The *Northwind,* drawing twenty-eight feet of water, felt her way among countless shoals on her way up treacherous Kvichak River, which discharges into the head of Bristol Bay. Since we had sailed from Nushagak Bay at 9:00 P.M., the chant of leadsmen in both chains had accented the click of our fathometer. Ordinarily I would not have attempted to grope our way between uncharted sandbars, but we were determined to meet the court's schedule. And there was another reason for this seeming rashness. We had been unable to engage a pilot, so I was taking a precaution learned the hard way in northeast Greenland. We were navigating on the lower half of the tide.

We had grounded once during the night. Commander Peter F. Smenton, my executive officer, had literally washed away part of the bar on which we rested and used a bower anchor to pivot the vessel free. It had been a brilliant piece of seamanship.

Our destination was the village of Naknek at the confluence of the

Kvichak and Naknek rivers. We were able to navigate to within seven miles of the settlement—a close approach for a deep-draft vessel in this part of Alaska.

The mean tidal range of the Kvichak and Naknek rivers is thirty feet—one which rivals that of the Bay of Fundy. These rivers cut channels through mud flats which are several miles from the docks at low tide. When the tide floods, rising water rushes over the mud flats and inundates the entire basin.

Half-flood for the village of Naknek is reveille. The village comes to life. Whistles blow and work begins. Boats cast loose from their moorings and get under way for upstream destinations which they try desperately to reach before high slack. When the tide starts to ebb the direction of traffic is reversed. Vessels move downstream, racing against the rapid draining of the basin. When low water leaves the moorings and piers high and dry it is time to quit. Boats settle into the mud, whistles blow, work stops and all hands turn in. Thus flows the semidiurnal cycle of life in Naknek. Everything moves on the tide. Clocks are worthless and there are no watchmakers in town.

Naknek marked the end of the court-cruise phase of the Bering Sea Patrol. The court disembarked to proceed to Anchorage by plane. The *Northwind* weighed anchor, slipped down the Kvichak River into Bristol Bay and shaped course for St. Paul Island in the Pribilofs.

On our first day out of Naknek the sea was smooth and the skies clear. A hail from the lookout directed the attention of those on the bridge to a herd of more than a hundred walruses crossing the vessel's bows. Their white tusks flashed in the early sunlight. Then the leaders, sensing the approach of danger, alerted the herd, and it plunged beneath the surface.

Walruses subsist chiefly on two Arctic species of clam which require the use of their tusks as shovels to dig the clams out of the sea bed. From my Greenland days I knew they seldom go far from sea ice and reasoned that, in spite of the absence of a blink, the ice could not be far north of our track. I had the ship hove to for an oceanographic station. Water salinity, temperature and the microplankton we found confirmed the proximity of the ice. Microplankton is microscopic floating life of the sea. Usually every drop of sea water is teeming with it. (I had completed a sparetime course in oceanography prior to the cruise.) In order to avoid dipping into the pack at night I had the navigator abandon the great circle along which we had been steering and set a rhumb-line course.

On the evening of June 7 the *Northwind* arrived at St. Paul Island.

The Pribilof group, of which St. Paul is the principal island, lies about 56° 50' North, 170° 00' West, roughly 200 miles north of the Aleutian Islands. St. Paul Island is about thirty-five square miles in area, while St. George Island, thirty miles southeast of it, has twenty-seven square miles. Like the other islands of the Bering Sea, the Pribilofs are of volcanic origin.

The Pribilofs were first sighted by Europeans in 1769 when John Synd, an English explorer, sailed by and recorded them without actually landing. In 1786 Gerasim Pribilof, a Russian trader, visited and claimed them for Russia. Seeing that the islands abounded in seal, which he called "sea bears," he recognized the herd's tremendous commercial value and established the fur industry as a crown monopoly.

Today there are U. S. government-owned factories on both St. Paul and St. George islands. The actual processing of furs taken by the U. S. Fish and Wildlife Service is done by the Foulke Fur Company of St. Louis, Missouri.

After the *Northwind* anchored the quiet of the evening was broken by the barking of bull seals, which were arriving by the thousands. The mating season was about to begin, and the cows would be here within a fortnight.

Each bull seal, as he arrives, hauls himself out in one of many rookeries and seeks a position which is advantageous in enticing cows to his harem. The competition for the most suitable places is keen and vigorous. Choice locations are fought over, and the outcome is often fatal to the loser. Therefore only the stronger bulls are able to establish on the rookeries' rocky beaches. The aged, the weak and the young bachelors are known as *idle* bulls because they are forced off the beach onto the grass beyond, where they cannot hope to win a cow.

It is amazing how patient bull seals are. Once ashore, they will cling to their positions without food and water until ready to leave the island after wearying of domestic life. This may be as long as two months, during which time a bull may lose half his weight.

Prior to and during the mating season it is not safe for man to venture too close to a bull. The two-ton monsters rear their shaggy necks, bare saberlike fangs and charge with determination. They have been known to kill men. Fortunately a bull will not venture far from his coveted position for fear of losing it.

On June 8 the crew we had brought to the Coast Guard loran station on St. Paul Island relieved the outpost and began its year of lonely duty. Shortly after midnight we sailed for Adak, a naval base in the Aleutians.

We arrived at Adak on June 11. I called on the commandant, Captain T. O. Dahl, USN, and took an immediate liking to him. Dahl was having his troubles. He had a party of naval research scientists on his hands who required transportation to several islands east of Adak and ultimately to Umnak. He explained something of the nature of their work. The group, known as the Harvard Expedition, had been engaged by the Navy to make an ethnological study of Aleuts. Each of its seven members was an expert in his own sphere of science, with co-ordination of the work vested in the leader, Dr. Laughlin of Peabody Museum.

The commandant could provide no safe water transportation for the expedition. His face brightened when I told him I would be glad to take it in the *Northwind,* since I was about to proceed to Scotch Cap via Atka and Umnak. The following day the expedition embarked on board the *Northwind,* and at midnight we sailed for Atka.

I always made a point of keeping my ear close to the galley grapevine in order to know the condition of my ship's morale. To this end I sometimes donned an apron and helped the cooks prepare breakfast when the ship was under way. I learned that in the opinion of my culinary staff, who digested and reflected the views of their shipmates, the Harvard Expedition was just so much monkey business.

"You see, Captain," one cook advised, "these here scientists are all cracked. They're just a bunch of bone hunters, and I can't see as bone huntin's got anything to do with the Navy."

"They never know what they want, Captain," another agreed.

"You've got to treat them like kids. Why, we'll end up doing all their work for them. Then they'll go back and write a book about lithnosis of the osmosis, or some such tripe, and all the long beards will say: 'Extraordinary! How did we ever get along without you all these years?' "

But generally, after sailors come face to face with scientists, they become curious and, after a few explanations, even enthusiastic These are two of the many virtues I love about sailors—their willingness to adapt to environment and friendliness toward everyone who shares their deck-bound world.

We paused at Atka to render medical and dental relief to the natives and to a U. S. Army outpost near by. Then the ship headed for Svienchinkof Harbor on Amlia Island which is separated from Atka Island by a narrow channel—Amlia Pass.

Approaching the narrows of Amlia Pass, we ran into a swift head current which increased in velocity as we progressed. On our port hand the rocky wall of Amlia Island hung high above us. We were obliged to hug this shore so closely a man could easily have cast a stone from ship to shore. On the starboard side, and very close aboard, breaking seas spread a boiling foam over ugly reefs.

When we reached the halfway point I had the impression of forcing our way up a millrace. We were turning over for eleven and a half knots and making good one knot. Then gradually the current slackened its pace, and the *Northwind* was soon free, plowing deeply into heavy North Pacific swells which showered the decks with bursts of spray.

Two miles offshore the vessel turned onto an easterly course. Because our track was unsounded I had the echo-ranging apparatus placed in operation against the possibility of submarine pinnacles being in our way. Looking beyond the white, pulsating ocean wash at the foot of crag-scarred cliffs, I could see storm clouds gathering about the hidden tops of ancient volcanoes. Clearly we were in for a blow, and I hoped we could make Svienchinkof before it struck.

It was not until 11:00 P.M. that we hove off the harbor's bottleneck entrance. Already a raw southerly wind was whipping the tops of heavy combers as they plunged shoreward. I believe we all experienced an eerie sensation as the *Northwind* raced before following seas toward what appeared to be just another crag in the sheer periphery. But inside its narrow opening the harbor was smooth and snug, with soft, grassy shores and sparkling streams.

No material improvement had been made to charts of Svienchinkof Harbor—or, for that matter, of Amlia Island—for more than a hundred years. The following morning, when the scientists left to dig for relics, I sent out hydrographic and topographic survey parties to chart the harbor and as much of the surrounding land as they could in one day.

The return of Dr. Laughlin and his colleagues at 8:00 P.M. gave me a chuckle. A day's excavation had produced blistered hands and stiff muscles, but no artifacts. I remembered Von Paulsen boarding the ship on a similar occasion five years before in Greenland: "Some damned grave robbers got there first!"

We sailed that evening for the Islands of Four Mountains.

When the morning fog unfolded we were anchored close under Kagamil Volcano. At the base of the mountain jets of steam spouted in tall, white columns through fumaroles between rocks. The place was known as the Steaming Springs of Kagamil. Dr. Laughlin reasoned that a year-round supply of steam heat would attract primitive man. He led his party ashore to investigate.

The day passed, and at suppertime the expedition had not returned. Fearing it had met with mishap, I sent Commander Smenton ashore with a patrol to make a search for the missing men. They were found digging among ruins of an ancient Aleut village, quite oblivious to the time of day. The party's excavations netted fragments of human remains and bits of antique handicraft.

On June 15 the ethnologists left the ship at Umnak, a little Aleut village. A mud-swathed tractor from the Coast Guard station on the southeast end of Umnak Island was on hand to pick up supplies and mail for overland transport five miles through a sea of mud to the loran station.

After leaving Umnak we stood eastward to Dutch Harbor, thence to Scotch Cap—so named because it resembles a Scottish bonnet in profile. In 1944 there had been a lighthouse and coastal lookout outpost at Scotch Cap with a complement of twenty men. Then without warning a tidal wave struck. When the wave surged away, lighthouse, barracks and men were gone. In 1945 the Coast Guard rebuilt the station, locating it high on top of the cliffs. We were here to deliver supplies to the two-man crew and make repairs to motorized and electronic equipment.

The only approach to Scotch Cap Lighthouse is by making a surf landing. And today a heavy surf was running in from southwest. Our shore party quickly learned that a Monomy surfboat is useless on this stretch of coast because of its tendency to sink deep into the porous strand of rhyolite ash. Rubber life rafts proved to be the answer to surf landing here.

On the return trip from Adak we paused briefly on the north side of Amlia Island to chart a nameless cove. It was a beautiful inlet with a sandy beach and an abundance of fresh water close by. I was greatly tempted to let our people try their luck at brook fishing, for I was sure no visitors had been here for years. But we were faced with a heavy schedule, and I was anxious to get about our business.

On June 24 the *Northwind* was once more at St. Paul Island Biological changes had plainly taken place during the two weeks we had been away. Now the soft barking of cows and pups mingled with louder roars of the bulls. The rookeries echoed like a mighty sounding board.

During our absence from the Pribilofs the cows had arrived, joined the innumerable harems scattered about the islands and delivered young who had been conceived during last year's mating season.

After her young is born the mother remains in the harem of her new husband until her pup is strong enough to look after himself. In the meantime she must nurse him, teach him to swim and to forage for squid and smeltlike fish.

Bull seals are decidedly polygamous. It is not unusual for one to have as many as seventy cows in his harem. To maintain suzerainty over his wives the male must be constantly on his guard. Sometimes a cow will attempt to leave the harem before she is served, in response to the ogling of some near-by Casanova. She is generally caught and dealt with gently but firmly by her master. Should she try again, he promptly stifles further disloyalty by flipping her over his body and allowing her to drop with forceable impact on the rocks. There are no divorces in the rookeries.

Each breeding cow bears one pup each year, the period of gestation being nearly a year. Nature so times migration of female seals to the Pribilofs that they deliver their young within six to forty-eight hours after arrival. Within a week they are bred again, a condition made possible by the biuteral anatomy of the cow. Therefore the cows are almost constantly pregnant from the time they are three years old until they are nearly twenty.

After a cow has been served she is free to depart from the harem. Leaving her pup, she swims to her favorite feeding ground. This may take her 150 miles from the Pribilofs. But she returns unerringly to her own pup, which she finds among perhaps a million others. No cow will suckle any but her own offspring. If the mother is killed, her pup also dies.

On the day of our arrival at St. Paul the killing season was in full swing. Each rookery has a slaughtering field which is used only one day before operations shift to the next rookery. The government specifies the number of three-year-old bachelors to be killed each day. This generally runs in the neighborhood of 300. The slaughtering is done by U. S. government employees, all of whom are Aleuts native to the islands. Seals are taken around 2:00 A.M., the coolest time of day, five days a week, and this continues until the annual quota established by biologists is filled.

Killer teams consist of the herders, clubbers and skinners. The herders must use great care to see that seals do not perspire immediately before they are killed. Perspiration spoils the fur. Clubbing seals requires a high degree of skill, and the clubbers are the best paid of the workers. Only an expert can distinguish a three-year-old bachelor from a cow at a glance. This the clubber must be able to do. Should he accidentally club a cow, he loses caste with the other natives. The skinners follow the clubbers socially as well as literally. They must work fast to keep pace with the kill. It requires a pair less than a minute to skin a seal.

Nothing is wasted on the Pribilofs. The offal is reduced to fertilizer or fed to the foxes with which the islands abound. The government's fox-fur industry has become a lucrative side line to the seal fisheries. Moreover the United States shares with no one in the sale of fox pelts.

In the sale of seal furs and by-products the United States shares with Canada twenty-five per cent of the annual yield. Both Japan and Russia have failed to renew their membership in the convention.

The *Northwind* stayed at St. Paul Island until its 250 inhabitants' medical and dental requirements were attended. Then on June 27 she turned her stem to the northeast and sailed from the land of the Aleut for the land of the Eskimo and the reindeer.

# Chapter 42

# INTO THE LAND OF THE
# ESKIMO AND THE REINDEER

ESKIMOS in Alaska number about 15,000 and live on the islands, coasts and principal rivers, generally north of Latitude 59° North throughout the Bering Sea and Arctic Ocean. They are closely related to the Aleuts in habits and in language, though their culture is less highly developed. Ethnologists do not know when the Eskimo migrated to the New World from Asia, but certainly he is the most recent of aboriginal settlers. We know they crossed from the Siberian mainland via the closely linked islands in the northern part of the Bering Sea.

In common with Eskimos in other parts of the Arctic and boreal regions the Alaskan Eskimo lives by hunting and fishing. Since there is no state religion in the United States, his manner of worship has followed the widely varied missionary trends. In the more isolated places, however, he still adheres to a half-belief in his traditional metaphysical philosophy.

Such an isolated settlement was the *Northwind's* first introduction to the Alaskan Eskimos. This was at Kwigmiut, near Cape Mendenhall on the southeast side of Nunivak Island.

Because Nunivak has been seldom visited by travelers, it was not until the coming of the Coast Guard to the Bering Sea that a usable chart of the island was produced. The identity of the cutters who

332

carried out cartographic contributions are preserved by such names as
Cape Mohican, Cape Mannin, Cape Corwin and Cape Rush. But
these ships had other missions, and even today many stretches of the
island's 157 miles of coast have not been accurately sounded.

The day of our arrival at Nunivak, June 28, was unusual in that it
was bright and clear with a brisk breeze sweeping across the tundra.
I had the landing force sent ashore for infantry drill. Later liberty
was granted to one watch to visit the settlement with the official party
and see how Eskimos lived before the coming of white men.

At Kwigmiut time had made little change in the inhabitants' primitive manner of livelihood. We found five families living in houses
that outwardly resembled a circular mound of earth, seven or eight
feet high and thirty or forty feet in circumference. These dwellings
were overgrown with grasses, littered with all sorts of handmade
utensils, weapons, sledges and other Eskimo furniture. From two of
the huts a small spiral of smoke rose from a hole in the apex. Hunks
of walrus meat were draped out of reach of the dogs on rude pole
scaffoldings near each house.

When our men marched into the village they were greeted by the
barking of several dog teams staked out close to the huts. The children, frightened by the sight of so many strange men, huddled close
to their mothers. The women stood apart from the men and giggled
at us like schoolgirls. Obviously no one in so primitive a place spoke
English, but I had brought a copy of *Glossary of Greenlandic Words
and Phrases* by Commander MacMillan with me.

My conversation with the villagers went something like this:

"*Naalagok?*" I asked for the chief.

The natives grinned and pointed to a man who had the appearance
of being elderly.

"*Kiurna,*" I greeted the chief. "How are you?"

He laughed heartily, joined by the rest of the men. I could not
translate his reply, but I knew he was pleased. An Eskimo appre-
ciates even an unsuccessful attempt to use his language. I wished,
however, that Snus Jensen had come ashore with me to help in the
conversation.

"*Suit! A-yorniar pagit,*" I said, pointing at Dr. Robert Price.
"Medicine, he will help you."

Again the men laughed, but somehow got the idea that a doctor was here to take care of any medical needs. I bared my teeth, pointed to them, then at Dr. William J. Braye to let the Eskimos know a tooth doctor was also present. More laughter.

"*Igdlu-takko-A?* . . . House, can he see?" I asked. No one seemed to understand this phrase, probably because my pronunciation was poor. I had to use signs to get the idea across, but the chief smiled and led us to the nearest hut. In the meantime Dr. Braye created not a little hilarity among the females by letting them know he would like to examine their teeth. They all appeared to be as anxious to let him look at their teeth as he was to see them.

To enter the hut we were obliged to crawl on our hands and knees through a tunnellike entrance about eight feet long. Inside, the atmosphere was heavy with the stench of burning seal oil. It took a minute or so before my eyes became adjusted to the feeble light cast by the crude seal-oil fireplace in the center of the house.

The earthen floor was damp with seeping water and the blood of animals. The perimeter on three sides was lined with wooden sleeping shelves about three or four feet wide and covered with reindeer hides. Near the entrance was a pile of seal bladders which were filled with oil. A few dishes carved out of wood and scattered about the sleeping shelves appeared to be the only eating utensils in the hut.

Leaving the house, I was glad to breathe the clean outside air and would have cheerfully delegated visiting the remaining four huts to the doctor, were I not afraid of offending their owners. I recalled that a primitive Eskimo will lose caste if a visit is made to one home and not to his. Moreover these villagers must know from the gold stripes on my uniform I was *naalagok* of the *oomiak puk* (big umiak) lying off their village. So, setting my teeth, I made the ordeal as hasty as I could gracefully accomplish it.

Living so far from white men, none of the twenty-odd natives of Kwigmiut required help from the Coast Guard. Dr. Price found their health to be perfect, without a trace of respiratory diseases that a cursory examination could reveal. Dr. Braye announced that, without exception, their teeth were free of decay. This he attributed to a natural diet of blubber, which kept the teeth conditioned by constant exercise. And I had no duties to carry out as a peace officer because there were no drunkards, bank robbers, embezzlers or murderers. There was not even a marriage to peform. Similarly Commander Smenton, who had been commissioned U. S. Marshal, was not required to make any arrests.

Most of the crew who made the trip to the village were fascinated by the novelty of seeing Eskimos. Only a few had ever seen one before. After we left Kwigmiut a party of officers and men hiked inland in the hope of finding a reindeer herd. While no reindeer were seen, the men were quite excited about some musk oxen they encountered.

In the summer of 1936 twenty-seven head of musk oxen were transferred from Greenland to Nunivak. So closely do the climate and flora of Nunivak resemble that of certain places in northeast Greenland that the herd is now said to number several hundred.

Meyoryuk is the principal settlement on Nunivak Island. It is situated on an inlet about two miles southwest of Cape Etolin, the northwesternmost point on the island. The population numbers about 100, which includes a government nurse and a Presbyterian missionary with his family.

When we visited Meyoryuk on the day following our call at Kwigmiut we were obliged to anchor at Cape Etolin, where the *Northwind* was sheltered from a strong westerly wind. The trip from cape to village was far from pleasant. With Dr. Price, Dr. Braye, Lieutenant Commander Joseph R. Fredette, the chief engineer, and Mr. Aubrey Scotto, a free-lance writer, I splashed across several miles of boggy tundra in order to make good the two direct miles to the settlement. Even the wind, the drizzle and low, dark clouds did little to dampen the aggressiveness of swarms of voracious mosquitoes. We made ineffectual passes at them throughout the journey.

Meyoryuk is a village of dingy shanties, unpainted and ugly on the outside but spotlessly clean on the inside. In common with Greenlandic women these Eskimos take a great deal of pride in keeping their floors scrubbed white and their walls ornate with pictures clipped from magazines and mail-order catalogues. Here hygiene stops. Doors and windows are habitually closed, and interiors are ill-smelling and poorly ventilated. Entire families eat, sleep and live in one room.

Also, common to Eskimo practice wherever I have been, the natives of Meyoryuk have no bathrooms or backhouses. The wealthier families have a chamber, but the poor must use a bucket, can or whatever will suffice. When these become full, they are taken to the fiord or bay and emptied. The chore is generally assigned to one of the females.

Making the rounds of the village with Dr. Price and the government nurse, I came to a dark, foul-smelling little shack which had barely enough room for one sleeping shelf. Three human shapes were huddled together on this shelf when we entered, but on seeing us they stood up. My eyes, adjusting to the darkness, rested first on a boy whose well-proportioned body, delicate features and erect bearing made him beautiful, even by white standards. Next to him was his twenty-seven-year-old mother. Her withered face and bent frame looked as though she had been mummified. She had the appearance of having lived through seventy winters. Next to her lay a shy little girl whom we took to be three or four years old, but whose age was actually twelve. Like her mother, she had been dwarfed by malnutrition. The father and several brothers and sisters had been carried away by tuberculosis. This family lived in characteristic fashion, sharing the same bed, the same eating utensils and the same close air.

An Eskimo is never happy away from home and those with whom he has been brought up. Hence banishment from his village is the worst fate that can befall a member of the race. One would rather share tuberculosis with his kinfolk than leave them or be isolated. For this reason the defeat of the Eskimos' worst enemy—respiratory diseases—is complicated. The Danish government, with its system of hospitals and compulsory treatment, has been able to cope with the problem in Greenland with a fair measure of success. But in Alaska neither the territorial nor the Federal government has been able to bring adequate medical aid to the Eskimos.

At Meyoryuk I saw my first Alaskan kayak and appraised it in contrast to the Greenlandic model. Outstanding among differences is the broader beam and less delicate lines of the Alaskan boat. The Greenland kayak is longitudinally symmetrical, with the cockpit centered at the waist. On the other hand the Alaskan kayak is more rakish forward, with the cockpit located abaft the waist. The stern is blunt, and at the stem a built-in becket or ring is provided to facilitate hauling onto a beach.

Each type of kayak, however, is adapted to its own region. On the ragged coast of Greenland the craft must be lifted rather than dragged clear of the water. This would be far less convenient to the Alaskan Eskimo, who finds sandy beaches no obstacle to dragging his kayak by the stem. The Greenlander is generally well sheltered from heavy seas by the pack ice and network of deep fiords. He does not require the built-up foresection, as does the Alaskan, who hunts more frequently in unsheltered waters.

On the return trip to Cape Etolin, I resolved to take the long route along the beach rather than cross the tundra again. The wind, blowing onto a lee shore, kept the beach free of mosquitoes and gave us an opportunity to investigate some of the native graves which stretch along the margin of the shore zone. We made no attempt to molest these graves, nor was it necessary. In the manner characteristic of Eskimos in this part of Alaska the dead had been buried in crude caskets perched on poles near the ocean to enable the spirit of the deceased to watch the seal herd. The ancient graves had been collapsed by wave action undercutting the bank and the coffins broken open. Doubtless, many bodies had been washed into the sea. The bones resting in these old graves could be plainly seen without uncovering them. From a rough calculation of the erosional rate of the wave-cut cliff I concluded that the more antique graves were about 200 years old.

On the evening of June 29 we were speeding north over a smooth sea, bound for St. Michael after a brief call at Nash Harbor, which lies about thirty miles west of Cape Etolin.

On the bridge Lieutenant (j.g.) Russell, our navigator, leaned over a chart and indicated a neat little circle with a fine dot in the center. "Here we are at twenty hundred, Mr. Murray," Russell said to the relieving officer of the deck. "Course zero-zero-zero, speed eleven and a half knots. Take a look in the RPPI [remote radar repeater] and you can see the east end of St. Lawrence Island bearing about three-four-five. The watch has been relieved, the eight o'clock reports have been made and the captain has granted permission to strike eight bells."

Ensign John Murray peered into the radar repeater, turned a few dials and studied the picture on the scope. At length he raised his head, glanced around the horizon and then saluted Russell.

"I relieve you, sir," Murray said.

Russell turned down the ladder, hesitated, eyed his relief over his shoulder and said: "Water temperature's dropping. We ought to run into ice soon. Tell the captain when you sight it."

"But how will I recognize it?" Ensign Murray asked.

"Don't worry," the navigator declared. "You'll know it. If in doubt, send for me."

Within a quarter of an hour the officer of the deck was studying a halo which loomed across the horizon before him. Soon he made out a solid white wall beneath it and wondered how the *Northwind* would ever assail it. By the time I stood beside him, little fingers of water could be seen weaving among the broken floes. It was a fascinating sight, but the pungent odor of Russell's pipe dampened the charm.

"Shall I reduce speed now, sir?" Murray asked anxiously.

During his years as cadet at the U. S. Coast Guard Academy and subsequent service as an officer Murray had been saturated with the doctrine: "Avoid striking anything with the ship. If you *must* collide, make it a glancing blow."

Now the captain and his navigator shattered precedent by a sequence of curt advice: "No, goose 'er, Mr. Murray." ... "That's right, Mr. Murray, head smack between those two floes!" ... "No, no, Mr. Murray, don't strike that ice a glancing blow! Hit it square on! ... That's right! Now steady her!"

"But it's hard stuff," Murray pleaded.

"Wait until we get into the real polar ice," Russell remarked dryly. "This is only Bering Sea ice—sissy stuff. Yet you have to respect it. If you strike it a glancing blow as your schoolbooks say, you'll swing your stern into it, and there goes a propeller. Whenever possible, hit it square on, and you will either smash through it or push it clear."

The young ensign set his teeth and did as he was told. It did not take him long to grasp the idea. Before the watch was over he was enjoying the sensation of crushing the floes, seeing them part and watching huge slabs break off and topple noisily.

And I felt the *Northwind* was enjoying it, too. To every sailor his ship is an entity who shares the emotions of those who sail her. Now she was again in her element, doing the kind of thing she had been created to do.

At midnight Lieutenant (j.g.) Orville C. Hinnen relieved Murray, and before he had opportunity to try his skill at conning the ship in ice the vessel popped into open water. To me open water at this time was disappointing. We were entering Norton Sound, a shallow bay about a hundred miles long. Throughout its entire length we could carry no more than two or three fathoms of water under our keel. Because this basin is so shallow, huge waves can build up with slight provocation—a most unhealthy predicament for a deep-draft vessel. Large quantities of ice would have damped out such waves. But the barometer held steady, and there was Egg Island, near the head of Norton Sound, which would offer a lee of sorts.

Our immediate destination was St. Michael, seaport of the Yukon.

# Chapter 43

# THE GOLD COAST

IT IS ONLY natural that the sole semblance of a seaport near the mouth of the Yukon should become a base from which to exploit the resources along one of the longest rivers in the world. First there were the furs sought by the Russian-American Company. In 1833 a fort and trading post were built on the shores of the little bay from which a channel affords access to the Yukon River. The place was named Fort St. Michael.

For sixty-five years Fort St. Michael continued to exist as a quiet little village. Then in 1898 gold was discovered in the Klondike. The rush was on! There were two ways of reaching the new bonanza. One was to land at Skagway and endure the hardships of the Klondike trail. The other was to go by steamer to St. Michael, thence up the Yukon River to the gold fields. Because the latter approach was far easier, St. Michael mushroomed overnight to become the principal seaport in the Alaskan territory.

On July 29, 1900, the White Pass and Yukon Railway, connecting Skagway with the upper Yukon, was completed. This railroad cut off over 3,000 miles of the St. Michael route—and St. Michael along with it. Overnight the thriving port became a ghost town.

Today a score or so of silent buildings stand crumbling and ghostlike along an antique wooden sidewalk which winds across the tundra. Most of these buildings were saloons and dance halls which echoed the babble of voices, the shrill laughter of chorus girls and the hoarse cries of bewhiskered prospectors. On the beach, washed by the tides, lie three gaunt skeletons of palatial river steamers, the *Susie, Hannah* and *Louise*, Mississippi River-type steamboats—all that remain of a fleet of fifty which plied the 2,000-mile stretch of the Yukon during St. Michael's short-lived prosperity. There are still a number of steamboats in use on the upper Yukon and the Green River, one of its tributaries.

At one end of St. Michael the deserted, rotting houses of shrewd merchants who made their fortunes far from the upper reaches of the Yukon are now packed with 140 sickly natives. The conditions in which these natives live—in poverty and filth—was a shock to Dr. Price as he made his rounds. Nearly every native in the village was infected with tuberculosis! In spite of a high birth rate, at the present rate of decline of the native population St. Michael will be completely depopulated within the short span of fifty years.

A "ninety-eighter" who had remained after the receding tide of the gold rush walked with me to the rickety old dock which served as a boat landing. His parting words were: "We're all glad the Coast Guard is back. There's no doctor in town, and no dentist has been here for years. It's not too bad for the whites, because they can go to the doctor in Unakaleet, and there's a dentist in Nome, but the natives can't afford the trip to either place."

At midnight we sailed for the Seward Peninsula.

Had the Seward Peninsula been named "The Gold Coast," it would have connoted a literal meaning. Gold is transported in the sediments of streams which drain the interior and deposited on the beaches. This is particularly true of Anvil Creek, which empties into Norton Sound at Cape Nome. Here was sounded the cry of "Gold!" which in 1899 drew a cosmopolitan crowd of 10,000 prospectors.

Certainly Nature never intended man to build a city on bleak Cape Nome. It requires little imagination to conceive of the chaos wrought by dumping so many adventurers onto a morass where weather is nasty and mosquitoes merciless. In a place so ill-prepared to receive them lawlessness might have decimated a large percentage of the population but for the timely arrival of the Coast Guard cutter *Bear* with her armed bluejackets.

Today Nome is the metropolis of northwestern Alaska, with a

resident population of 1,500, most of whom are whites. While it has plank sidewalks, graveled streets and all conveniences, many buildings are warped by alternate freezing and thawing of the soil on which they rest.

We arrived off Nome on the morning of July 4 after calls at Elim and Golovnin on the southeast side of Seward Peninsula. It was a cheerless day with a sleety rain driven by a brisk southerly wind spreading a deep haze over the blurred outline of buildings.

"By the deep eight!" The leadsman's report told us we were a mile off the Coast Guard lookout tower and close enough to shore—too close if the wind should increase. It was time to anchor.

A few minutes after anchoring I could see a motor surfboat leaping and plowing into the seas which swept into the inner harbor between jetties. This would be the crew of the Nome Coast Guard station fetching our mail to us. My own men stood on deck, watching every heaving motion of the boat as it struggled toward us. Mail was uppermost in their minds—as it is with all men and boys away from home.

The boat came alongside. A lone seaman in glistening wet oilskins cut the motor, scrambled forward and cast the painter to our deck.

"Swede!" a crew member shouted at the boatman. "What did you do that you had to come to Nome?"

"Cayse! You old river rat!" the boatman flung back. "Why did you get kicked off your old side-wheeler?"

Neither question was answered. James Cayse, our chief boatswain's mate asked another—one I might have asked. "Where's the rest of your crew, Johnson?"

"I'm it!" Johnson replied. "I'm captain, cook and crew. It's really a good job, Jim. Now if it wasn't for the rescue business, the housekeeping, the radio and the damned paper work, I'd lead the life of Riley." Nome lifesaving station had enjoyed a complement of an officer and eight men. Lean postwar years had trimmed it to a one-man crew.

Several sacks of mail were hoisted on board, and I had the boat ordered away. I did not like the looks of the weather. The barometer was falling fast and the wind plainly on the make-up. I must get under way and claw off this lee shore into deeper water.

By noon the wind was howling, and even at slow speed the *North-wind's* bows were scooping up tons of green water which burst into spray against the forward turret and was blown over the vessel's entire length. I had read in the *Alaskan Coast Pilot* that in heavy southerly winds deep-draft vessels at anchor in Nome roadstead usually seek shelter behind Sledge Island, about twenty-five miles west of Nome. I recalled having read of the *Bear* riding out a hurricane behind that island in 1913.

The hurricane of 1913 had severely damaged Nome. Raging seas had uprooted the cemetery and washed away many coffins. It is said that an old prospector returned to his hut after the weather moderated and found an open coffin at his very doorstep. He peered inside. It contained the remains of a dance-hall queen named Goldie, who had died nearly a decade before. The "ninety-eighter" shook his head sadly and said: "Goldie, you're still the best-lookin' gal in town!"

I laid course for Sledge Island and, as we drew near the bight on the north side, began sounding our way cautiously to an anchorage in the approximate center.

"Mark seven!" the leadsman shouted.

Lieutenant (j.g.) Robert I. Price, who had the deck, reached for the control handles and threw them astern to check headway.

At this point the vessel lurched violently. The bows rose slightly to a swell that backlashed in the bight. The forefoot settled with a terrific jolt. The bows rose again—and the ship backed clear.

The damage-control party flew into action. It found water spouting into the forward shaft alley through a neat, round hole about the size of a dinner plate. The compartment, which was of no consequence because of its small size, was quickly blanked off and shored.

I concluded that the flat keel had been punctured by a needlelike submarine pinnacle. My ardor for Sledge Island was cooled, and the *Northwind* again put to sea.

The wind moderated on July 5, and we returned to Nome, loaded Army freight and passengers, then sailed for St. Lawrence Island, 120 miles in a west-southwesterly direction from Nome and only twenty miles from Siberia.

The St. Lawrence Eskimo is clearly Siberian and appears to differ from the Nunivak. It may be recalled that an Eskimo will never travel out of sight of land if he can avoid it. From Gambell, our first village, we could see the bold Siberian mainland.

Adherence of the St. Lawrence Islanders to Siberian culture is reflected in their manner of living and traditional beliefs. The Asiatic influence can be seen in a few of the older houses. These huts consist of walrus hide draped over a circular framework, lashed down by strips of reindeer hide. Although most of Gambell's 260 inhabitants are Presbyterians (there are also a few Seventh Day Adventists), there are some who retain a half-belief in the legends of their forefathers. In one of the old-style houses I visited there was a wood-carved totem, along with magazines and mail-order catalogues.

In general the health of Gambell is good. Hygienic conditions here probably stem from the regard of the Presbyterian missionaries for such matters, the presence of a government nurse and the isolation of the settlement from exploitation by white men.

Natives at Gambell live chiefly by hunting and ivory carving. The latter craft is highly developed because of the abundance of walrus which thrive about the island in the winter. But walrus ivory is not the only kind used by St. Lawrence Islanders. They also have what the natives call "rotten ivory," which they dig out of the soil in the summer—when it is not frozen. This ivory is the fossil tusks of woolly mammoths which roamed over St. Lawrence Island during the last glacial age, more than 25,000 years ago.

The landing craft, returning from Gambell to our anchorage, had an armada of skin boats in tow. They were filled with natives who sought to sell carved ivory on board the *Northwind*. However a few of them were patients whom Jimmy Otiyohok, the native dentist, was fetching to the ship.

Jimmy had learned dentistry in the *Northland* when she was under the command of Commander (now Vice Admiral, USCG) E. D. Jones in the late 1920's. While Gambell could not support the full-time services of a dentist, Commander Jones conceived the idea of training a likely young native in first aid and dentistry. Jimmy was intelligent and ambitious, and he wanted the opportunity. He was taken on board the *Northland* and trained as a dental assistant while the vessel was on an Arctic cruise. When Jimmy had received sufficient instruction to carry on by himself the commander left a portable dental unit in his care. Otiyohok is still signed for it.

Dr. Braye inspected Jimmy's work, gave it his professional blessing and treated only the cases which required dental surgery.

In the meantime the natives were scattered over the deck with ivory spread out on display before them. The sailors enjoyed passing from trader to trader, appraising their wares and making an occasional purchase. Like Greenlanders, these natives were reluctant to establish a price. The customer must initiate the bargaining, and the trader scrupulously avoids "high pressure" in making a sale. In Greenland sales must be made in the presence of a Danish official, and transactions are in cash, but in Alaska cigarettes or other commodities of negotiable value may be used as a medium of exchange.

Snus Jensen, who stood apart, his pockets abulge with cans of Copenhagen snuff, appeared to be unhappy about something. His face brightened when Jimmy came over and greeted him warmly.

"What's the matter, Snus?" Jimmy asked.

"Someone's wised up the natives here, Jimmy," Snus grumbled. "I used to get some pretty fancy ivory for a few cans of snuff. You can't even get an ivory toothpick for it no more."

"We got a co-operative now, Snus," Jimmy replied. "Eskimos run the trading post, and we fix our prices. The Alaskan Native Service sees that everybody gets a fair deal."

"Well, I'll take the good old days," Snus complained. "A sharp man could make a lot of dough on these cruises, but now he can't make a dime."

Jimmy laughed and gave Snus a slap on the shoulder, and soon the Dane was chuckling with him.

We sailed for Savonga the following day. This village is the second largest on St. Lawrence Island and is located about thirty miles east of Gambell. Our surfboat scooted through the breakers of a heavy surf which pounded a sandy stretch of beach near the village. Everyone in Savonga had assembled there to meet us, thinking their "soldier umiak, big, white" (man-of-war) *Northland* had at last returned. They seemed much surprised when I told them that this was the *Northwind*, which had come to take the *Northland's* place.

Savonga is a village of frame houses, most of which are in a remarkably good state of preservation. In many ways they reminded me of the neat, wooden houses of Greenlanders in the larger settlements. The houses were tidy and clean inside, and the natives were clean, healthy and neatly dressed. Miss Olive Matthews, the government nurse, pointed out only seven cases of t.b. in the entire village, and these were well isolated. Quantities of walrus meat, suspended on racks here and there throughout Savonga, brought a smile of satisfaction to Dr. Braye. It was clear to the dental officer that a walrus diet would minimize demands for his professional services.

Wherever we trudged we were surrounded by a score of boys who appeared to be between the ages of seven and fourteen. A like number of giggling girls, all of them robust, comely and in the bloom of health, trailed along a discreet distance behind.

I showed the children some American games, which they joined, shyly at first, but enthusiastically as we played on. When it was time to return to the *Northwind* the children begged me not to go.

"Why can't they play without us?" I asked Mrs. Williams, the schoolteacher's wife.

She replied that the children like to play games but have no initiative in organizing sports. "The children have given you a name," Mrs. Williams added. "It will probably stick with you wherever you go among Alaskan Eskimos. You are called 'The-man-who-walks-with-the-springy-legs!' "

Eskimos love to bestow descriptive names on persons and things. To do this they join their nouns, verbs and adjectives into one complex word.

I had heard persistent mention among St. Lawrence Islanders of a person known as "The-woman-who-walks-and-acts-like-a-man." I wondered what sort of woman she was.

# Chapter 44

# CLIFF-DWELLING ESKIMOS

I MET "The-woman-who-walks-and-acts-like-a-man" at Nome.

The *Northwind* anchored again in the Nome roadstead on July 10. I was determined to push north as soon as possible, but decided to delay our departure until midnight to give the crew a liberty and to have dinner with Judge and Mrs. Joseph Kehoe.

The Kehoes' party was formal. One of the guests was introduced as Miss Mildred Keaton, but the others called her "Buster." She was tall, slender and graceful, with a youthful face beneath well-groomed gray hair. Her personality was charming and buoyant, and her conversation reflected a wealth of knowledge about Alaska.

During the evening Judge Kehoe explained to me aside that "Buster" Keaton was known among the Eskimos as "The-woman-who-walks-and-acts-like-a-man." So this was she! The name, I thought, was quite incongruous with her feminine bearing.

The judge went on to say that Miss Keaton was commonly known as the "Dog-drivingest, hard-bittenest, cigar-smokingest, best doggone person in Alaska." This was a reputation she had earned in more than twenty-five years' service as a U. S. government nurse in Alaska. She had sledged from village to village across northern Alaska, bringing medical care to Eskimos throughout the trackless wastes. Usually she traveled alone, save for her dogs and stalking wolves. In her official capacity she had made several cruises to Point Barrow in the *Northland.*

347

Miss Keaton was now retired from active duty in the U. S. Public Health Service. The judge suggested that she would be a valuable asset to us on our way to Barrow because she knew the natives and they knew and respected her. Moreover she spoke their language fluently.

I thought a *nurse* with these qualifications was exactly what we needed. But there was the matter of regulations. "The book" forbids the presence of a female on board a Coast Guard cutter overnight without the permission of the commandant. I pondered whether or not to send a dispatch, but discarded the idea. I was afraid the answer would be "NO!" So I decided to act first and ask questions afterward.

When I asked Miss Keaton if she would like to sail with us and carry out the same duties she had had in the *Northland* her answer was a question: "When do we sail?" .

"Midnight," I replied. I looked at my watch and added, "It is only an hour from now, but we will hold on until you are ready."

"Fiddle," Buster exclaimed disdainfully. "I'll excuse myself and meet you at the Coast Guard station in forty-five minutes."

Smenton and I arrived at the Coast Guard station at 11:45 to find Miss Keaton drinking coffee with Snus Jensen. I had to look twice to recognize her. She wore Army OD trousers with the legs tucked into shoepacks and had on a woolen Army shirt. Her parka was draped over the arm of a chair, and on it rested a little canvas bag.

"When will the rest of your luggage be coming down?" I asked.

"What luggage, Captain?" Buster demanded brusquely. "Snus knows I never traveled around with hatboxes and wardrobe trunks. Everything I need is either on my back or in here." She patted the canvas bag.

Buster politely refused Commander Smenton's offer of assistance and sprang into the boat with the agility of a sailor. I thought: *This is indeed "The-woman-who-walks-and-acts-like-a-man"—and the Eskimos might have added "—and-talks-like-a-man."*

The *Northwind* hove her anchor at midnight and shaped course for King Island.

King Island is a mere basalt rock one mile square which rises abruptly to an elevation of nearly 800 feet. The shore is bold, the cliffs and slopes steep and the top domed so gently that it is virtually a plateau. The unique thing about this island is the village, where about 140 natives live. The village straddles a little creek which cascades down from the south edge of the table top. The houses are built on a haphazard array of platforms which are supported by high poles. They are laid out in tiers, one above the other, in such a manner as to suggest the homes of cliff dwellers. A hodgepodge of ladders and catwalks connect the various huts from the schoolhouse near the shore to the neat little white church hundreds of feet above.

On the morning of our arrival a heavy, frothy sea lashed the rocks below the village. A dense fog hung over the island, veiling everything except the lowermost tier of buildings. It was impossible to land at the village. I took the motor surfboat in close to shore and spoke through an electronic megaphone to a group of natives who had gathered on a patch of snow.

"We will meet you on the other side of the island," I shouted.

The Eskimos waved an acknowledgment and raced off to fetch their families and their ivory.

By the time we made anchorage on the northwest side of King Island the natives, young and old, had gathered near the water's edge and were waiting for our boats. It is hard to understand how they could cross this rugged island so quickly. Many women brought infants on their backs in the deep hoods of their parkas.

The decks soon swarmed with the entire population of King Island, except for the very aged who were too weak to climb over the mountain. Miss Keaton soon proved her efficiency in organizing medical and dental treatment. To the crew the novelty of seeing Eskimos was beginning to wear off, but the men were interested in the exquisite carved ivory the King Islanders had for sale.

Like St. Lawrence Island, King Island contains many fossil tusks, which are confined to a small area on the dome. The natives ingeniously etch their carvings by inserting bits of fossil ivory stained green by olivine deposits. Whalebone is also used to color the etched lines in ivory.

Whenever possible I made a practice of inviting the chief or principal citizen of each village to have a sandwich and coffee with me in my cabin. When I asked the chief of King Island he hedged and explained that his party had just been swept into power by a recent election. The old chief was on board and was entitled to the same social prestige as the new chief. I sent for the old chief, and they both eagerly accepted my invitation. Even bleak King Island is not free of politics.

We arrived at Teller on the Seward Peninsula not far from King Island early on the morning of July 13. I was glad to anchor in Port Clarence Bay, on which Teller is situated. This is an almost land-locked basin with good holding ground—our first sheltered port since leaving Adak.

The day was crisp and cheerful. I stood on the quarter-deck and watched the crew clear away and lower boats. Miss Keaton announced that she would take Dr. Price to Imuruk Basin on the Mary River about twenty-five miles inland from Teller. She explained that, now the salmon-fishing season was in full swing, natives from all over the peninsula would be congregated there to fish. Doubtless some would be in need of medical attention.

I told Buster she could use the Greenland cruiser for the trip.

"The Greenland cruiser is too deep and slow," the nurse said. "We will commandeer Father Tom Cunningham's skiff when we get ashore."

"How do you know you'll find Father Tom and his skiff at Teller?" I asked.

"Captain," Buster answered, "everyone on the peninsula knows where *you* are, where *I* am and where Father Tom is. The only thing we don't ask is *why*."

In the evening Father Tom Cunningham's skiff hove into sight, towing a skin boat filled with nine natives. Buster sprang up the accommodation ladder and announced: "We'll have two surgical cases tonight."

It was 3:00 A.M. before the patients were treated and surgery completed. At 7:00 A.M. the doctor and nurse went to the village to round up the local patients. They worked on these, together with another batch from Imuruk, until 8.00 P.M. Dr. Price was obviously weary, but Miss Keaton was still going strong.

"She's twice as old as I am," Dr. Price' muttered sadly.

When the *Northwind* sailed out of Port Clarence that night she carried an additional passenger—Irving Newell, Ph.D., associate professor of biology at the University of Oregon. Dr. Newell was under an Office of Naval Research contract to study marine *mites* for the Arctic Institute of North America.

I sensed that word was already flying about the ship that another crackpot scientist was on board. But to me Dr. Newell was a welcome asset to the oceanographic information I was striving to collect. I felt that each minute sea creature was virtually a tiny drift bottle when properly classified by a biologist. They would serve as a check on my faltering physical oceanographic investigations.

The next stop on our agenda was Cape Prince of Wales, near the westernmost tip of the Seward Peninsula. Here I was treated to my first ride in an umiak, or skin boat. Because our surfboats could not slide over the offshore bar, we were obliged to wade, waist deep, the remaining distance to the beach. I decided to ride back to the ship with a group of Eskimos who were going out for medical treatment.

Natives poured into the umiak until I counted twenty-nine women and seven men. I thought the boat would surely sink under such a load. The men chattered about something, and I believed they were trying to decide who must remain behind. But it turned out they were waiting for three more passengers—all women who carried babes in their parka hoods.

The umiak was launched. As it met each breaker the bows were tossed upward, causing the craft alternately to sag and hog at the waist. It seemed that the skin boat would surely break in half. But none of the Eskimos were in the least perturbed. When the umiak reached the bar the men shipped their paddles, jumped out and pushed the boat into the deeper water beyond. At this point the romance of the ride ended. The native who had held the steering paddle lowered an outboard motor over the stern and spun it a few times. The motor purred, and the umiak leaped ahead.

*The machine age has gone too far,* I told myself.

In the late afternoon we sailed for Little Diomede.

The Diomede Islands consist, properly, of a chain of three barren, rocky islets which stretch like stepping stones across Bering Strait. The largest and most western is Big Diomede, about three miles long and one mile wide. It lies on the Russian side of Bering Strait and is 1,759 feet in abrupt elevation from the water. Its sister island, Little

Diomede, is about half as large. It is separated from Big Diomede by less than two miles of strait.

Little Diomede, though 500 feet lower than Big Diomede, is no less rugged than the Siberian island. Viewed from a distance, it resembles in profile the back of a gigantic, spiny dinosaur. The neural parts are enormous, jagged rocks. Because there is very little mantle on the island, vegetation is almost entirely lacking.

Vitus Bering discovered and named the Diomedes on St. Diomede's Day, August 16, 1725. Fifty-three years later the intrepid Captain Cook visited the islands and recognized their geographical significance as the boundary between two hemispheres. On the straits in which they lie he generously bestowed the name "Bering."

From our anchorage between the two Diomedes, we could see the little village nestled on the lower slope near the north end of the American island. A narrow, cobblestone-paved street forms the principal thoroughfare and links a system of stairs. These stairs serve the upper dwellings and the white Catholic church which stands at the highest point of the village. This little church is the seat of Father Cunningham's parish. Here he ministers to the natives' spiritual needs and shares their hardy life of hunting seal, walrus and auks.

Auks form a material part of the Diomedans' diet, for the island abounds with hundreds of thousands of these little birds. They live among the sharp rocks which cover the sides of the island. To take them, Eskimos cast nets over a bevy with unerring skill. The meat of auks is quite palatable, and their skins are used in making parkas.

The Little Diomedans are closely related to the Big Diomedans. Until a few years ago the natives on both sides of the strait maintained constant communication with one another, but now a Soviet military outpost on the Russian island forbids intercourse between the two Diomedes. This is a restriction the natives cannot understand and one which the American Eskimos learned the hard way after being placed under arrest by the Soviet authorities. On this occasion Father Cunningham used his persuasive powers on the Russians and secured the natives' release without having to resort to diplomatic channels.

Mr. Heinricks, the schoolmaster, led us to a hut which we entered through a tunnel. Notwithstanding the stench of burning seal oil, the hut was remarkably clean. I noticed the sleeping shelves were spread around the perimeter of the single room in Siberian style. A withered old woman was scrubbing the floor. Save for a few words in Eskimo, spoken to Mr. Heinricks, she appeared not to heed our presence.

"This old woman is completely blind," the schoolmaster declared. "Thirty years ago she was a girl of striking beauty—the belle of the village. She had marriage proposals from three white men, one of them wealthy and handsome, yet she spurned them all to marry a native. Probably it was just as well."

I remembered that blindness is common among elderly Eskimos. Doubtless this accounts for the practice so prevalent until a few years ago of casting away the aged and infirm. It was customary to lead these poor souls to a secluded spot outside the village, where they were left to die of cold and starvation. Barbarous as the custom appears, it served Eskimo economic needs. Food is seldom plentiful among them, and the aged could only consume without being able to produce. The Eskimo reasoned it was far better to feed his children, who had a useful career ahead of them. This fate of the aged was one they accepted as inevitable with complete understanding and complacency.

On the mountainside beyond the village outskirts I stumbled upon an ancient burial place. It was evident that driftwood is scarce on the Diomedes, for only the more recent remains were encased in coffins It was formerly customary to inter the deceased beneath huge slabs of flat rock without benefit of casket. Through the interstices I could plainly see skeletons which peered vacantly upward. Weapons and other favorite possessions of the natives were deposited in orderly array beside them. Coffins, a post-nineteenth-century luxury, were likewise deposited among the huge rocks.

Beside each of the modern graves is a smaller casket which contains the possessions the deceased may require in the spirit world. Even inanimate objects have a spirit. Eskimos reason that the spirits of spears, knives and other objects necessary to hunt seal should accompany the dead on their journey into the beyond.

There seemed to be a consistency in the orientation of these graves in that the bodies were laid out normal to the shore line. But I noticed that within the past decade it had become a practice to plant the head toward the mountain, while earlier graves had the head-marker toward the sea. I later asked Miss Keaton the reason for this incongruity.

Buster's answer was prefaced by hearty laughter. She confessed that she had been responsible for this reversal of tradition and explained how it came about.

One day a few years ago Miss Keaton attended the funeral of a great hunter. Immediately after the casket was covered with rocks and stones the nurse asked innocently: "Why did you bury him with his head to the sea?"

"So he keep watch over seal herd, Woman-who-walks-and-acts-like-a-man," a spokesman replied.

"Can a man see out of the top of his head?" the nurse inquired.

"No," came the answer.

"Then he should be buried with his feet toward the sea so he can see across them to the waters beyond," Miss Keaton commented.

This remark puzzled the Eskimos. They paused, then plunged into a heated discussion. At length they seemed to reach an accord and, disinterring the coffin, swung it through a semicircle, lowered it, then heaped rocks on it again.

The *Northwind* sailed from Little Diomede on July 16 and came to Shishmaref the following morning.

Shishmaref is situated on the north central shore of Seward Peninsula. Here we made one of those wretched offshore anchorages in a strong, northeasterly wind which drove biting sleet over ugly, licking seas. I begrudged having to call at this village, but it had no medical facilities, so we could ill afford to pass it by.

I went ashore with the rest of our party to investigate the feasibility of discontinuing the Coast Guard light during the frozen winter months. This mission naturally led me to Mr. George Goshaw. George was commissioner, postmaster, light keeper, justice of the peace, mayor and U. S. deputy marshal. On top of this he ran the local trading post.

"Winter's when we need the light most, Captain," Goshaw declared. "Folks use it as a beacon to home on while sledging. You might still call it an aid to navigation, because they sledge on Shishmaref Bay when it's frozen, and that's navigation, isn't it?" George continued without waiting for an answer. "Big ships never come close enough to see the light in the summer because this stretch of coast is bad. Now take weather like we have here today—why, a northeast wind always carries the water away from the coast and——"

My mind flashed back to the *Northland* . . . Walrus Island . . . the movement of particles relative to the wind . . . Corioli's force. A northeast wind would push the water offshore—out from under the *Northwind's* keel!

"Toll the bell!" I interrupted. "I've got to round up my party and get back to the ship at once!"

The surfboat splashed alongside the heaving icebreaker. I rushed to the bridge and felt the ship quiver as her stern settled in the trough. Russell had the deck. He had already hove up the anchor, and the engines were churning astern. The ship failed to budge. We were obviously aground!

I realized with alarm that the wind was increasing. If we didn't get the *Northwind* off the shoal, she would soon be pounded to pieces! "Goose 'er, Russ!" I ordered.

"I am, Captain," Russell replied.

"Then reverse your engines," I yelled. "Goose 'er ahead."

Russell obeyed, shoved the control handles forward and motioned the leadsman to cast ahead. The lead flew out—beyond the bow. The ship failed to creep up to the line. The leadsman cast an appealing glance toward the bridge.

"Keep your engines full ahead," I warned the OOD.

"Fathometer still does not register, sir!" a quartermaster reported. I wished the man wouldn't remind me of it. But, after all, the ship's routine must go on.

A series of onrushing breakers, larger than their fellows, spilled their crests against the bows. I felt the decks swell upward as each wave struck. The ship struggled ahead a few fathoms, then settled with a violent jolt. I wondered if our bottom could take it. Four times the ship was lifted high and bashed onto the sea bed. Then we were free.

Our course was laid for Kotzebue Sound. I left the bridge, feeling glad the medical party had finished its work at Shishmaref. I had no yen to return.

Then through a PA outlet the screech of a boatswain's call was followed by an announcement:

"Now hear this! The uniform of the day for lowly ice worms is dress hats, long underwear and Arctic boots!"       .

We were about to cross the Arctic Circle. To be a Polar Bear an ice worm must undergo the same kind of ordeal as a pollywog who crosses the equator to become a Shellback.

# Chapter 45

# INTO THE ARCTIC

THE Arctic coast of 'Alaska is generally flat and monotonous, with low bluffs fronting the ocean shore. In places, north of Cape Lisburne, veins of coal are exposed where the sea has carried away the overlying mantle. (The Revenue cutters *Corwin* and *Thetis* mined their own steaming coal from these outcrops in order to extend the scope of their operations north of the Arctic Circle.)

Coastal navigation is made hazardous by catastrophic shoaling. Every year ice crowds against the coast and builds up to such a thickness that it presses deeply into the sea bed. In this manner the bottom sands and gravel are pushed about and redeposited in such an unpredictable pattern that hydrographic data changes radically from year to year. Charts and sailing directions are therefore unreliable.

When we dropped anchor in the middle of Kotzebue Sound on the early morning of July 18 it was as smooth as a millpond. The LCVP had no more than begun its fifteen-mile trip to Kotzebue when a northwest wind began to blow into the sound. Because the waters were shallow, heavy seas made up quickly. They commenced breaking over the eight-fathom depths in which we were anchored. The craft was hastily recalled, and we lost no time getting under way. Before the *Northwind* reached the open sea and deeper water, her bottom was beginning to slump onto the sea bed each time she sank into the trough.

The voyage from Kotzebue to Point Barrow was marked by consistently bad weather which made navigation a nightmare and boating miserable. With the exception of our first two points of call, Kivilina

357

and Point Hope, all anchorages were made on lee shores. Because the wind was apt to moderate by night, there was a continuity of activity which blended days and nights into a dreary, diurnal whole that lasted nearly a week.

Day or night, whenever weather conditions permitted surf landing, we sent our boats ashore. In the raw cold, rain, snow and sleet everyone worked with a cheerfulness that spoke well for his sportsmanship and devotion to duty. But the weather which made the voyage difficult was also keeping the ice clear of the coast—especially at Point Lay and Wainwright. As Snus aptly put it: "It's an ill wind that doesn't dry somebody's breeches!"

Long before the ship reached Point Barrow the natives had lost their dramatic appeal to my crew. Monotony made each village a repetition of the one before and stripped it of glamour. Settlements became an incubus of smelly huts, of grinning men, of women climbing the steep accommodation ladder with babes in their parka hoods, of giggling teen-age girls and curious children who followed us about the village like shadows.

As the *Northwind* pushed northward her popularity snowballed. Children looked forward to the ice cream they were sure to receive. Adults were eager to see the movies, though unable to understand the words. Dr. Braye's reputation sped northward before him. Word flew from village to village that it was no ordeal to undergo dentistry in his chair. This was no exaggeration. Dr. Braye treated the most humble of natives in the same gentle manner he would a wealthy dowager on the point of making her will. It is little wonder one Eskimo girl was heard to remark: "I hope I have something wrong with my teeth next year, too."

The activity of Dr. Newell, on the other hand, was beginning to arouse widespread interest among the crew. He used a dredge to scrape fauna off the bottom and plankton nets to catch floating life. Each haul he made brought men flocking aft to the oceanographic wench. The "Professor," as everyone now called Dr. Newell, always took pains to describe the creatures and tell something of their life cycle. Many of our seamen soon took pride in being able to classify marine organisms.

The *Northwind* arrived at Point Barrow on July 23 in a driving snowstorm. Shore-fast ice, stretching along the coast, jutted out a distance of a mile or more. Between Wainwright and beyond Point Barrow only one void in this ice wall showed on our radar. It, luckily, was immediately off the U. S. naval station a few miles northeast of Barrow village. We entered this ice-walled harbor and secured with ice anchors.

Point Barrow lies about fifteen miles northeast of the naval station. It is fringed with treacherous shoals and shifting bars with heavy, compact ice, but when summer breakup comes shore-fast ice remains anchored to shoals to mark them until it, too, is broken loose and swept offshore.

The principal mission of the U. S. naval station at Barrow was to collect Arctic scientific information. The Office of Naval Research maintained a huge, well-equipped laboratory there. During our visit the station was under the direction of Dr. Laurence Irving. Dr. Irving had earned degrees in medicine as well as in basic sciences. He was well qualified for his post by reason of temperament and personality. To stimulate interest among his colleagues he held a seminar every night.

The night of our arrival Dr. Newell and I attended this seminar. The lecturer of the evening was an eminent authority on blood typing and nutrition, Dr. V. Levine.

"... and so you will find," Dr. Levine concluded his lecture, "Eskimo blood is either type A or type B. If the subject's blood is of any other type, he is not an Eskimo!"

Immediately after the lecture I asked Dr. Levine if he would be kind enough to show me how blood typing was done. His consent showed both enthusiasm and delight.

"First," the scientist explained, "I will show you how type A or B blood reacts to the reagent we use." He drew a drop of blood from a vial and spread it on a slide. Then he added his reagent and placed the slide under a microscope. "Now look into the microscope," Levine directed. "You will see the blood turn color."

I looked—but nothing happened.

Dr. Levine saw that I was perplexed. He bent over the microscope. "Well, now, that's odd," the doctor declared. "This blood is type O. Wait! I'll get a sample that *is* Eskimo blood!"

Dr. Levine tried another sample and repeated the process. The result was the same—type O.

"The third try is always successful," said the doctor, laughing. "This one is sure to be Eskimo blood."

It was type O. So were the fourth and fifth samples.

Dr Levine was growing more and more embarrassed. After the fifth experiment he jumped to his feet and exclaimed, "Damn! All I can say is, there's a *white man* in the woodpile!"

This last statement was a half-truth. In 1875 a schooner manned by a Negro crew was wrecked near Point Barrow. The survivors sought refuge in the village, and it was several years before they could be evacuated. But this was not the sole contributing factor to the mingling of blood at Point Barrow. Charlie Brower, a white man, established a trading post at Point Barrow in 1885. During a regime which lasted more than fifty years he became a sort of patriarch in a filial as well as a temporal sense. But Charlie was a wise ruler, and throughout his lifetime Barrow village prospered.*

After Brower's death his suzerainty passed to his competent, though less forceful, college-educated, half-caste, legitimate sons. Perhaps if Charlie were still alive, an economic crisis which now faces the village might have been averted.

This problem was expressed to me by one of the village elders. He summed it up this way: "Our sons work for Navy. Get much money. Too much money no good for Eskimo. Our sons no learn hunt. Someday Navy get white man work or maybe Navy go way. Then Eskimo get no money. Him no get seal, no whale, no walrus. Him starve!"

The old man referred to the employment of the young men of the village by the Navy at the wage scale established by the government—the fabulous sum of $5,000 a year. That this money was not always invested wisely by the native workers is reflected in a story which persists at Barrow.

A worker ordered a shipment of twelve cases of canned pineapple, so the report ran. When the pineapple arrived the worker opened the cases, removed the labels from the cans, plastered them on his

* *Fifty Years Below Zero* by Charles Brower.

walls and discarded the remainder of the shipment.

We remained at Barrow until the medical and dental requirements of both naval personnel and natives had been satisfied. It was now July 29, and I was anxious to push into the Beaufort Sea and work the north coast of Alaska. We knew this, particularly Oliktok Point, was a mecca for natives from the interior who flocked to the coast to fish. A plane which had flown in from Point Simpson early in the day reported the coast ice-free that far, at least.

At 6:00 A.M., July 30, I sailed for Point Simpson. Our plan was to make oceanographic investigations along the fifty-fathom curve on the north coast. Dr. Laurence Irving was interested in our mission and accompanied us as guest observer.

We had no difficulty following the fifty-fathom curve because a southeasterly wind held the ice well off the coast. At noon we were off Point Simpson. I observed the wind haul abruptly to the westward. This was bad! It would pack the ice close to shore! I ordered two more engines on the line, reversed course and made haste to get out of the Beaufort Sea.

The wind increased to a howl, and a heavy snowfall closed the visibility to less than one mile. Soon the ice was upon us—an enormous field which seemed to be endless. Moreover this ice was hard and had the color of weak coffee. It had obviously formed during the winter along the north coast of Alaska, where rivers discharge tons of sediment into the Beaufort Sea.

By 2:00 P.M. the fathometer was clicking off twenty fathoms! It was plain that the field along which we raced was forcing the *Northwind* into shallow water! I hoped any minute to find a lead through which we could work offshore, but there was none. An hour later, soundings had dropped to ten fathoms, and they decreased rapidly to eight fathoms! The stern was already beginning to squat.

I turned over in my mind the idea of blasting a hole into which we could jam the ship, but discarded the notion. It would take too much time. Then through the haze I saw—or thought I saw—a lead. A few more propeller beats confirmed it. A narrow, ribbonlike shadow wound northward until it was swallowed by the haze. Without waiting for orders Hinnen, who had the deck, headed for it.

Presently we crashed into a brash-filled crack which separated the

forty-two-mile-long hunk of ice that had threatened us from the adjacent field. Prying first one way, then another, we worked along
slowly until the channel began to widen and tiny pools of water peeked
through the brash and slush which covered it.

Throughout the afternoon and night we battled it out with the ice.
At 6:30 A.M., July 31, we reached our mooring off Barrow.

Our ice anchor was barely planted before we received dispatch
orders to return to the Bering Sea without delay. This, of course,
meant I must cancel my plans for bringing medicine and law to the
natives along the north coast of Alaska.

In telling my officers and Miss Keaton about this change in our
itinerary I added lightly that there would be no marriages this trip.
The north-coast natives would have to live in sin for at least another
year.

"That's no joke, Captain," the nurse commented. "About twenty
years ago some well-meaning citizens heard about illicit cohabitation
among Eskimos in the far north. They became alarmed that such li-
centiousness should exist under the American flag and put the heat on
the government to stop it—and quick-like!"

Miss Keaton went on to say it would be difficult to explain the
institution of the wedding ceremony to Eskimos who had never heard
of such a thing. But she had an idea and got a justice of the peace to
sign a ream of blank marriage certificates. When winter came she
took the certificates with her and began her dog-sledge rounds of
northern Alaska. All along her route she filled the certificates with
appropriate names and peddled them to unwed cohabitants. On her
return to Nome after her journey Miss Keaton reported that there
were no natives of opposite sex living together who did not have duly
executed certificates to prove their marital status.

Sailing from Barrow into a sea which was covered with close-
packed floes of old ice, I recalled there was still one more job to be
done. Sea ice had never been sampled and analyzed below the three-
meter layer (about ten feet). I had a scheme for sampling ice much
deeper.

At length the vessel plunged into an ice lake. Several floes of heavy
polar ice were drifting from windward to leeward in this lake. Se-
lecting one, I relieved the deck and put the ship into a full charge at

the ice. The *Northwind* crashed into the left end of the floe, with full right rudder applied at the proper instant. The ice split under the impact, and the shaved-off portion plunged beneath the surface and emerged with a roar as tons of water poured off the top. A full cross-section was exposed.

The crew, no doubt, thought the old man had at last gone completely ice-happy. And when I boarded the floe fragment and began chipping samples at the four and eight-meter layers the sailors probably shook their heads and concluded that the skipper, like his ice, was "cracked." Samples of chipped-off ice were stored in the ship's refrigeration compartment for future analysis.*

Throughout the night we battled our way westward, where I hoped we would find a favorable lead, clear of the ice which crowded the coast. But none was found until noon, August 1, nineteen hours after we left Barrow. The navigator fixed the ship's position and found we had made good only nine miles offshore. We had been swept twenty-one miles farther from our destination during the night!

The next day it became clear why we had been ordered back to the Bering Sea. I was asked by Rear Admiral J. E. Stika, to whom I was immediately responsible, if we could step up our schedule and make rendezvous with Governor Ernest Gruening at Ketchikan on September 1. Knowing this mission was one of considerable importance, I replied in the affirmative.

In the Aleutians a heavy logistic program awaited us which I had hoped to accomplish in two months. Now we must carry out the task in two weeks.

There would be landings at Theodore Point, Attu; at Sarichef and Scotch Cap. These would be hazardous and difficult under heavy conditions of sea and surf. Then there would be numerous bays and harbors to enter in fog and darkness. But somehow I felt we would be successful.

To the doughty *Northwind* and her company there was no such word as "can't."

---

\* With the following results:

| Layer | Chlorinity (ppm) | Oxygen (Ml/L) | pH |
|---|---|---|---|
| 4 meter | 0 613 | 6.79 | 6 25 |
| 8 meter | 0.459 | 10 51 | 6.60 |

# Chapter 46

# OF ICE TOMORROW

*Clang, clang!* Again the procession of hourly reports, the saline whisper of ruffled wave caressing the heavy steel hull, the hum of wind in the rigging, the muffled escape of exhaust smoke, the patter of sleet on my parka hood. I had heard these familiar sounds hundreds of times, but, occurring together, they must have provided the cue that carried my mind back to the *Northland,* to the thrill of entering on a new and adventurous chapter of life. Across the panorama of years my memory flew in a review of many little incidents which had made this phase of my career spicy. Now I sensed that the end was near. The thought made me a bit frightened—and unhappy.

Behind us the blink of Arctic ice was blending into a lone strip of clear sky just above it. In another half-hour that, too, would be swallowed by the black clouds overhead. Somehow in my present mood this seemed foreboding. Would there be a next year? I wondered. If so, things might be different. Perhaps we would have aircraft—a plane or helicopter, maybe both. Such devices would mean an end of precarious anchorages off treacherous shores, of blind groping for leads in pack ice. With plane and helicopter the *Northwind* could smash her way to the very Pole. It is always tomorrow for which the dreamer lives and plans. But dreams are forerunners of progress.

And what of tomorrow in the world of men, ships and ice? Will

364

there be a place for the ice sailor, the icebreaker and iceworthy vessels?

The answer is simple. To seek it one need only turn to a polar projection of the earth's surface and plot the shortest distances between the great metropolitan centers of North America, Europe and Asia. These are the air routes of the future—the lanes which will be most hotly contested commercially in time of peace and militarily in the event of hostilities between two powerful enemies. They will be seen to pass over the Arctic and boreal regions.

For instance, suppose the United States faced a European enemy whose ships, men and equipment were adapted to operations in frozen seas and on icy terrain. This foe would likely hit us where we are least prepared to parry the blow—in the Arctic.

By a series of lightninglike thrusts our enemy might readily occupy Spitzbergen, Jan Mayen, Iceland, East Greenland and Northern Canada. Then, from base to base, across icy seas he could pour his might in troops and war materials. An operation of this nature would place the enemy athwart our northern flank—today our vulnerable one—a calamitous situation.

In order to secure this vulnerable flank, we must deny any enemy— real or potential—steppingstones which span a likely invasion route. This means we have to get in there first with our bases. Thus we are assured a well-supported defense chain that will force the fighting close to the enemy's shores and provide us a springboard from which to deal short, powerful jabs at the enemy's homeland.

Overseas bases always require support by ships. If ships can't operate in sea ice, polar bases are worthless. In the Arctic, two fundamental ship types are essential: (1) Transports for troops, supplies and fuel, and (2) heavy icebreakers to escort them. Transport vessels must be iceworthy—sturdily built, maneuverable, economical, relatively small in size and produceable in quantity. Heavy icebreakers must be powerful and well armed to insure the safe and timely arrival of an ice convoy.

Unlike costly long-range bombing planes, iceworthy transports are good for many years. They can carry a pay load in all latitudes—in peace as well as war.

The basic geological structure of the Arctic and Antarctic does not differ materially from that of the great mineral and petroleum-producing regions which are now being exploited. Moreover, there is an abundance of potential energy in the polar regions.

For example, it required energy on an unprecedented scale to take water from the sea and deposit it on the Arctic and Antarctic icecaps. The good Lord has stored this water high and in frozen form for man to use—as soon as he desperately needs it.

Our resources in raw materials and energy are rapidly being drained. The time is not too far away when we will be forced to turn northward for new, unexploited sources.

The economic as well as the political destiny of the United States and other nations of the world will creep ever pole-ward. Rear Admiral Richard E. Byrd has recognized this for many years. He has dedicated his career to proving that man can make a friend of ice— make it serve him rather than deter him. Admiral Byrd has been many generations ahead of his time.

So in war and in peace, the role of the ice sailor, the icebreaker and iceworthy vessel is one of growing importance. Unquestionably, there will be a place for the submarine and other vessel types as civilization pushes northward.

Technical improvements in ice navigating and breaking are inevitable—even to the point of disintegrating ice. But throughout the polar world there will always be good ice years and bad ice years. It is with the bad ice years the United States and her peace-loving friends must be prepared to cope.

For *ice is where you find it.*

**THE END**

INDEX

# INDEX

CPSIA information can be obtained
at www.ICGtesting.com
Printed in the USA
LVHW020625221218
601183LV00019B/1102/P